Dictatorial Power and States of Exception in the Weimar Republic

This book is an account of the tension between the need for order and the desire for freedom during the tense years of the Weimar Republic. It explains how various groups interpreted Article 48 of the Weimar Constitution and utilized it to reinstate peace and tranquility. While Article 48 is usually associated with the so-called Preußenschlag—the taking over of the Prussian government by the order of Reich Chancellor Kurt von Papen—it had been introduced as a necessity during earlier "states of emergency."

This investigation delves into the relevant works by many of the leading constitutional scholars in Germany. This list includes Hugo Preuss, Carl Schmitt, Hans Kelsen, Gerhard Anschütz, Richard Thoma, Erwin Jacobi, Hans Nawiasky, and Richard Grau. This book is a clearly written and detailed account of the history surrounding the debate about the appropriate emergency measures to be taken under Article 48. The work is important for its historical interest, and also because the conflict between authority and freedom has continuing relevance.

The book will be a valuable resource for researchers and academics working in the areas of Legal History, Legal Philosophy, Legal Theory, Constitutional History, and German Studies.

Christopher Adair-Toteff is a philosopher and a social theorist whose research has been in social economics and in political liberalism. He is a Fellow at the Center for Social and Political Thought, University of South Florida, USA.

Routledge Research in Legal History

Socialism and Legal History
The Histories and Historians of Law in Socialist East Central Europe
Edited by Ville Erkkilä and Hans-Peter Haferkamp

A History of Divorce Law
Reform in England from the Victorian to Interwar Years
Henry Kha

The League of Nations and the Development of International Law
A New Intellectual History of the Advisory Committee of Jurists
Edited by P. Sean Morris

Transforming the Politics of International Law
The Advisory Committee of Jurists and the Formation of the World Court in the League of Nations
Edited by P. Sean Morris

Transitional Justice in Italy and the Crimes of Fascism and Nazism
Paolo Caroli

Slavery, Indenture and the Law
Assembling a Nation in Colonial Mauritius
Nandini S. Boodia-Canoo

Justice and International Law in Meiji Japan
The María Luz Incident and the Dawn of Modernity
Giorgio Fabio Colombo

Dictatorial Power and States of Exception in the Weimar Republic
The Controversial Article 48, 1919–1933
Christopher Adair-Toteff

See more at https://www.routledge.com/Routledge-Research-in-Legal-History/book-series/RRLEGHIST

Dictatorial Power and States of Exception in the Weimar Republic

The Controversial Article 48, 1919–1933

Christopher Adair-Toteff

Routledge
Taylor & Francis Group
LONDON AND NEW YORK

First published 2025
by Routledge
4 Park Square, Milton Park, Abingdon, Oxon OX14 4RN

and by Routledge
605 Third Avenue, New York, NY 10158

Routledge is an imprint of the Taylor & Francis Group, an informa business

British Library Cataloguing-in-Publication Data
A catalogue record for this book is available from the British Library

Library of Congress Cataloging-in-Publication Data
Names: Adair-Toteff, Christopher, author.
Title: Dictatorial power and states of exception in the Weimar Republic : the controversial Article 48, 1919–1933 / Christopher Adair-Toteff.
Description: Abingdon, Oxon [UK] ; New York, NY : Routledge, 2025. | Series: Routledge research in legal history | Includes bibliographical references and index.
Identifiers: LCCN 2025002589 (print) | LCCN 2025002590 (ebook) | ISBN 9781032320823 (hardback) | ISBN 9781032320830 (paperback) | ISBN 9781003312796 (ebook)
Subjects: LCSH: Germany. Verfassung (1919) | Constitutional history—Germany. | Proportional representation—Germany—History. | Dictatorship—Germany—History. | Germany—Politics and government—1918–1933. | Germany—History—1918–1933.
Classification: LCC KK4710 .A73 2025 (print) | LCC KK4710 (ebook) | DDC 342.43/062—dc23/eng/20250118
LC record available at https://lccn.loc.gov/2025002589
LC ebook record available at https://lccn.loc.gov/2025002590

ISBN: 978-1-032-32082-3 (hbk)
ISBN: 978-1-032-32083-0 (pbk)
ISBN: 978-1-003-31279-6 (ebk)

DOI: 10.4324/9781003312796

Typeset in Galliard
by Apex CoVantage, LLC

Contents

1 Dictatorship, State of Exception, and Article 48

Introduction

The years between the end of the First World War and Adolf Hitler's rise to power is a period that is often misunderstood. There are many reasons for this; they include historical, political, and sociological issues that render this time to various interpretations. Was this a time of historical renewal and for political optimism, or a time of economic upheaval and social change? What about this period's legal position? Was it a liberal democracy based upon the rule of law or was it something of a composite and was fundamentally political? Again, there are questions concerning German laws during the 1920s: were they relatively permissive or were they almost reactionary? Closely aligned with these legal issues is the question of Germany's constitution. Was the constitution of the Weimar Era liberal or did it contain the basis for the Nazi regime that succeeded it? Of all of the articles found in the Weimarer Reichsverfassung (Weimar Reich Constitution), Artikel 48 was, and is, the one that appeared to have led to the dictatorship of the Third Reich. That is because Art. 48 contained paragraphs that encompassed the "state of exception" ("Ausnahmezustand") and suggested that dictatorial "power" was legitimate. Before turning to Art. 48 itself, some of these terms call for clarification.[1]

The purpose of this book is to provide an account of the origins, meaning, and history of Art. 48. The title of this book is intended to indicate the focus of the work: *Dictatorial Power and States of Exception in the Weimar Republic.* This book's subtitle announces the central subject and the time frame: the controversial Art. 48 and its beginnings in 1919 to its end in early 1933. This book is not just of historical and legal importance; it underscores the tension between security and freedom; between dictatorship and law. Above all, it illustrates the tension, if not conflict, between politics and the law.

While there is a temptation to think of an "Ausnahmezustand" as a "state of emergency," that is not the literal translation of the term. A "state

1 Translations are notoriously difficult because the struggle to find the right word often reflects the tension between what is literal and what is readable. This problem is compounded here because many of the terms have a historical context and many of them are specific legal terms.

DOI: 10.4324/9781003312796-1

of emergency" would be the translation of "Notstand." There is no doubt that Art. 48 covers "states of emergency"; however, it does not refer to "Notstand" but always to "Ausnahmezustand." It is also helpful to keep in mind that several of the people engaged in this debate also spoke only of exceptions. Carl Schmitt was not the only one, but is likely the most famous one. This is the reasoning behind the use of "state of exception" in the title of this book. Dictatorial "Macht" also requires some comment. It is usually rendered as "power" and the word "Gewalt" is most often translated as "force." But as it is used in Art. 48, "Macht" means both "power" and "force." Both terms are connected to "Zwang" or "compulsion"; all three imply the use of power, force, and even violence to compel someone or some group to either stop doing something or perform some action. "Zwang" is not often found in this book, but "Macht" and "Gewalt" are: the translation of them as dictatorial power or dictatorial force is largely dependent upon their contexts.

Dictatorship, States of Exception, and Article 48

> "On the basis of Article 48, paragraph 2 of the Reich Constitution the following are implemented in order to defend against the Communist state-threatening acts of violence:"
>
> "Auf Grund des Artikels 48 Abs. 2 der Reichsverfassung wird zur Abwehr kommunitischer staatsgefährdender Gewaltakte folgendes verordnet:"
>
> Hindenburg 2018: 370

This quotation is from the order that Paul von Hindenburg issued on February 28, 1933, which justified the suspension of seven articles of the Weimar Constitution. In effect, Hindenburg was using the Weimar Constitution in order to abolish it. The basis for this political move was Article 48 of the Weimarer Reichsverfassung, which gave the Reichspräsident the power to suspend certain rights. Hindenburg's order then led to the beginning of the Third Reich and all that it would entail until 1945. It was also the end of the Weimar Era, which had lasted from August 1919 until its collapse in early 1933. The Weimar Era had begun with a burst of optimism that signaled the break with the beliefs and policies that went back to the original Reich's founding in 1872.

While no one apparently refers to the Weimar Era as the Second Reich, its founders and most Germans during that 13-year period referred to it as the Reich. It followed the original "Reich"—the one founded by Bismarck—and would precede the notorious "Third Reich" ("Drittes Reich").[2] During the Weimar Era, the railroad was referred to as the "Reichsbahn," money was called "Reichsmark," and the government was the "Reich." Most important for this book was that the constitution was named the "Reichsverfassung."

2 That the "Drittes Reich" followed the Weimar Reich was not the reason for it being regarded as third. Rather, the Nazis claimed that the first "Reich" was the Christian "Reich" and Bismarck's was the middle or second one. The "Drittes Reich" alluded to the thousand-year Christian era.

The "Reichsverfassung" guaranteed rights that were not given under Bismarckian rule; among them was general equality and the rule of law. Democracy was the key, and the constitution was designed to protect it. However, those who approved the Weimarer Reichsverfassung also recognized the need for "public security and order" ("öffentlichen Sicherheit und Ordnung"), and that was the original intent of Art. 48 of the Weimarer Reichsverfassung. It did not seem possible to Hugo Preuß, the man who drafted the constitution, that politicians would use that law to undermine and end the Weimar Reich. Preuß and many others believed that the new Germany of the Weimar Era would adhere to the spirit and the rule of law. The use and then abuse of Art. 48 both emphasize the belief in law and the refusal to accept that those who disliked democracy and wanted a strong rule would use that law to end Weimar. This book is intended to tell the story of Art. 48 of the Weimarer Reichsverfassung. This introduction contains three sections: the first indicates the nature of the book and the second indicates what the book intends to cover and what it omits. The third section provides a brief overview of the individual chapters.

"Artikel 48 Der Weimarer Reichsverfassung"

This book is one attempt to detail the origins and the history of Art. 48 of the Weimarer Reichsverfassung. It is not a definitive account, even if such an account could be written. This limitation is not just because such an account is likely to be beyond my abilities, but is also because of the huge scope of such a project. This book was originally intended to be close to 60,000 words; it is now 80,000 words. I now recognize that it could be double that number and would still not cover all aspects of the history that should be covered. There are further limitations to this book. It is important for understanding the nature of Art. 48 to begin each chapter with a historical overview. This provides a much-needed historical context for the specific years. This brief historical background has had to be kept to a minimum; books have been written about single years—there are several devoted just to 1923. In addition, lengthier accounts should be written by historians; and I am not one. This brings me to the final point. An ideal account of the origins and history of Art. 48 should be written by a constitutional scholar. While I have had an abiding interest in the Weimar Constitution, I am not regarded as an expert. My earlier research for my previously published work on Max Weber, Carl Schmitt, Hans Kelsen, Hermann Heller, and Georg Jellinek has been helpful in writing this book. But I recognize that a constitutional scholar would understand some particular legal nuance that I failed even to notice. By training I am a philosopher and by inclination I am a social theorist, and it is with a combination of the two that I approached this project. It has been longer in the making than I had anticipated and, as noted earlier, is lengthier than I had intended. I ended this project even more secure in this conviction. It is my hope that this account will convince some readers.

Chapter Overviews

Chapter 2 begins with a brief historical overview. It is longer and more detailed than the historical overviews of the later chapters because of the complexity of the post-war situation in Germany and the uncertainty about the future. The loss of the war meant a break with the past, and many who still revered Bismarck were fearful of the future. For many others, the break with the past meant hope for a new and better future. Most all of those who were involved in forming the new German government and were associated with the drafting of the Weimarer Reichsverfassung were among those who held democratic values and liberal sentiments. But there were many who wished to return to the "good old days" under the monarchy and others who were revolutionaries intent upon establishing a new Communist order in Germany. These struggles between Right and Left would continue throughout the Weimar Era. The main parts of Chapter 2 are devoted to detailing the birth of the Weimar Constitution, and that involves discussions of the many sessions of the Constitutional Committee. The chapter then focuses on the development of Art. 48—how it was originally divided into two articles and only later in discussions was decided to bring them together into one article. The single Art. 48 contained five paragraphs—each of these five "Absätze" varied in importance and in length. The first two (Abs. 1 and Abs. 2) dealt with matters of exceptional importance and were several sentences in length. Ab. 5 was one brief sentence but really offered no real sense of what Art. 48 meant and what its scope and its limitations were. Chapter 2 is similar to Chapter 6 because both chapters contain accounts of actual debates. In contrast, Chapters 3, 4, and 5 focus less on personal discussions and more on scholarly debates.

Chapter 3 is devoted to the political turmoil of the years 1920–1922. It begins with a brief overview of some of the main political issues. It then contains a discussion of Carl Schmitt's *Die Diktatur.* That 1921 book does not contain much discussion of Art. 48 of the Weimarer Reichsverfassung but it does contain a number of crucial points about the legal and political justification of a dictator and the extent and limitations of the powers of a dictatorship. The chapter then offers a limited discussion of Gerhard Anschütz's commentary on the Weimarer Reichsverfassung. *Die Verfassung des Deutschen Reichs vom 11. August 1919* was first published in 1921 and would undergo three more major editions between then and the beginning of 1933. Anschütz was not only a well-respected professor at Heidelberg; he was also regarded as one of the leading constitutional scholars in all of Germany. Anschütz would not only produce 13 further versions of his commentary, he would also co-edit with Richard Thoma a massive two-volume book on the Reichsverfassung. Finally, Anschütz would play a leading role in the October 1932 trial that was the result of the "Preußenschlag." The remainder of Chapter 3 is devoted to an extensive investigation of Richard Grau's book on dictatorship. This lengthy discussion is justified on two grounds: first, his book was the only one devoted to Art. 48 and contains an exhaustive analysis of the five "paragraphs" of Art. 48. As such, it is crucial to understand what Art. 48 was intended to do and to comprehend the range and limits that it entailed. Second, Grau would go on to write numerous articles and essays exploring Art. 48 and justifying its implementation. The names Schmitt, Anschütz, and Grau will resurface often in the following chapters and will continue to play defining roles in the debates about dictatorship and states of exception.

Chapter 4 is focused on the years 1923–1926. This chapter has three sections. The first section is a brief historical overview and serves to identify the problems in economics, foreign policies, and politics in Germany during this four-year period. The other two sections are considerably longer. The second section covers the terrible years of 1923 and 1924. The political ramifications of economic crises, especially hyperinflation, were introduced into some of the important debates about Art. 48. This was true regarding the lengthy debate about Art. 48 that occurred in the spring of 1924. This debate involved Gerhard Anschütz, Karl Bilfinger, Carl Schmitt, and Erwin Jacobi. Granted, much of this debate centered upon such matters as what "setting aside" meant, but these apparently scholarly discussions about the meanings of words do not obscure the fact that much of that debate was political. The third section covers the years 1925 and 1926 and while there was no conference held that had Art. 48 as its focus, it was the center of several essays. Richard Grau published one in 1925 and another the following year. As the expert on Art. 48 his opinion carried considerable weight, but the fact that his arguments were often difficult to follow probably minimized his impact. Hans Nawiasky provided the third essay and his 1926 paper is lengthy and complex. However, his questioning of the terms of Art. 48 and his suggestion that that article is more limited than people like Schmitt and Jacobi claimed meant that his opinion was going to be welcomed by such legal defenders such as Gerhard Anschütz and Richard Thoma. Nawiasky would later assist Anschütz and Thoma in their defense of Prussia in the later "Preußenschlag" trial.

Chapter 5 is devoted to the years 1927, 1928, and 1929, and while the first two years of this period were relatively peaceful, 1929 saw the beginning of the real demise of the Weimar liberal state. This chapter has six parts. As with previous chapters, Chapter 5 begins with a brief historical overview. Most of those three years were peaceful and prosperous, at least in comparison with most of the previous years. But the increase in unemployment was accelerated by the aftereffects of the collapse of the United States' economy following the "Black Friday" of October 1929. The second section is a close examination of the second effort by Richard Grau to explain and defend his interpretation of Art. 48. It can, and should, be read as a response to Carl Schmitt's various comments and complaints about Grau's interpretation. What makes this debate interesting is that there are few grounds for this conflict because Grau and Schmitt were mostly in agreement about the meaning and the scope of Art. 48. The third section is the discussion between the eminent constitutional expert Hans Kelsen and the young legal scholar Wolfgang Flad. Flad's criticism is not always clear or correct, but he follows others who had objected to Kelsen's formalistic legal philosophy and how that "purity" affected Kelsen's understanding of Art. 48. The fourth section is a return to Anschütz's discussion of Art. 48 but in its expanded form. This version included in the 1929 edition is lengthier and more complex than his discussion in the earlier edition, but it was still not as long or as contentious as that given in the final edition of 1933. The fifth and sixth sections are devoted to the "Hüter der Verfassung" debate between Kelsen and Schmitt. This debate revolved around the question of who should be regarded as the legitimate or legal guardian of the Weimar Constitution. For Kelsen, the courts were the only appropriate body to be the guardian of the Constitution; for Schmitt, it was the president of the Reich. Schmitt's emphasis on executive power was a further instance of his decisionism and his embrace of an almost absolute ruler. Schmitt continues to be regarded as a constitutional scholar, and that has some basis since he published a book on the constitution and wrote on constitutional issues. However, his writings during the Weimar Era and those during the Nazi period reflect his ongoing acceptance of the leader over any court. Chapter 5 concludes with some final comments.

Chapter 6 covers the years 1930 through 1932, but it also looks back to 1929 and it does discuss some issues that occurred during the first two months of 1933. It is composed of five major sections. The first section provides the historical context. While not as extensive as that found in Chapter 2, this account is longer than the other chapters. Its length is needed to explain the thinking and the events which led up to the "Preußenschlag," and that means discussing not just the political conflicts between Right and Left but also the "Altona Bloody Sunday." Much of this chapter is devoted to the actual Reich intervention into the Prussian government with a discussion of the decrees and statements used by the Reich to justify the removal of many of the high-level officials of the democratically elected Prussian government. This involved a description of the political conflict between the Right-leading Reich government and the left-leaning SPD government of Prussia. Then there is the lengthy exploration of the legal battles—the first one right after the Reich's intervention and the second with the October trial in which Prussia again tried to show that the Reich had misused Art. 48. The Prussians insisted that the Reich had wrongly used legal means to accomplish a political goal. This section covers the analyses of speeches by Arnold Brecht, Gerhard Anschütz, Richard Thoma, and others for Prussia and those speeches by Carl Schmitt, Karl Bilfinger, and Erwin Jacobi and others for the German Reich. The remainder of Chapter 6 involves further debates between Hans Kelsen and Schmitt as well as a brief account of the trial and debate by Ernst Fraenkel. This lengthy chapter is intended to give an adequate account of the time leading up to the "Preußenschlag," the actual intervention, and the legal and political aftermath of the trial of "Prussia contra Reich."

Chapter 7 contains three sets of concluding comments. The first set is retrospective and provides a brief summary of the preceding five chapters. It is intended to provide a thread that unifies all of these chapters. The second set provides a brief account of four books. These books have addressed the Weimarer Reichsverfassung in differing degrees and provide diverse perspectives on the role that Art. 48 played during the Weimar Era. Although the time span covers from less than a decade to more than 50 years, they may still be regarded as present accounts. The final set contains some reflections on the origin and history of Art. 48. But this set is forward looking. These concluding comments are warnings about how legal documents can and will be used to undermine constitutional law. This set emphasizes the fundamental tension between the need for order and security and the desire for flexibility and freedom.

This book can be read in several ways. The primary way, and the one intended, is to read the book in its entirety. This way the reader can trace Art. 48 from its origins in 1919 through its history during the Weimar Era and to its demise with Hindenburg's February 1933 declaration. The alternative way is to choose individual chapters which may reflect an individual reader's desire to understand certain years during the Weimar Era. Whichever way readers choose, it is my hope that this book will serve to inspire others to read about the Weimar Era and to seek a fuller understanding of Art. 48 and its importance for the Weimarer Reichsverfassung. The goal is to further our comprehension of the notion of "dictatorship" ("Diktatur") and to gain a better understanding of the concept of the "state of exception" ("Ausnahmezustand").

References

Dreier, H. und Waldhoff, C., Herausgegebern (2018) *Das Wagnis der Demokratie: Eine Anatomie der Weimarer Reichsverfassung*. München: Verlag von C.H. Beck.

Hindenburg, Paul (1933) "Verordung des Reichspräsidenten zum Schutz von Volk und Staat. Vom 28. February 1933 [Reichstagsbrandverordung]." In Dreier und Waldhoff. 2018. 370–371.

2 1918–1919

The Years of Struggle and Renewal

The Weimarer Reichsverfassung did not spring fully formed like Athena from the head of Zeus. It did not just have a seven-month gestation period; prior to that, it had a period of several months that impacted its gestation and its birth. Christoph Gusy and Jörg-Detlef Kühne are two scholars who think it crucial to remind us that Germany had lost the war and that Germany needed to deal with the repercussions of that recent defeat while attempting to formulate a view of the near future (Gusy 2018: 11–12; Kühne 2000: 124–125).

The Reich that Otto von Bismarck established in 1871 lasted until early November 1918, but when the end came, it came quickly. Within a matter of days, the old Reich had fallen, the Kaiser had abdicated, and there was no government. Into this vacuum came six political people: three from the Sozialdemokratische Partei Deutschlands (SPD) and three from the Unabhängige Sozialdemokratische Partei Deutschlands (USPD)—the SPD would play a longer role in the formation of a new government while the more radical USPD would not (Boldt 1987: 44). However, there were also revolutionary governments in power in a number of major German cities.[1] Most of them did not last long, yet a few of them did.[2] But there was a concerted effort by a small and dedicated group to establish a new and more permanent

1 Hundreds, if not thousands, of books have been written about Germany in the First World War and the revolutionary days of 1918. What is provided here is only a bare sketch, so many points are either minimized or left out, but that should not be taken to mean that they are unimportant. One of these is the reintroduction of unrestricted U-boat warfare. Many politicians and scholars warned that if Germany allowed its submarines to attack any boats, then the United States would intervene and that would spell Germany's defeat. Another one is the propaganda that the German government used repeatedly to convey the sense of immediate and definitive victory. That became harder to maintain, but the German authorities continued to proclaim that victory would soon be achieved. A third instance is connected to both of these and that is the "dictatorship" of Eric Ludendorff and Paul von Hindenburg. Both had been appointed as leaders of the war effort because of their early victories in the East in 1914. Both would play crucial roles during the Weimar period. See Dreier 2016: 2–3.

2 This is not to minimize the conflicts and even uprisings that occurred between late November 1918 and January 1919. That certainly includes the Spartakus uprising and the subsequent murders of Rosa Luxemburg and Karl Leibknecht. Nor should this minimize the impact of the Munich "Räterepublik" and its violent suppression. See Winkler 1993: 57–61, 79–82.

DOI: 10.4324/9781003312796-2

government. This government would be democratic and would be founded upon a fundamentally new and radically egalitarian constitution. While there were many people involved in the political process of late 1918 and even more throughout much of 1919, there was only one genuine author of this new constitution. That author (and "Vater") of the Weimarer Reichsverfassung was Hugo Preuß.[3]

This chapter is devoted to setting out the history of the end of the old Reich and the beginnings of the new one and has two parts: the first part covers the final months of 1918 and the second part is devoted to the entire year of 1919. Both parts have two sections. The first section is the history of the end of the old Reich and the beginning of the new, and the second section is devoted to Hugo Preuß. The second part has a section covering the development and meaning of the Weimarer Reichsverfassung, and the final section is devoted specifically to the controversial Article 48. It is this article that is the main theme of this entire book, so in order to understand its history throughout the Weimar Era, it is crucial to understand its origins. The Weimar Constitution was designed by Preuss, but it did not spring forth out of nothing; it came out of the end of the Bismarckian era.

Part One

Late 1918

Whatever one thinks of Otto von Bismarck, one has to concede that he was a military expert as well as a political genius. Between 1866 and 1871, Bismarck was able to create the German empire. During these five years, Bismarck won three different wars: against Denmark, against Austria, and finally, against France (Weichlein 2015: 291). There were numerous problems and tensions within Bismarck's Germany—some he started himself, like the "Kulturkampf" that pitted his Protestant state against the Roman Catholic Church—and some he did not want, like the push for agrarian reforms. In the end, he lost the trust of Wilhelm II in 1890. Thomas Nipperdey described Wilhelm's rule from 1890 until the outbreak of hostilities in August 1914. These years were often a time of crises, both externally and internally (Nipperdey 1998: 621–729). Nipperdey referred to the First World War as the "Urkatastrophe" ("original catastrophe") (Nipperdey 1998: 758; Mommsen n.d.: 14, 150) and it was, not just for the world, but especially for Germany. Nipperdey maintained that the central experience in Germany was hunger and that thousands of people died during 1917 from starvation. That is why Friedrich Meinecke referred to it in 1930 as the "Hungerwinter" (Meinecke 1930: 101). The lack of food

3 Preuß's name is spelled differently in different places. In many of them it is spelled with the "sharfes s" as in Preuß, whereas in others it is spelled with a double "s" as in Preuss. Preuß himself occasionally used the double "s." In the interest of accuracy, I use the spelling of the original document and that accounts for the different spelling throughout this book.

caused not just malnutrition but contributed to the number of deaths caused by tuberculosis (Nipperdey 1998: 855–856). The lack of food, the rise in illnesses, and the defeats all caused many Germans to lose faith in its war efforts.

Benjamin Ziemann has argued that while there was a massive outpouring of support for Germany in August 1914, this support quickly faded. Working-class women were among the first to challenge the need for the war—grocery prices were going higher and rationing was introduced. Food riots occurred in the fall of 1915 (Koerner 1968a I: 121–122). It was likely that the six-month battle for Verdun may have been the deciding battle—the Germans and the French lost more than 700,000 soldiers. It was likened to Dante's *Inferno* by some and was regarded as hell on earth by others (Koerner 1968b II: 24–36). By 1918, many Germans had not only lost the belief that the war could be won; they also lost the belief in the legitimacy of the Wilhelmine government (Ziemann 2015: 386–387, 389–391). Thomas Kühne noted that more people died during the First World War by other human beings than ever before and that many people were horrified by the senseless battles over small portions of land. By 1917, many Germans had given up hope for peace and soldiers wanted only to survive and to return home (Kühne 2015: 528–529, 532; Ziemann 2015: 391; Nipperdey 1998: 865–866). By late 1918, the war had been mostly lost and the "October reform" from "above" had clearly failed; the only alternative appeared to be revolution from "below" (Nipperdey 1998: 868–869; Stammen 1992: 64–65; Winkler 1998: 25–26).

The German revolution of 1918 and 1919 counts as one of the most disputed times in Germany's modern history (Bernecker 1992: 87, 90). Its causes and its effects are still debated. The was no single revolution, but there were revolutionary movements that broke out in a number of German cities (Rosenberg 1973: 236–238; Koerner 1968c III: 114–117). Ursula Büttner insisted that the basis for the revolution was already present during much of 1918; people were tired of starving, they were sick of soldiers dying, and they just wanted to have normal lives again. But by November, people were in a revolutionary mood (Büttner 2008: 33, 43). This is confirmed by Friedrich Ebert's final speech to the Wilhelmine Reichstag. Ebert warned that they were living through the destiny-determining hours and that they needed to make critical decisions (Ebert 1926: 72, 91). Christopher Dillion argued that the first burst of revolutionary fever occurred on the October 30 in Wilhelmshaven and then spread to Kiel. These were sailors who mutinied (Dillon 2022: 29–30). The revolution broke out in Munich on November 7, 1918, and was brought on mostly by workers (Ay 1968: 10–14). It broke out in Hamburg and Kiel a day or two earlier by workers as well as sailors. It also broke out in Berlin; this time it was instigated mostly by left-leaning workers and Communist politicians (Nipperdey 1998: 872–874). It was on November 8 that Kaiser Wilhelm II abdicated and left Germany. That was the end of the old and the beginning of the new. Saturday, November 9, has been named the "birthdate of new Germany" ("Geburtstag des neuen Deutschland") (Heilfrom n.d. 1: 103). Philipp Scheidemann proclaimed the "Deutsche Republik" from a balcony of the Reichstag in the early afternoon of November 9 (Winkler 1998: 33). He made the announcement in the evening edition of the *Vossische Zeitung* on November 9: "the old is no more. Ebert is appointed Reich Chancellor" ("das Alte ist nicht mehr. Ebert ist zum Reichskanzler ernannt") (Scheidemann 2018: 357). But this was only the beginning of the struggle to determine Germany's future, and the following day Ebert issued a plea to all citizens to support the efforts to feed the people and to establish a new government.[4]

One can argue that there were three radical factions aiming for power in the months and even years after the November revolutions. One faction was composed of those who tried to radicalize the citizens from the Left, and this was done primarily by the Spartakus faction.[5] Another faction was composed of those who sought to radicalize the citizens, but only in the sense of going back to the old system. These people were composed of former military officers and entrenched political types. If the people on the Left wanted a radical future, the people on the Right wanted a radical return to the past. Then there was a third group who wanted a transition to a better future; one in which there would be greater freedom and more equality. These were people like Ebert and Hugo Preuß. Many of these wanted to maintain some semblance of continuity between the Wilhelmine period and the new one (Bernecker 1992: 101–105; Mommsen 2001: 54–59; Lehnert 1999: 27–31; Dillon 2022: 36–38). During November and December of 1918 and then into much of 1919, the revolutionaries of the Left seemed to have most of the influence. This was certainly true in Munich but also in Berlin (Neubarer 1967: 173–174).

There were also the radicals on the Right, and while they engaged in conflicts and battles in 1918 and early 1919, they would become more prevalent and more powerful in the 1920s. Then there were those who seemed to be in the center between the two extremes—while it was not explicitly radical as the revolutionary movement was, in its essence it was just as radical. It was a movement started largely by Ebert and others and was intended to create a new and democratic Germany (Meinecke 1930: 117–119). On November 12, Ebert issued a proclamation that lifted the military regime, eliminated the laws restricting freedoms, and proclaimed further measures that would be introduced no later than the first of January 1919 (Ebert 1926: 96–97). These were all critical measures, but the first and most important task of the national assembly was to produce a new constitution (Apelt 1946: 46). Walter Jellinek provided one of the most accurate and most concise account of the national assembly. Writing in 1930 he acknowledged that the last chancellor of the Bismarck constitution, Prince Max von Baden, had proposed changes to allow for greater voting rights, but

4 Ebert 1926: 93–94. The call was made verbally to bureaucrats on November 9 and was printed in the "Reichsanzeiger" on November 12 (Stammen 1992 1: 110). Ebert's appeal on the same day to the citizens of Germany is printed in Stammen (1992 1: 111).

5 See the documents by Kurt Eisner, Ernst Toller, and other members of the Left in Stammen (1992 1: 111–115).

it was not until after the November revolution that the new assembly began to take up this issue (Jellinek 1930a: 119–121). It was in his second article in the *Handbuch des deutschen Staatslehre* that Jellinek provided an equally accurate and important account of the development of the Weimarer Reichsverfassung, and he began by setting out the crucial role that Hugo Preuß played.

Friedrich Ebert had been selected just after Wilhelm's abdication to set about forming a government, and he selected Preuß to be "interior minister." As "Staatssekretär des Reichsamts des Innern" Preuß was instructed to issue orders for new elections, and his proclamation contained 62 paragraphs (Heilfron n.d. 1: 111–118). On the partial basis of this, Ebert later appointed Preuß to be the first interior minister and to draw up drafts for a new constitution. Jellinek noted that prior to the revolution, Preuß had been a member of the "Progressive Peoples' Party" ("Fortschrittlichen Volkspartei") but after that he had been a founding member of the "German Democratic Party" ("Deutsche Demokratischen Partei"). Ebert also selected him because he was aware that Preuß had already prepared a detailed suggestion for a new constitution in the spring of 1917 (Preuss 2006: 290, 296–298). At the time, he was the most left-leaning legal theorist, but Ebert chose him on November 15, 1919, because he was convinced that Preuß would be able to provide a bridge to the citizens (Jellinek 1930b: 127).

Hugo Preuß

Hugo Preuß (1860–1925) was a professor, writer, and politician, but above all, he is regarded as the "father of the Weimar Constitution" ("Vater der Weimarer Verfassung") (Boldt 1987: 47, 53; Stammen 1992: 4; Jasper 1992: 120; Friedrich 2000: 183; Lammert 2015: VII). Christoph Gusy begins a section of his book with the title "Am Anfang war Hugo Preuß" ("In the Beginning Was Hugo Preuß) (Gusy 2018: 41–42) Given Preuß's importance for Weimar in general and for the Weimar Constitution in particular, he is scarcely studied and rarely acknowledged: Michael Stolleis's *Juristen. Ein biographisches Lexikon von der Antike bis zum 20. Jahrhundert* has hundreds of entries but not one devoted to Hugo Preuß and then only in passing as a follower of Otto von Gierke (Stolleis 1995: 234). There are a number of possible reasons for this neglect: he was Jewish and his books were banned as "Undeutsch" in 1933.[6] He is regarded as the author of the Weimar Constitution but since it failed he should be ignored. Then there is the rather strange fact that he never signed the actual constitution since he had resigned from the government at that time. Yet, Hugo Preuß was the driving force behind the constitution, the author of several drafts, and must be regarded as the "Vater" of the Weimarer

6 My personal copy of Preuß's *Die Entwicklung des Deustchen Städtewesens* has two stampings inside the front cover and one on the title page. The first showed that it belonged to the bureau of the city of Freiburg im Breisgau. The second one indicated that "Book number 50" was removed from circulation on September 1, 1935, and stored in cabinet number 1. The stamping on title page simply stated "invalid" (Ungültig) (Preuss 1906).

Reichsverfassung. Preuß's constitution was a legal document and it reflected his understanding of constitutional principles. However, it was as much a political document because Preuß was as much a political thinker as he was a constitutional scholar. Accordingly, it is important to understand Preuß's political thoughts as well as his legal concepts. That is what Theodor Heuss wrote in 1926, and it was echoed by Gillessen in 1955 and repeated by Michael Dreyer in 2018 (Heuss 2006: 1, 11; Gillessen 2000: 17; Dreyer 2018: XI–XII).

Hugo Preuß was born on October 28, 1860, in Berlin to Louis and Minna Preuß, but Louis died the same year. The widow married Louis's brother, Leopold, who raised Hugo as his own son. It was not until he was almost an adult that he was told that Leopold was not his biological father (Albertin 2007: 2). According to Günther Gillessen, we know very little about Hugo's early years; we know that he attended the Sophia Gymnasium in Berlin and regarded himself as a genuine citizen of Berlin's Westend, complete with its particular humor, intelligence, and tendency towards self-irony (Gillessen 2000: 19). We do know that he attended the university at Heidelberg where he attended courses of the famous neo-Kantian Kuno Fischer. Hugo was impressed by Kuno Fischer's manner of speaking, but he did not share the master's inclination towards philosophical abstraction. Hugo also attended the university in Berlin where he heard Rudolf von Gneist; he graduated from Göttingen in 1883. Hugo Preuß "habilitated" in 1889 and in the same year he married Else Liebermann. They resided in the same house on the west side of Berlin for most of the rest of his life; he and Else had four sons. Because he was Jewish, the typical path to a professorship was not open to him and he remained a "Privatdozent" for 30 years. He was finally made professor in 1906 at the newly opened private "Handelshochschule" in Berlin (Gillessen 2000: 20; Albertin 2007: 3).

The same year Preuß published the first volume of his *Die Entwicklung des deutschen Städtewesens* and despite its historical nature, it provides a rather clear picture of his political and legal beliefs. He regarded the city as being something between the medieval age and modernity (Preuss 1906: 78–87). He also suggested that it contained the seeds of revolution (Preuss 1906: 106–108). This happened especially just after the French Revolution when the French ideals were imported into Germany. Preuß emphasized the role that Karl von Stein had in developing these ideals (Preuss 1906: 198–211). Preuß concluded the book by suggesting that in the years after the turn of the century there might be a reform of urban government (Preuss 1906: 377–378). What type of reform he had in mind cannot be really known because he never wrote a second volume.

There is a shared conviction that Karl von Stein was the political figure that Preuß held in the highest regard and considered as a model to follow. There is also a general agreement that the biggest influence on Preuß's legal thinking came from Otto von Gierke and his theory of "Genossenschaft" (Schmoller 1922: 24; Jellinek 1930b: 128; Heuss 2006: 5; Groh 2010: 28, 35). However, as Gillessen pointed out, Preuß did not always agree with him and he was rarely hesitant in pointing out where his master was wrong. In particular, Preuß strenuously objected to von Gierke's use of the concept of sovereignty.

While Preuß acknowledged that this concept had a long and rich history going back to Jean Bodin, he regarded it as an unfortunate relic of the monarch's claim to absolute authority (Gillessen 2000: 23–24; see Gerhardt 2012: 3).

Preuß's target was any form of government that was authoritarian, and he was against it whether it was monarchial or socialist. He was convinced that people needed and wanted freedom and that that could come about only in a democratic type of government (see Heuss 2006: 13). He believed in reform and that is why he regarded Freiherr von Stein as a hero—not only did Stein introduce much needed reforms in Prussia, but he was also the "greatest counter-player" to Napoleon (Heuss 2006: 14; Gillessen 2000: 36; Lammert 2015: VII; see also Preuß's own praise of Stein in "Stein-Hardenbergsche Neuorientierung" 1917 (Preuss 2006: 109, 119–121, 124)). Stein was also the opposite of Bismarck—Stein believed in freedom; Bismarck insisted on order (Albertin 2007: 3, 5, 8). Bismarck was a member of the Junker class and as such was a reactionary; he represented militarism, nationalism, and even anti-Semitism (Albertin 2007: 19–21, 24). Lothar Albertin ended his lengthy "Einleitung" ("Introduction") to the first volume of Hugo Preuß's collected writings by describing Preuß as the "pioneer of our democratic constitutional state" ("Pionier unseres demokratischen Verfassungsstaats"), thereby implying that Preuß was Bismarck's opposite (Albertin 2007: 65).

On November 14, 1918, Hugo Preuß published an article in the *Berliner Tagesblatt* that Michael Dreyer suggested belongs to the "classical documents of democracy in Germany" (Dreyer 2018: 334). Preuß's article had the title "Volksstaat oder verkehrter Obrigkeitsstaat?" and it generated considerable controversy (Gillessen 2000: 103). This title is somewhat resistant to translation for at least three reasons. First, part of the problem is that the German concept of "Volk" encompasses far more than the English term "people." A second problem is the term "Obrigkeitsstaat" and again that is a rather familiar concept in German history and one that "authoritarian state" only approximates. A third difficulty is Preuß's use of the term "verkehrter." Perhaps the closest translation to the use that Preuß had in mind might be "topsy-turvy" or "inverted." He noted that some people had apprehensions about the revolutionary movement and had a longing for the old authoritarian system; however, there was no going back and if there were, it would be to a system that had been turned upside down (Preuss 2006: 365, 2008: 73). The old system had failed and Germany now stood at the crossroads. It could choose another form of servitude under the "brutal forms of Russian fanaticism" ("brutaler Formen des russischen Fanatsimus") or it could choose to develop a democracy along the lines of the American system. "One must choose" ("Man muß Wählen"). It is either class warfare or a unified people: the question is "democracy or Bolshevism" ("Demokratie oder Bolschewismus") (Preuss 2006: 367–368, 2008: 74–75). Dreyer also indicated that this was an old theme of Preuß, but that the audience to whom it was addressed had changed overnight (Dreyer 2018: 335). Instead of being aimed at other intellectuals, it was now aimed at the German people. It was, as Dreyer notes, a remarkable success, and no one was more surprised that Preuß himself. It was regarded by the readers as a powerful counterpoint to the appeals by the Communists. But it was certainly noticed by Ebert because on the following day he named Preuß as interior secretary. Ebert had also considered Max Weber but had chosen Preuß (Dreyer 2018: 336). There are a number of possible reasons why Ebert selected Preuß over Weber: these include the fact that Preuß was a more committed democrat and was more ready to compromise than Weber (Dreyer 2018: 338; see Groh 2010: 41). There is also the fact that Preuß had been serving as an elected member of Berlin's government since 1895 (Dreyer 2018: 260–261, 339). Regardless of the reason or reasons, Ebert placed his trust in Preuß. Ebert was convinced that Preuß was not only the right person to help democracy succeed in Germany but to provide the necessary guidance to do so. One of the most difficult and most important tasks that Ebert immediately set for Preuß was to begin work on a draft for a new and far more inclusive constitution (Lehnert und Müller 2015: XI–XII).

Preuß was ready to write a draft but he wanted input from people whom he respected. He suggested to Ebert that he arrange a conference in which some of the leading democratic-minded thinkers could discuss the most important issues regarding the founding of a new Reich. The participants included Max Weber, Ludo Moritz Hartmann, and Alfred Verdross (Gillessen 2000: 106). The conference took place in Berlin between the 9th and the 12th of December 1918. One of the primary questions concerned the issue of monarchy or republic, but that was easily answered in favor of the latter. A more vexing question was whether this republic should be centralized or more of a federation (Gillessen 2000: 106–108). The final decision was for a federal state—a "Bundestaat" (Gillessen 2000: 115). The new constitution was intended to reflect this. How Preuß managed to do that will be discussed in the second part of this chapter.

Although Preuß is regarded as the father of the Weimarer Reichsverfassung, by the time it had been accepted he had resigned his official position. Michael Dreyer indicated Preuß's strong argument against the Versailles Treaty—the conditions were too harsh and Germany would be unable to function, much less prosper, under such penalizing conditions.[7] As a political leader who took his office seriously and believed in responsibility, Preuß believed he had no genuine alternative than to leave the government rather than be party to signing a document that he contended would seriously harm Germany for years into the future.

7 Dreyer 2018: 388–395. Winkler provided one of the briefest but most powerful accounts of the massive demands that the Versailles Treaty imposed upon Germany. Germany not only lost much of its territory in the East and the West, but also it was prohibited from joining with Austria to form a composite country. Finally, Germany's armed forces were to be massively reduced with no regard given to what the now unemployed soldiers and sailors were supposed to do. One can argue whether the Allies were entitled to impose such conditions; one cannot argue that those conditions caused massive problems for Germany. Winkler suggested that the notion that Germany alone was responsible for the war was like a "twin sister" ("Zwillingsschwester") to the "stab in the back legend" ("Dolchstoßlegende") with similar negative effects on the Weimar Republic. Winkler 1998: 89–98.

It was during the months between the end of 1918 and the summer of 1919 that Preuß wrote the five drafts of the Weimarer Reichsverfassung. He delivered the first one on January 3, 1919, the second on January 20, and the third on February 17. The fourth followed four days later while the fifth was not delivered until June 18. Much of the month of July was devoted to its discussion by members of the National Assembly. The final draft was submitted for approval on August 11, 1919. The various drafts will be discussed in the second part, but there are a few comments that will be made here.

Michael Dreyer pointed out that Preuß was not the only person writing drafts for a new constitution. There were numerous others who were engaged in this effort, but as Dreyer indicated, those drew little interest (Dreyer 2018: 347). One of the central problems for Germany's future was the long-standing problem regarding Prussia. Prussia was not only the largest "Land," its prestige was greater than the others and its power was significantly greater than any other. More importantly for Preuß, Prussia represented the feudal past and it glorified the military. All of these factors were obstacles for a new, decentralized democracy (Gillessen 2000: 121–122; Dreyer 2018: 352). Yet as the final draft indicates, the new Republic was primarily a centralized government (Giese 1925: 18). It may have been somewhat of a compromise, but it was clearly Preuß's achievement of a lifetime.

When Preuß resigned in 1920, he was 60 years old and too young to retire. More importantly, he had no interest in receding from public light. While he returned to teaching in Berlin, he continued to publish. The fifth volume of his *Gesammelte Schriften* has a half dozen writings from 1920 until his death in 1925 while the fourth volume has some 70 articles, essays, and monographs from the same period (Preuss 2012, 2008). Many of these are beyond the scope of this book, but there are a number that are crucial for understanding Preuß's view of what was happening in Weimar and how he thought his constitutional work should be considered. These essays will be examined in later chapters. Suffice it to say, Hugo Preuß may have lost his official capacity to involve himself in Weimar's history, but he still had his powers of observation and his political skills of persuasion.

Hugo Preuß died on October 9, 1925, just a few weeks before his sixty-fifth birthday. When he died he was slightly older than some of his fellow liberals such as Max Weber, Walther Rathenau, and Fredrich Ebert at their deaths. One wonders what course Weimar might have taken if these men had not died during the early years of the Weimar Republic. It is especially true regarding Ebert—the first president of the Republic and Preuß—the "Vater" of the Weimar Constitution.

Part Two

The Weimarer Reichsverfassung

The story of the writing of the Weimarer Reichsverfassung is complicated and lengthy. It was complicated because it was revolutionary. Peter C. Caldwell has recently argued, "The constitution was the product of revolution," but he also suggested that the constitution itself was revolutionary. It rejected the old regime's insistence on the necessity of a monarchy, the importance of the military, and the unequal rights to vote (Caldwell 2022: 120–121). Preuß himself insisted that his constitution was a product of the November Revolution (Preuss 2008: 308, 2015: 2). He needed to win over as many people as possible, not just those like him who were committed to democratic principles. The process was also lengthy: the time from when Preuß submitted his first draft on January 3, 1919, until its acceptance on August 11, 1919, was slightly more than seven months. In order to convince people, Preuß needed to adjust his drafts to take into account the national assembly members' opinions. But as a historian, he also recognized that he could claim that his draft was built upon other drafts—he had in mind the "Paulskirche" draft from 1848–1849. This would give his work more legitimacy. Preuß was not the only person wanting to remind people of the historical connections and not just with the revolutionary movement of 1848. In the first part to the first volume of the history of the national assembly during 1919 and 1920, Eduard Heilfron provided a 120-page history of the constitutional national assemblies, beginning with France in 1789 to the German national assembly of 1848 and then to the Paris assembly of 1871 and then to the German assemblies in 1866 and 1871 (Heilfron n.d. 1: 3–120). Heilfron emphasized the importance of freedom in the Frankfurt Proclamation of April 28, 1848 (Heilfron n.d. 1: 18–19). However, he also noted that the assembly which met during the spring through fall was anything but quiet and peaceful (Heilfron n.d. 1: 21–26). The constitution that was proposed also emphasized force—see in particular §§ 10–19, 21, 24, 32, 41–47. In particular, § 54 dealt specifically with "inner security and order" ("inneren Sicherheit und Ordnung") (Heilfron n.d. 1: 27–32). The proposed constitution of 1848 provided a template for Weimar's "public security and order" ("öffentliche Sicherheit und Ordnung"). This phrase would become both famous and infamous; even today the phrase is often used in certain parts of Germany.

Preuß delivered the first draft for consideration on January 3, 1919. It was labeled as a draft of the general parts of the future Reichsverfassung, thus indicating that Preuß recognized that this draft was only a draft and that there would likely be a number of revisions. This first draft had three main sections: first, on the Reich and the German free states ("Das Reich und die deutschen Freistaaten"), second, on the Reich, and third, on the president and the Reich government ("Der Reichspräsident und die Reichsregierung"). The first draft was relatively brief and consisted of a total of 68 paragraphs. The majority were found in the first two parts (I. Abschnitt §§ 1–23 and II. Abschnitt §§ 24–52), while the third part contained only fifteen (§§ 53–68). The first two parts contained general comments, such as the importance of self-determination (§ 1), but they also contained numerous specific points, such as on customs and tolls as well as on boats (§ 3; § 5). Preuß's largest problem was to balance the power of the Reich with that of the individual states. That is why six of the paragraphs are devoted to the power and rights of the "Freistaaten" (§§ 11–17). But it is also clear that Preuß insisted on the superiority of the Reich: "§ 5. Reich laws take precedence over state law" ("§ 5. Reichsrecht bricht Landesrecht") (Preuss 2015: 533–540).

Preuß rewrote his effort and submitted the second draft on January 20. While there were similarities between the first and second draft, notably the title to the first section, there were notable differences. The second draft now had four parts: Part Two on the Reichstag became Part Three and the second draft's Part Two was devoted to "The Basic Rights of the German People" ("Die Grundrechte des deutschen Volkes"). There were twelve paragraphs in this new section, and they guaranteed important rights for all German citizens: § 18 equal rights before the law; §19 religious freedom of belief; § 20 right to education; § 21 freedom of expression; and § 22 freedom of association. There were also guarantees for housing, property, and post: authorities needed justification to search any of these (§§ 23–27; Preuss 2015: 543). The four parts now contained 73 paragraphs (Preuss 2015: 541–547). This draft was again composed of general rights and specific issues, but there were more than just the changes in numbers of parts and the increase in paragraphs. The number of paragraphs devoted to the states had decreased but the number of specific freedoms guaranteed to each citizen of Germany reflected a remarkable increase. If the first draft seemed to try to walk a fine line between the central government and the states, Preuß's second draft came down solidly on the side of the Reich. But that should not be taken to mean that he had given up his opposition to central authority; his enumeration of individual rights demonstrated his championing of the individual. But both the first and second drafts make it clear that Germans were not Robinson Crusoe individualists; rather, they belonged to the German "Volk."[8]

On January 21, 1919, the national assembly determined that Berlin was not the proper location to continue its work. There were many reasons to change the location: Prussian history, the threats from the streets, and the distrust by members from other states. Eisenach, Erfurt, and Weimar were proposed; Ebert chose Weimar (Apelt 1946: 53). It was at Weimar that the third draft was submitted in early February. Between January 20, when Preuß delivered the second draft, and February 10, when he submitted his reworked third draft, several things had happened. Perhaps the most important, and more likely the most relevant, was the meetings of the National Assembly. The background and the proceedings were gathered into the seven volumes that Eduard Heilfron produced. They are fascinating documents that contain much more than reports of dry political meetings. Heilfron provided detail histories of the political parties; he also reproduced pamphlets that the various parties produced from 1918 through 1920. The right-wing German National People's Party (Deutsch National Volkspartie) emphasized the impending disaster if Germans did not vote for it. One expressed this danger clearly: "Who will

8 Somewhat surprisingly, the second draft is included as an appendix to the second volume of Heilfron's history of the National Assembly (Heilfron n.d.b II: 513–521).

save us from demise? ("Wer rettet uns vor dem Untergang?") (Heilfron n.d. I: 150). The Christian Peoples Party (Christlichen Volkspartie, or Centrum [Zentrum]) warned against class conflict and anarchy and counseled fathers and mothers to vote for this party in order to safeguard the well-being of the children (Heilfron n.d. I: 153–155). The Social Democratic Party Germany (Sozialdemokratischen Partei Deutschland) argued much the same: one sign showed a troubled youngster insisting "Mother! Think about me!" ("Mutter! Denk an Mich!"). But the SPD also appealed to women: "Women! Same Rights—Same Duties: Vote Social Democratic!" ("Frauen! Gleiche Rechte—Gleiche Pflichten. Wählt Sozialdemokratisch!" (Heilfron n.d. I: between 156 and 157). Heilfron revealed not only the parties' preferences; he also provided much of the context for the speeches and the votes that occurred in the meetings of the National Assembly.

The first session of the Weimarer Nationalversammlung was held on February 6, 1919, and was opened by Friedrich Ebert. He began by repeating some of the ideas that he had said and written during November and December, that the revolution had ended the old and the new was going to be different. The monarchy was gone and the war was lost but the revolution was responsible for the former but not for the latter. He proclaimed that the new Germany would be for justice, equality, and a lasting peace. It would be one nation made up of different people with various dialects but it will embody a new spirit. It would no longer be devoted to imperialism but now to idealism; from a "Weltmacht" to the Weimar of great philosophers and poets. Ebert reminded his audience that the Nationalversammlung was facing a fateful decision and he implored them to embrace the notion of freedom and to follow the fundamental principle of "all for the people and all through the people!" ("alles für das Volk und alles durch das Volk!") (Heilfron n.d. I: 3–11).

The third session of the National Assembly took place two days later, and on this occasion Preuß played a critical role. He emphasized that the development of the constitution was a task for all of the members of the National Assembly and he stressed the historical connections to the "National Assembly of the German people in the Paul's church in Frankfurt" ("Nationalversammlung des deutschen Volkes in der Paulskirche zu Frankfurt"). He insisted that they would succeed where the members of the 1848 assembly had failed because of the success of the revolution and the embracement of the concept of the "sovereignty of the people" ("Souveränität des Volkes"). He concluded with the acknowledgement that the parties have their own wishes, but he reminded the members that what is most important is the "love of the entire fatherland" ("Liebe zum gesamten Vaterland") and he ended with "Deutschland über Alles" (Heilfron n.d. 1: 27–28, 31, 35).[9] It was at this session of February 8

9 It is worth repeating that while there was a major break between the Second and the Third Reich and that there is no comparison between the mostly peaceful Weimar period and the destruction that was prompted by the Nazis, there are phrases that are associated with the later period but have their origins in the earlier ones. "Deutschland über Alles" is one.

that Preuß submitted his notice regarding the drafting of the constitution. Most of the ten numbered paragraphs focused on the responsibilities of the Reichspräsident: §§ 6, 7, 8, 9 (Heilfron n.d. 1: 26–27).

The fourth session occurred on Monday, February 10, and the account revealed that it was a rather contentious session with a number of members insisting on changes in the draft of the constitution. Preuß felt compelled to intervene and he warned of "bad consequences" ("schlimmen Folgen") in the attempt to avoid using foreign terms. The quarrel was over the phrase "absolute majority" when what is "meant is that in any case at least one vote above the half, thus absolute majority." ("Gemeint ist jedenfalls mindestens eine Stimme über die Hälfte, also absolute Mehrheit.") (Heilfron n.d. 1: 69). The discussion finally ended and the document was accepted with the most notable change being the addition of § 10 regarding the empowerment of the previous nine paragraphs (Heilfron n.d. 1: 82–84; Preuss 2015: 547–548). In contrast to the lively discussion of the fourth session, the fifth was made up of two matters: congratulatory messages and the election of Friedrich Ebert as Reichspräsident. Of the many points that Ebert made, three stand out: he admitted to being a "son of the working class" ("Sohn des Arbeiterstandes") and a social democrat; that "freedom and law are twin sisters" ("Freiheit und Recht sind Zwillingsschwestern"), and "freedom [is] not the freedom to beg but rather cultural freedom" ("Freiheit nicht Bettlerfreiheit sondern Kulturfreiheit") (Heilfron n.d. 1: 85–89, 93–94).

Regarding the ninth session which took place on February 17, there seems to be some discrepancy. According to the editor of volume three of Preuß's *Gesammelte Schriften* as well as Preuß's recent biographer, the third draft was submitted and read during that session. However, there is no mention of this third draft for February 17, 18, 19, or 20 in Heilfron's chronical. Whatever the reason for the omission, Preuß's third draft was significantly different and larger than the second draft. The third draft had seven parts: I. was now the Reich and its member state; II. Remained the Grundrechte; III. The Reichstags; IV. The Reichspräsident and the government; but V. was finance; VI. was post, telegraph, and transportation; and VII. was on law. Besides these many changes, the draft had expanded to 109 paragraphs (Preuss 2015: 549–560).

Preuß submitted a reworked draft number four on February 21, and it is documented in Band 3 of the *Gesammelte Schriften* as well as in Dreyer's table (Preuss 2015: 561–573; Dreyer 2018: 349). Given that Preuß had only three days to alter the draft, it is mostly unchanged. The major exception is the addition of an eighth part containing four paragraphs. Two of these were in response to matters from the 1871 Constitution, one was from 1918, and final one was devoted to insurance administration (Preuss 2015: 561–573).[10]

10 The fourth draft is given in the second volume of Heilfron's history. Reference to it is given in a footnote to the fourteenth session on Monday, February 24 (Heilfron n.d.b 2: 522–541).

Almost three months passed before Preuß submitted draft number five. It was on June 18, but according to Heilfron's account, there was no session between May 12 and June 22 (Heilfron n.d. 3: 406–407). For much of the intervening sessions, the discussions centered on the treaty for peace, the economic problems, and other domestic issues. But on July 2, during the 44th session, attention was turned to the latest draft of the constitution and the focus was on the first part of the Reichsverfassung. In particular, great attention was directed to Artikels 1 and 3.[11] Artikel 1 in this draft read, "The Deutsch Reich is a republic. The power of the state stems from the people" ("Das Deutsche Reich ist eine Republik. Die Staatsgewalt geht vom Volke aus") (Preuss 2015: 574). There was considerable debate about particular words—what do "republic" and "unified state" mean? Finally, Preuß felt it again necessary to interject. He was reacting to Dr. Oskar Cohn of the Independent Social Democratic Party Germany (Unabhängige Sozialistischen Partie Deutschland) who argued that there cannot be any talk about "constitutional change" between the old constitution and the new one because there was the historical revolutionary break. Preuß countered that he had not suggested such a continuity between the two; in fact, he reminded the members that the old regime was referred to as the "Deutsche Reich," but the new "Deutsche Reich" is also the "Deutsche Republik." The second point that Preuß made showed that Cohn was misusing the term "Einheitstaat." Cohn seemed to want to wait until sometime in the future when most everyone could agree on what it meant. Preuß responded by noting that the majority of the members wanted a constitution now, not in the future. That meant that the constitution needed to be revised so as to be a document that could have legal force (Heilfron n.d. III: 540, 550–551, 556–559). It was towards the end of the 44th session that Dr. Eduard David, Preuß's successor as interior minister, spoke about the democratic basis of the new republic, and that was enshrined in the draft of the constitution (Heilfron n.d. III: 581–582, 585). In contrast, the discussion over the second part of the draft was relatively brief and without much of the rancor that plagued the debate over the first part (Heilfron n.d. III: 633–640).

The National Assembly devoted most of the next 26 sessions to the fifth and then sixth draft of the constitution, thus almost all of July was devoted to this debate. Many of these sessions were focused on the second main half of the draft, and most all of those paragraphs lay outside of the scope of this book. However, there are a number of articles from the first main half that are pertinent to this study. Articles 1 and 3 have already been commented on but

11 Artikel 3 determined the colors of the flag and that stirred considerable debate—the so-called Flaggenstreit (Boldt 1987: 59). See, for example, Apelt's account (Apelt 1946: 75). Winkler clarified that the more liberal parties wanted the colors to be black-red-gold in honor of the 1848 attempt at liberalism, while the more conservative parties wanted to carry over the Bismarck colors of black-white-red (Winkler 1998: 103–104). Despite its interest, this debate is not relevant here, but it will surface briefly in the next chapter.

Article 47 is important because it gives the Reichspräsident the control over the entire military force of the Reich: "The Reichspräsident has the supreme command over the entire military of the Reich" ("Der Reichspräsident hat den Oberbefehl über die gesamte Wehrmacht des Reichs") (Preuss 2015: 579, 598). This article justifies the use of force in Artikel 48; how and why Artikel 48 was invoked was determined by the Reichspräsident: it was used primarily by Ebert to restore order; it was employed largely by Hindenburg to further political ends. This is a strong claim to make but will be justified in the later chapters.

The Weimarer Reichsverfassung was adopted on July 31 and then put into effect on August 11, 1919. This is the date that the contemporary commentators tended to use.

The Controversial Art. 48 of the Weimarer Reichsverfassung

Article 48 of the Weimarer Reichsverfassung was not entirely new. As Hugo Preuß had noted in his 1917 proposal, its antecedent was found in Art. 68 of the Bismarck constitution.[12] There it stated, "The Kaiser can declare a state of war if the public security is threatened in a part of the state" ("Der Kaiser kann, wenn die öffentiche Sicherheit in dem Bundesgebiete bedroht ist, in jeden Teil desselben in Kriegszustand erklären"). Preuß offered an alternative that read:

> In the case of a war or an uprising against the law of the Reich of the state or part of it can be a state of war be declared. The law determines the move away from the normal state of law in particular: however, the extraordinary measures may be withdrawn by the highest rung of the responsible Reich's rulers. [In the case that] the Reichstag is not gathered and the danger is such, the Kaiser can delegate to and under the responsibility of the Reichskanzler the necessary determinations can be permitted temporarily until the assembly of the Reichstag can be immediately called.[13]

However, Preuß did not propose what he had written in 1917 but something quite different.

12 Hans Boldt argued that the antecedents of Art. 48 were found in Art. 19 of the 1871 constitution and its origins could be found in a constitutional order from 1820 (Boldt 1993: 290).

13 "Im Falle eines Krieges oder Aufruhrs kann durch *Reichsgesetz* das Reichsgebiet oder Teile davon in Kriegszustand erklärt werden. Das Gestz bestimmt die Abweichungen von dem ordentichen Rechtszustand im einzelnen: jedoch darf durch keine Bestimmung die oberste Leitung der außerordentlichen Maßnahmen der Reichstage verantwortlichen Reichsregierung entzogen werden. Ist der Reichstag nicht versammelt und ist Gefahr im Verzuge, so kann der Kaiser auf Antrag und unter Verantwortlichkeit des Reichskanzlers die nötigen Bestimmungen vorläufig erlassen bis zum Zusammentritt des Reichstages, der sofort zu berufen ist" (Preuss 2006: 322–323).

The first draft (Jan. 3, 1919) of the constitution did not specifically contain the Artikel 48 of the later versions; rather, that Art. 48 was devoted to voting in parliament (Preuss 2015: 538). The antecedents to the contentious Art. 48 were found in Art. 57 and Art. 58 and neither was close to what the final Art. 48 said.

§ 57. "Wenn deutschen Freistaaten die ihnen nach der Reichsverfassung oder den Reichsgesetzen obliegenden Pflichten nicht erfüllen, kann sie der Reichspräsident dazu mit Hilfe der bewaffneten Macht anhalten" (Preuss 2015: 540).

§ 57. If the German free states do not fulfill the duties required by the Reich constitution or the Reich laws, then the Reich president can stop it with the help of weaponized power.

§ 58. Der Reichspräsident kann, wenn in einem deutschen Freistaat die öffentliche Sicherheit und Ordnung in einem erheblichen Umfang gestört oder gefährdet wird, mit Hilfe der bewaffneten Macht einschreiten und zur Wiederstellen der öffentliche Sicherheit und Ordnung erforderlichen Anordungen treffen. Er ist verpflichtet, hierzu unverzüglich die Genehmigung des Reichstags einzuholen und seine Anordungen aufzuheben, wenn der Reichstag die Genehmigung versagt (Preuss 2015: 540).

§ 58. The Reichspräsident can, if in a German free state, the public security and order is severely disturbed or threatened, with the help of weaponized power intervene and restore public security and order. He is unreservedly bound to request the permission of the Reichstag and is required to withdraw his order if the Reichstag denies his request.

These two paragraphs were carried over into the second draft (Jan. 20, 1919). They were changed for the third draft (Feb. 17, 1919) both in their numbers and in their contents. Both new versions left out any mention of "Freistaaten" and both were shortened. Both lost the paragraph sign § and, as with the others, were now preceded by the term Artikel. § 57 became Artikel 65 and § 58 became Artikel 66. There are, however, certain factors that remained unchanged. There are crucial phrases that are retained in the third draft. These include the function of the Reichspräsident, the use of weaponized force, and the critical phrase "public security and order" ("öffentliche Sicherheit und Ordnung"). Here are the two articles:

Artikel 66. Wenn deutsche Gliedstaaten, die ihnen nach der Reichsverfassung oder Reichsgestzen obliegenden Pflichten nicht erfüllen, kann sie der Reichspräsident dazu mit Hilfe der bewaffenten Macht anhalten.

Artikel 66. If a member state has not fulfilled its obligated duties under the Reichs Constitution or Reich laws, then the Reichspräsident can stop it with the help of weaponized power.

Artikel 67. Der Reichspräsident kann, wenn in einem deutschen Gliedstaat die öffentliche Sicherheit und Ordnung in einem erheblichen Umfang gestört oder gefährdet wird, mit Hilfe der bewaffneten Macht einschrieten und die Wiederstellung der öffentiche Sicherheit und Ordnung erforderlichen Anordungen zu treffen. Zu diesem Zweck darf er vorübergehend die in Artikeln 32, 33, 35 bis 38 festgesetzen Grundrechte ganz oder sum Teil außer Kraft setzen. Er ist verpflichtet, zu diesen Anordnungen unverzüglich die Genehmigung des Reichstags einzuholen und seine Anordungen zu aufzuheben, wenn der Reichstag die Genehmigung versagt. Das Nähere bestimmt ein Reichgesetz.

Artikel 67. The Reichspräsident can, if in a member state the public security and order is severely disturbed or threatened, with the help of weaponized force intervene to restore public security and order. For this purpose, he may temporarily suspend either entirely or partially the basic rights found in the articles 32, 33, 35 through 38. He is bound to announce this to the Reichstag and to withdraw his order if the Reichstag denies its permission. Specifics will be provided by a Reich law.

There are several points that require elaboration. First, the contents of these two articles (66 and 67) were combined into Art. 48 with 66 becoming Abs. 1 and 67 becoming Abs. 2. Second, the last sentence of 67 became Abs. 5 of Art. 48. Third, while there were continuing debates about these ideas, the major debate about the need to include such an article had largely been decided in favor of including it.

There was the fifth draft of June 18 and is the following:

Artikel 48. Wenn ein Land die ihm nach der Reichsverfassung oder den Reichsgesetzen obliegen Pflichten nicht erfüllt, kann der Reichspräsident es dazu mit Hilfe der bewaffnete Macht anhalten (Preuss 2015: 579).

Artikel 48. If a land does not fulfill its duties in accordance with the Reich Constitution or a Reich law, then the Reichspräsident can stop it with the help of weaponized power.

The debate over Artikel 48 and Artikel 49 took place during the 47th session of the National Assembly. This was on Saturday, July 5, 1919. The discussion regarding Artikel 48 was not very lengthy but was somewhat heated. In between was a discussion of Artikel 41 (Heilfron n.d. IV: 78–79).

After the National Assembly president Constatin Fehrenbach (Zentrum) brought up Art. 48, he introduced two proposed changes. The first one was proposed by Lore Agnes (SPD), and she wanted to add the words "with the responsibility of the entire Reich ministry" ("unter Verantwortlichkeit des gesamten Reichsministeriums"). The second proposed change was put forth by Erhard Auer (SPD), and he suggested that a clause be included at the conclusion of Art. 48 spelling out that the Reichstag has the authority to reject the Reichspräsident's order. Both were intended to put restraints on the Reichspräsident's powers; Agnes's clause that insisted that his authority needed to be backed by the ministry and Auer's addition that demanded that his decree be rescinded if the Reichstag insisted upon it. Agnes's amendment was rejected but Auer's was incorporated in a different format.

There was some discussion; Simon Katzenstein (SPD) reminded the members that there was a similar phrase to what Auer was suggesting found in Art. 49 and that it might be appropriate to insert it into Art. 48. But he also reminded them that Prussia was no longer the most powerful part of Germany and that its army was now part of the German army. In closing, he suggested that it should be considered as an addition in order to further law and freedom. After Preuß had briefly clarified that this addition was not needed, Karl Rudolf Heinz (Deutsche Volkspartei) objected to it because it would limit the Reichspräsident's power and that was something that he did not want; in fact, it was something that "We do not want" ("Das wollen wir nichts"). William Koch (Deutsche Demokratie) spoke in favor of it because he did not want anyone, even the Reichspräsident, to have the power to dispense with any law. Oskar Cohn warned that in most cases, people with weapons are able to set aside the law (to which his fellow USPD members added "right!"), and he additionally warned that the ability of the Reichspräsident should be constrained—especially if the Reichspräsident turns out not to be trustworthy. Preuß responded rather dismissively of such an idea. Fehrenbach asked for a vote on Agnes's amendment but it failed.[14] He moved to the second amendment and that too failed. The National Assembly voted on accepting the proposed Art. 48 and it was accepted (Heilfron n.d. IV: 77–79).

After the brief discussion about Art. 41, the National Assembly took up Art. 49. The president Konstantin Fehrenbach announced that the National Assembly had already rejected the motion by Agnes to reject Art. 49. The first person to speak was Konrad Anton Beyerle (Zentrum), who cautioned that adopting Art. 49 might lead to a conflict between the national government and an individual state. He also took exception to the idea that the army could be used to restore order when that should be the duty of the police (Heilfron n.d. IV: 79–80).

Katzenstein again spoke briefly and made two brief points. First, he spoke in favor of the amendment that had not yet been discussed and he expressed concerns about how the Reichspräsident might delegate authority to the states during a time of unrest. Katzenstein was followed by Cohn, who spoke for a long time. He began by mentioning that the books that he had in front of him should not shock his fellow members. These were books containing previous German constitutions. Cohn indicated that the proposed Art. 49 had its antecedents in the proposed 1848 constitution, and it also was a directive on how to respond to disorder. Cohn also suggested the introduction of a law from June 4, 1851, which also addressed the need to restore public order. However, Cohn warned that the proposed Art. 49 went beyond both the proposed

14 Heilfron has "Auer" listed but it is clear it was the first suggestion—hence, Agnes's (Heilfron n.d. IV: 76–77).

constitution and the 1851 law because it gave the Reichspräsident almost carte blanche to do what he wanted for an arbitrarily determined time. More troubling was that the military could act in any way that it believed it needed to act, which would very likely threaten democracy. Cohn then attempted to appeal to the more conservative members by pointing out the tension between the proposed Art. 150 and the proposed Art. 49. He read the entirety of the proposed Art. 150, which was drafted to protect property from confiscation. However, Art. 49 would suspend Art. 150 and not only would allow authorities to search a person's home but also could allow them to take possession of it. In light of this, Cohn insisted that the proposed Art. 49 was a step backward compared to the previous constitution. However, he added that there were even graver dangers lurking in the proposed article; namely, the government would also have authority to read, censor, and confiscate letters and telegrams and would be permitted to listen in on telephone conversations. In essence, the government would be licensed to act totally arbitrarily, and Cohn warned that there would be no means to prevent these actions. He asked that the members consider this matter carefully and be fully willing to take responsibility for the consequences. Cohn ended by warning them that if they accepted this Art. 49, then they would be acting in a way that would be contrary to democracy (Heilfron n.d. IV: 80–81).

Preuß again responded to Cohn and asked rhetorically how Cohn would want to draft the constitution; after all, he had not been anywhere close to those cities such as Bremen and Munich that could be governed without a declaration of a state of emergency. More to the point, Preuß suggested that no one would be confiscating housing and no one would be censoring correspondence. But his final point was to emphasize that what he wanted was to make Germany such a place that "public security and order" ("öffentliche Sicherheit und Ordnung") would be secured without ever having the need to declare a state of emergency (Heilfron n.d. IV: 82).

The Graf Anton zu Dohna (Deutsche Volkspartie) found it understandable that Cohn was troubled by the proposed Art. 49 and especially how it would negatively impact the rights guaranteed in Art. 150. Zu Dohna suggested that they simply strike Art. 49 from applying to Art. 150 (Heilfron n.d. IV: 82). Ludwig Haas (Deutsche Demokratische Partie) did not comment on zu Dohna's suggestion but turned to Cohn's comments. Haas expressed his concern that Cohn was so eager to protect correspondence, telegrams, and telephone calls. Haas found those concerns to be somewhat peculiar since Cohn was so convinced that the constitutional clauses from the previous century were better—given that telephones had not yet been invented (Heilfron n.d. IV: 83).

Peter Holl (Sozialistische Partie Deutschlands) also spoke against Cohn. Holl commented on how enthusiastically Cohn spoke against imposing restrictions on mail and correspondence and Holl noted also that his city of Passau had been ruled by the Independent Socialist Party Germany for seven days and, during that week, they had no qualms in instituting such measures that Cohn as a member of the USPD now finds troubling (Heilfron n.d. IV: 83).

Vice President Conrad Hausmann (Deutsche Demokratische Partie) then announced that Katzenstein again had the floor and he also directed his comments to Cohn. Katzenstein wondered how the "holiness" of property could be regarded as being more important than civil order, so he saw no reason to strike out the reference to Art. 150 (Heilfron n.d. IV: 83–84). Clemons von Delbrück (Deutsche National Volkspartie) took the floor and expressed surprise that there was so much criticism of Art. 49. He pointed out that the Spartakus members were demonstrating and plundering and that the government would have had an instrument in which to deal with them—namely Art. 49. A state which is prohibited from intervening is one which has handcuffs ("Handschellen") on it. Any state that cannot maintain "public order" ("öffentliche Ordnung") is not really a state (Heilfron n.d. IV: 84).

Wolfgang Heine (Sozialistische Partie Deutschlands), who was minister of the interior, advised the assembly members to accept Beyerle's recommendation but to reject Katzenstein's proposal. He clarified that the "disturbance of public order" ("Störung der öffentlichen Ordnung") and the "public security" ("öffentlichen Sicherheit") belong together; therefore, Katzenstein's advice to eliminate "und Ordnung" is misplaced. In addition, if the suggestion to dismiss "und Ordnung" is approved, then every single rule will have to be checked to see whether it applies. Just as important is the issue about how Art. 49 will be enforced. Cohn's claim that it would allow soldiers with machine guns is rather farfetched and the likelihood of misuse is rather small. Heine concluded by appealing to the majority and to ignore these demands from the Independent Socialists (Heilfron n.d. IV: 84–86).

After brief clarifications by Cohn and zu Dohna, the discussion was closed. Haußmann moved to the process of voting. After a few housekeeping comments, he noted that the assembly voted against Agnes's motion to eliminate Art. 49. Graf zu Dohna's motion to eliminate the reference to Art. 150 also did not pass. A second motion by Agnes to replace the masculine reference to the constitution also failed. Katzenstein's motion to strike "und Ordner" after "Sicherheit" also failed. But the motion to add "or the Reichstages" did pass. Finally, Haußmann asked for a final vote on Art. 49 and, with the additions about combining it with Art. 48, it passed and was given its place in the final draft of the Weimarer Reichsverfassung (Heilfron n.d. IV: 86–87). When the National Assembly made its final decision on it on July 31, 1919, it was suggested that Artikel 48 and Artikel 49 be combined into one, and this proposal was accepted (Heilfron n.d. V: 369–370). Artikel 48 now consisted of five paragraphs (Absätze):

Artikel 48. Wenn ein Land die ihm nach der Reichsverfassung oder den Reichsgesetzen obliegen Pflichten nicht erfüllt, kann der Reichspräsident es dazu mit Hilfe der bewaffnete Macht anhalten.

Der Reichspräsident kann, wenn im Deutschen Reiche die öffentliche Sicherheit und Ordnung erheblich gestört oder gefährdet wird, die Wiederherstellung der öffentliche Sicherheit und Ordnung nötigen Maßnahmen treffen, erforderlichenfalls mit Hilfe der bewaffneten Macht einschreiten. Zu diesem Zwecke darf er vorübergehend die in den Artikeln 114, 115, 117, 118, 123, 124 und 153 festgesetzten Grundrechte ganz oder teil außer Kraft setzen.

Von allen gemäß Abs. 1 oder Abs. 2 dieses Artikels getroffenen Maßnahmen hat der Reichspräsident unverzüglich dem Reichstag Kenntnis zu geben. Die Maßnahmen sind auf Verlangen des Reichstags außer Kraft zu setzen.

Bei gefahr im Verzuge kann die Landesregierung für ihr Gebiet einstweilige Maßnahmen in der Abs. 2 bezeichneten Art treffen. Die Maßnahmen sind auf Verlangen des Reichspräsidenten oder Reichstags außer Kraft zu setzen.

Das Nähere bestimmt ein Reichsgetzes (Preuss 2015: 598–599; Heilfron n.d. V: 711–712).

Here is the translation:

Artikel 48. If a land does not fulfill its obligations in accordance with the Reich Constitution or a Reich law then the Reichspräsident can stop it with the help of weaponized power.

The Reichspräsident can, if in the German Reich the public security and order is substantially disrupted or endangered, take the necessary measures to restore it even with the help of weaponized power. For this purpose, he is allowed to temporarily suspend the specific basic rights in Articles 114, 115, 117, 118, 123, 124 and 153 fully or partially.

First and foremost, according to Abs. 1 or Abs. 2 of this article regarding the affected measures, the Reichspräsident must immediately notify the Reichstag. These measures can be suspended by the request from the Reichstag.

With the danger of its suspense, a Land government can take the necessary temporary measures as specified in Abs. 2 which are appropriate for its region. The measures can, upon the desire of the Reichspräsident or Reichstag, be suspended.

Specifics will be determined by a Reich law (Preuss 2015: 598–599; Heilfron n.d. V: 711–712).

There are again a number of brief comments on this final version of Artikel 48. First, paragraph 1 is identical to the previous draft. Second, paragraph 5 is carried over from the several previous drafts. Third, the "temporariness" of the measures is even more emphasized. Fourth, the "decisionism" of the Reichspräsident is also underscored. Fifth, notification of the Reichstag is also further demanded. Sixth, some of the numbers of paragraphs that the invocation of Artikel 48 sets aside have been changed. The first three remain the same: personal freedom can be restricted (§ 114); living quarters may be searched (§ 115); communications may be intercepted (§ 117). However, the final four have their numbers altered to reflect the overall change in articles: freedom of expression in any form is restricted (§ 118); carrying weapons is limited as well as the right to assemble (§ 123); the right to form any type of club, association, or society is restricted (§ 124); a person whose property is damaged need not be compensated (§ 153).

Most commentators have tended to focus on Paragraph 1 ("Reichsexekution/Reich execution") and Paragraph 2 ("Dikaturgewalt/dictatorial power") (Boldt 1987: 52, 57) because the first two provide the Reichspräsident with the authority to unilaterally determine whether a "Land" has failed to fulfill its duties and whether there is sufficient disruption and, in either case, order an intervention with weapons. Yet, the final three also need to be discussed and are in the following chapters.[15] In this manner, a more complete account of Art. 48 can be given and a fuller appreciation of its strengths and its weaknesses can be determined.

Conclusion

This chapter was intended as an overview of Article 48. The final months of the old Wilhelmine Regime were recounted as well as an indication of the revolutionary months of November and December of 1919. The main focus of the chapter was on this history of Art. 48; how it grew out of Preuß's ideas about the new constitution and the extent and the limitations of the Reichspräsident. This entailed a discussion of the development of the new constitution in general and then to the specific account of the changes to the relevant articles of the Weimar Constitution. This entailed a discussion of the first three drafts and how the articles concerning stability and order were changed from the numbering in the 60s to the numbers of the 40s. It then entailed a discussion of the various versions of Articles 48 and 49 and how they were altered in the fourth, fifth, and sixth versions of Preuß's drafts. The chapter concluded on a rather high note; the contents of Articles 48 and 49 were combined into Artikel 48. Preuß's optimism seemed to permeate much of the National Assembly and its members were hopeful that the Weimarer Reichsverfassung would provide a democratic and equalitarian template for Germany's future. The next five chapters will show that this hope was sometimes misplaced and that Art. 48 engendered a number of unintended effects.

References

Albertin, L. (2007) "Einleitung." In Preuss. 2007. 1–69.

Anschütz, G. (1933) *Die Verfassung des Deutschen Reichs. vom 11. August 1919*. Berlin: Verlag von Georg Stilke. 14. Auflage.

15 Anschütz's commentary is perhaps the best example because his was among the most scholarly and remains immensely important. His account of Art. 48 is 32 pages long: the bottom of page 267 through 271 is introductory; pages 271 to the bottom of 275 is on Paragraph 1; from the bottom of 275 until the top of 300 are all devoted to Paragraph 2. Paragraphs 3, 4, and 5 do not get any specific discussion (Anschütz 1933: 271–300). Although most commentators refer to Paragraph 2 as "Diktaturgewalt," Friedrich Giese referred to it in his commentary as "Ausnahmezustand" (Giese 1925: IX, 163–169).

Apelt, W. (1946) *Geschichte der Weimarer Verfasssung.* München: Biederstein Verlag.
Ay, K.-L. (1968) *Appelle einer Revolution. Das Ende der Monarchie. Das revolutionäre Interregnum. Das Rätezeit.* Mit einem Vorwort von Carl Amery. München: Süddeutscher Verlag.
Bernecker, W. (1992) "Die Revolution 1918/1919. Von der Monarchie zur Republik." In Stammen. 1992. 87–116.
Boldt, H. (1987) "Die Weimarer Reichsverfassung." In Bracher, Funke and Jacobsen. 1987. 44–62.
Boldt, H. (1993) "Der Artikel 48 der Weimarer Verfassung." In *Die Weimarer Republik.* Herausgegeber Michael Stürmer. Frankfurt am Main: Hain. 3. Auflage. 288–309.
Büttner, U. (2008) *Weimar. Die überfoderte Republik 1918–1933. Leistung und Versagen in Staat, Gesellschaft, Wirtschaft und Kultur.* Stuttgart: J.G. Cotta'sche Buchhandlung Nachfolger.
Caldwell, P.C. (2022) "The Weimar Constitution." In Rossol and Ziemann. 2022. 119–140.
Dillon, C. (2022) "The German Revolution of 1918/1919." In Rossol and Ziemann. 2022. 27–47.
Dreier, H. (2016) "Die deutsche Revolution 1918/19 als Festag der Nation? Von der (Un-) Möglichkeit eines republikanischen Feiertags in der Weimarer Republik." In Jestaedt und Paulson. 2016. 1–48.
Dreyer, M. (2018) *Hugo Preuß. Biografie eines Demokraten.* Stuttgart: Franz Steiner Verlag.
Ebert, F. (1926) *Friedrich Ebert. Schriften, Aufzeichnungen, Reden. Mit unveröffentlichten Erinnerungen aus dem Nachlaß.* Dresden: Carl Reissner Verlag. Zweiter Band.
Flad, W. (1929) *Verfassungs-Gerichtsbarkeit und Reichsexekution. Beiträge zur Lehre von den Steritigkeiten Zwischen Reich und Ländern und deren Entscheidung.* Heidelberg: Carl Winters Universitätsbuchhandlung.
Friedrich, M. (2000) "Nachwort." In Gillessen. 2000. 183–188.
Gerhardt, P. (2012) *Die Entstehung der Weimarer Reichsverfassung. Hugo Preuß als Wegbereiter einer modernen parlamentarischen Demokratie?* Norderstedt, Germany: GRIN Verlag.
Giese, F. (1925) *Die reichsverfassung vom 11. August 1919.* Berlin: Carl Heymanns Verlag. Sechste ergänzte und verbesserte Auflage.
Gillessen, G. (2000) *Hugo Preuß. Studien zur Ideen- und Verfassungsgeschichte der Weimarer Republik. Erstveröffentichung der Dissertation von 1955. Mit einem Nachwort von Manfred Friedrich.* Berlin: Duncker & Humblot.
Groh, K. (2010) *Demokratische Staatsrechtslehrer in der Weimarer Republik. Von der konstitutionallen Staatslehre zur Theorie des modernen demokratischen Verfassungsstaats.* Tübingen: Mohr Siebeck.
Gusy, C. (2018) *100 Jahre Weimarer Verfassung. Eine gute Verfassung in schlechter Zeit.* Tübingen: Mohr Siebeck.
Heilfron, E., Herausgeber (n.d.a) *Die Deutsche Nationalversammlung im Jahre 1919 in ihrer Arbeit für den Aufbau des neuen deutschen Volksstaates.* Berlin: Norddeustche Buchdruckerei und Verlagsanstalt. 1. Band.
Heilfron, E., Herausgeber (n.d.b) *Die Deutsche Nationalversammlung im Jahre 1919 in ihrer Arbeit für den Aufbau des neuen deutschen Volksstaates.* Berlin: Norddeustche Buchdruckerei und Verlagsanstalt. 2. Band.
Heilfron, E., Herausgeber (n.d.c) *Die Deutsche Nationalversammlung Jahre 1919/1920 in ihrer Arbeit für den Aufbau des neuen deutschen Volksstaates.* Berlin: Norddeustche Buchdruckerei und Verlagsanstalt. 3. Band.
Heilfron, E., Herausgeber (n.d.d) *Die Deutsche Nationalversammlung Jahre 1919/1920 in ihrer Arbeit für den Aufbau des neuen deutschen Volksstaates.* Berlin: Norddeustche Buchdruckerei und Verlagsanstalt. 4. Band.

Heilfron, E., Herausgeber (n.d.e) *Die Deutsche Nationalversammlung Jahre 1919/1920 in ihrer Arbeit für den Aufbau des neuen deutschen Volksstaates.* Berlin: Norddeustche Buchdruckerei und Verlagsanstalt. 5. Band.

Heuss, T. (2006) "Hugo Preuß." In Preuss. 2006. 1–24.

Jasper, G. (1992) "Improvisierte Demokratie? Die Entstehung der Weimarer Verfassung." In Stammen. 1992. Band 1. 117–145.

Jellinek, W. (1930a) "Die Nationalversammlung und ihr Werk." In Anschütz und Thoma. 1930. 119–127.

Jellinek, W. (1930b) "Inbesondere: Entstehung und Ausbau der Weimarer Reichsverfassung." In Anschütz und Thoma. 1930. 127–138.

Jestaedt, M. und Paulson, S.L., Herausgegebern (2016) *Horst Dreier. Staatsrecht in Demokratie und Diktatur. Studien zur Weimarer Republik und zum Nationalsozialismus.* Tübingen: Mohr Siebeck.

Koerner, P. (1968a) *Der Erste Weltkrieg 1914–1918. Band I. Vormarsch und Stellungskrieg.* München: Wilhelm Heyne Verlag.

Koerner, P. (1968b) *Der Erst Weltkrieg 1914–1918. Band II. Trommelfeuer und Massenangriffe.* München: Wilhelm Heyne Verlag.

Koerner, P. (1968c) *Der Erste Wektkrieg 1914–1918. Band III. Kriegswende und Kriegsende.* München: Wilhelm Heyne Verlag.

Kühne, J.-D. (2000) "Demokratisches Denken in der Weimarer Verfassungs-diskussion—Hugo Preuß und die Nationalversammlung." In Gusy. 2000. 115–133.

Kühne, T. (2015) "*Todesraum:* War, Peace, and the Experience of Mass Death, 1914–1945." In Smith. 2015. 527–547.

Lammert, N. (2015) "Von der Überwindung des deutschen 'Andersseins'. Zum Abschluss der Hugo-Preuß-Edition." In Preuss. 2015. VII–IX.

Lehnert, D. (1999) *Die Weimar Republik. Partienstaat und Massengesellschaft.* Stuttgart: Philipp Reclam. June.

Lehnert, D. und Müller, C. (2015) "Vorwort." In Preuss. 2015. XI–XII.

Meinecke, F. (1930) "Die Revolution. Ursachen und Tatsachen." In Anschütz und Thoma. 1930. 95–119.

Mommsen, H. (2001) *Aufstieg und Untergang der Republik von Weimar 1918–1933.* München: Propyläin Taschenbuch. 2. Augabe.

Mommsen, W.J. (n.d.) *Die Urkatastrophe Deutschlands. Der erste Weltkrieg 1914–1918.* Stuttgart: Klett-Cotta.

Neubarer, H. (1967) "München 1918/19." In *Die Münchner Räterrepublik. Zeugnisse und Kommentar.* Herausgegeber Dorst Tankred. Frankfurt am Main: Suhrkamp. 171–188.

Nipperdey, T. (1998) *Deutsche Geschichte 1866–1918. Band II. Machtstaat vor der Demokratie.* München: Verlag C.H. Beck.

Preuss, H. (1906) *Die Entwicklung des Deutschen Städtewesens. Erster Band. Entwicklungsgeschichtende Deutschen Städteverfassung.* Leipzig: Druck und Verlag von B.G. Teubner. (all that appeared).

Preuss, H. (2006)[1926] *Staat, Recht und Freiheit. Aus vierzig Jahren deutscher Politik und Geschichte. Mit einer Einleitung von Theodor Heuss.* Hildesheim, Zürich and New York: Georg Olms Verlag.

Preuss, H. (2008) *Gesammelte Schriften. Vierter Band. Politik und Verfassung in der Weimarer Republik.* Herausgegeben und eingeleitet von Detlef Lehnert. Tübingen: Mohr Siebeck.

Preuss, H. (2012) *Gesammelte Schriften. Fünfter Band. Kommunalwissenschaft und Konnunalpolitik.* Herausgegeben und eingeleitet von Detlef Lehnert, Christoph Müller und Dian Schefold. Tübingen: Mohr Siebeck.

Preuss, H. (2015) *Gesammelte Schriften. Dritter Band.* Das Verfassungswerk von Weimar. Herausgegeben und eingeleitet von Christoph Müller. Tübingen: Mohr Siebeck.

Rosenberg, A. (1973) *Entstehung der Weimarer Republik.* Herausgegeben und eingeleitet von Kurt Kersten. Frankfurt am Main: Europäische Verlagsanstalt. 15. unveränderte Auflage.

Rossol, N. and Ziemann, B., Editors (2022) *The Oxford Handbook of the Weimar Republic.* Oxford: Oxford University Press.

Scheidemann, P. (2018) "Ausrufung der Deutschen Republik." In Dreier und Waldhoff. 2018. 357.

Schmoller, G. (1922) *Walther Rathenau und Hugo Preuß. Die Staatsmänner des Neuen Deutschland.* München and Leipzig: Verlag von Duncker & Humblot.

Smith, H.W., Editor (2015) *The Oxford Handbook of Modern German History.* Oxford: Oxford University Press.

Stammen, T., Herausgeber (1992) *Die Weimarer Republik. Das Schwere Erbe. Band 1. 1918–1923.* München: Bayerische Landeszentrale für Bildungsarbeit. 2. Auflage.

Stolleis, M., Herausgeber (1995) *Juristen. Ein biographisches Lexikon. Von der Antike bis zum 20. Jahrhundert.* München: C.H. Beck'sche Verlagsbuchhandlung (Oscar Beck).

Weichlein, S. (2015) "Nation State, Conflict Resolution, and Culture War, 1850–1878." In Smith. 2015. 281–306.

Winkler, H.A. (1998) *Weimar 1918–1933. Die Geschichte der Ersten Deutschen Demokratie.* München: Verlag von C.H. Beck. Durchgesehene Auflage. 1998 15. Bis 20. Tausend der Gesamtauflage.

Ziemann, A. (2015) "Germany 1914–1918: Total War as a Catalyst of Change." In Smith. 2015. 378–399.

3 1920–1922

The Years of Political and Economic Turmoil

The years 1920 through 1922 can be described as years of political turmoil. One can suggest that the Kapp Putsch of March 1920 was the beginning and that the political effects from the increasingly out-of-control inflation in December 1922 point to the end of this period. However, both time frames are misleading because the political unrest from the Right was a continuation from the previous year and inflation would not begin to recede until 1924. As political and economic problems continued to multiply, these years saw an increasing debate regarding the notion of dictatorship. This debate was both political and legal, and two books that were published during this time considered both aspects. The one by Carl Schmitt was regarded at the time as being of importance and has been part of Schmitt's legal legacy ever since. In contrast, the one by Richard Grau did not attract much attention at the time, nor has it drawn much interest since then. However, Grau was one of the first legal scholars to focus on Art. 48 and he became one of the most important experts on the dictator paragraph (Absatz 2). Carl Schmitt and especially Richard Grau will continue to play crucial roles in this investigation into Art. 48 of the Weimarer Reichsverfassung. This chapter has five parts: the first provides a brief historical overview of the years 1920 to 1922. The second is a lengthy discussion of Schmitt's early writings on the dictator concept and of his "dictator" book. The third is a focus on Article 48 as explained by Gerhard Anschütz in the first edition of his commentary on the Weimarer Reichsverfassung. The fourth part is a detailed examination of Grau's 1922 book on the concept of the dictator. The fifth part is a brief summary and an indication of the themes for the next chapter.

1920–1922

If the German people had hoped that by agreeing to the conditions of the Treaty of Versailles and by adopting the Reichsverfassung it would lead to a period of "inner consolidation," they were disappointed (Winkler 1993: 109; Geyer 2022: 49). Instead, 1920 through 1922 (and beyond) was a time in which the very existence of the Weimar Republic was under attack (Kolb 2002: 37). There were a number of reasons for the discontent and even anger,

DOI: 10.4324/9781003312796-3

but the two most likely causes of this dissatisfaction were right-wing agitation and increasing inflation. While both would continue well into 1923 and later, they were both already problematic in the early part of 1920.

Karl Dietrich Erdmann reminds us that the political upheavals and conflicts did not arise in 1920 but were continuations of conflicts from the previous year (Erdmann 1982: 80–82). There is no doubt about this; the reason that they were not mentioned often in the previous chapter was that there was no constitution until August 1919. Therefore, there was little justification for discussing them. But Ebert was sworn in on August 21, 1919, and after that he was bound to follow the Weimarer Reichsverfassung (Dillon 2022: 42).

January 1920 was when the Versailles Treaty came into effect, and it provoked widespread dissatisfaction and anger. Those who were most steadfast against the Treaty were the conservatives. Although Protestants and Catholics were often at odds, the two center-right parties were united in their opposition to the Treaty. While the Catholic Center Party (Zentrum) would end up having a number of members who became influential, the Protestant German National People's Party (Deutschnationale Volkspartie or DNVP) was largely antigovernment (Baranowski 2022: 363–364). But it was not only the party members who were dissatisfied with the Versailles Treaty and with the government; many workers were also deeply disappointed in the government (Bernecker 1992: 233). There were two manifestations of some of this disappointment: one lasted only a few days while the other occurred over several months. But both stemmed from the belief that the Ebert government not only failed many former members of the German military but also was actively working to construct a Jewish state.

The first and shorter occurrence is often referred to as the Kapp Putsch but it involved not only Wolfgang Kapp but also Walther von Lüttwitz, so some scholars refer to it as the Kapp-Lüttwitz Putsch.[1] One of main and most onerous conditions of the Versailles Treaty was the demand that Germany reduce the number of its troops. Heinz Hürten has suggested that this demand meant that three quarters of the military would be eliminated. Not only would this cause a massive increase in unemployment but it would also be a blow to the military's prestige (Hürten 1987: 87–88). One of the most prominent generals who objected to this demand was Lüttwitz. On March 10, General von Lüttwitz demanded that Ebert reject the Treaty's demand that much of the army and navy be disbanded. When Ebert refused, the Kapp-Lüttwitz Putsch began on March 13 when Lüttwitz proclaimed Kapp as chancellor and at first it seemed like the Putschists had achieved their objectives. Ebert and others

1 Heinz Hürten provided a condensed but important account of the Kapp-Lüttwitz Putsch. Karl Dietrich Erdmann offered an equally important but much longer one. Heinrich August Winkler's account is also to be recommended, but he treated the Putsch as a small but critical part of the counter-revolution. An interesting but unreliable account is embedded in Klaus Gietinger (Hürten 1987; Erdmann 1982; Winkler 1998; Gietinger 2020). It is odd that there is no chapter devoted specifically in *The Oxford Handbook of the Weimar Republic*.

fled Berlin to Dresden and then to Stuttgart. Furthermore, the Putschists received backing not only from many in the military but also from governments in East Prussia (Büttner 2008: 138–139; Gietinger 2020: 108–111). However, the military itself was split between those wanting to restore the old order and those who were defending the new one. It was not just many in the military who sided with the government; the bureaucrats in Berlin refused to accept the Putsch (Hürten 1987: 88–89). Ebert invoked Art. 48 to restore "public security and order" (Hürten 1987: 90). After four days of evident failure, Kapp resigned and hours later so did Lüttwitz. Defeated, the Putschists left Berlin (Erdmann 1982: 136–137; Hürten 1987: 90; Bernecker 1992: 234). One might have suspected that this failed Putsch would have discredited the right-wing factions but, as Klaus Schabe argued, that period of discreditation was short-lived (Schabe 1987: 95–96).

The second situation occurred in the Ruhr region (Ruhrgebiet) and the beginnings can be traced to January 11, 1919. According to Klaus Gietinger, Ebert invoked Art. 48 to restore order in the areas of Dortmund, Münster, Minden, and Arnsberg (Gietinger 2020: 281). Two days later, the so-called security police (Sicherheitspolizei/SiPo) fired on the crowd that had been demonstrating against the government. Forty were killed and a hundred wounded and as a result Ebert invoked Art. 48 for most of Germany (Gietinger 2020: 281).

Jonathan Wright's article in *The Oxford Handbook of the Weimar Republic* is devoted to foreign policy but, as his subtitle indicates, Weimar was constrained by what the victors would accept. Wright pointed out that after the Kapp-Lüttwitz Putsch was put down, Ebert used the army to deal with the uprising in the Ruhr region. Because this was a demilitarized area, this was a violation of the Versailles Treaty and Ebert's actions prompted France to impose sanctions until the military withdrew. Wright's point is, "It was a perfect illustration of how limited the room for manoeuvre of the German government was" (Wright 2022: 246). This was true not just about force; it was also true about finance.

The year 1923 is often regarded as the beginning of inflation but that is not exactly accurate for two reasons. First, it was the period of hyperinflation, and second, the period between the beginning of 1919 and the end of 1922 was a period of inflation.[2] The causes of inflation and then hyperinflation have been debated for decades. Germany not only lost people and land after the war ended; it was saddled with debts and forced to pay reparations. Martin Geyer noted that even after protests cut the reparations in half,

2 The issue of inflation was already being discussed during the war. Much of that discussion focused on the replacement of gold by paper currency. Economists debated whether paper money had any worth and involved such scholars as Georg Friedrich Knapp, Robert Liefmann, Friedrich Bendixen, and others. Some critics contended that it lacked any real value, that is why some referred to the paper economy as a "Zettelwirtschaft." "Zettel" is a small note and not even a genuine piece of paper. See Bendixen 1917: 7–9, 31, 1918: 24–25.

Germany was still expected to pay 132 billion gold marks on May 1, 1921, with 2 billion annual interest and repayment charge (Büttner 2008: 170; Kolb 2002: 46–47). All of this contributed to the massive financial instability and ultimately to the increases in inflation. In a table, Berg-Schlosser gave the income index: it was given as 100 in 1913 but in 1919 it had dropped to 67.1. While it rose slightly in 1920 to 74.0, it only barely increased in 1921 to 79.3. It would rise again the following year before dropping back in 1923. It would finally rebound in 1924, and these figures are addressed in the next chapter (Berg-Schlosser 1992: 323, 325). In a second table, Berg-Schlosser gave the rate of inflation. Again, the numbers for 1922 and 1923 will be discussed in the following chapter. Using 1913 as the benchmark of 1.0, 1920 saw a rate of 15 for most of the year. It remained around 15 for the first half of 1921, but by September it had hit almost 25 and by November it had risen to 62.64 before dropping to 45.72 in December. The year 1922 was particularly bad, and mid-year is often described as the beginning of the hyperinflation. January and February saw the rate remain in the upper 40s, but the three months of March, April, and May saw it rise into the upper 60s. It went from 75.62 in June to 117.49 in July while it more than doubled in August to 270.6. During September it rose to almost 350 before reaching 757.73 in October. It then hit 1711.08 in November, and closed out the year at 1807.83 (Büttner 2008: 169). These are not numbers like those in 1923 and 1924, but they affected most Germans and contributed to their sense that Ebert's government was either incompetent or worse, intent on destroying Germany (Meyer 2022: 55, 66).

The point is that while 1923 and 1924 would be terrible for Germany, 1921 and 1922 had their share of problems, both politically and economically. A number of German jurists on the Right were concerned enough about the lack of stability and order that they wondered whether it was time for a dictatorship. Carl Schmitt was one of the leading jurists and he published *Die Diktatur* in 1921. It would be reprinted in 1928 with a lengthy and crucially important "Appendix" ("Anhang") and would be reprinted eight more times. For now, the focus is on the first edition.

Carl Schmitt's Dictator Writings 1916–1922

The book *Die Diktatur* was not Carl Schmitt's first work on dictatorship (Adair-Toteff 2020). During the First World War Schmitt published an article on dictatorship entitled "Diktatur und Belagerungszustand" ("Dictatorship and the State of Occupation") that was intended as a legal work, as indicated by the subtitle "Eine Staatsrechtliche Studie" ("A State Legal Study"). Schmitt's purpose in this essay was to differentiate the state of war ("Kriegszustand") from the state of occupation ("Belagerungszustand") from dictatorship ("Diktatur"). He pointed out that during the French Revolution, the notion of occupation was not regarded as a dictatorship but was the executive's means to protect the republican principle (Schmitt 1995: 7). Schmitt maintained that the state of occupation differs from a dictatorship because the former gives orders and is unconcerned with legislating. In addition, a military believes itself entitled to use force in order to put down any unrest (Schmitt 1995: 18–19). However, the main purpose of the military is to safeguard the state from external enemies and not to be involved in internal disputes (Schmitt 1995: 13). Regardless of whether they are a military state, a state of occupation, or a dictatorship, they all are "states of exception" ("Ausnahmezuständen").

Carl Schmitt returned to the notion of dictatorship in his work *Die Diktator*. But unlike his earlier work, Schmitt was not as concerned with the "state of exception" as he was with the concept of the dictator. His interest in Art. 48 of the Weimarer Reichsverfassung was also rather minimal and became a focus only in the final pages of this work. However, Art. 48 became a central focus in the "Anhang" that he included in the second edition of 1928, but since that "Anhang" was first published in 1924 it will be discussed in the chapter devoted to that year. For now, there is need only for some remarks on the 1921 edition of *Die Diktatur*.

Despite the title, the first edition of *Die Diktatur* did not provoke much controversy. In part it was because the author's name was confusing—before this book and after, most everything Carl Schmitt published was under the name Schmitt. But the first edition of *Die Diktatur* carried the name Carl Schmitt-Dorocit. Another and more important cause for the confusion was that it was not really clear what Schmitt's book was really about. The title seemed clear enough—the book was about dictatorship—but the subtitle served to confuse the issue because it was *From the Beginnings of the Modern Sovereignty Thoughts Until the Proletarian Class Conflict* (*Von den Anfängen des modernen Souveränitätsgedanken bis zum proletarischen Klassenkampf*). Then there is the preponderance of history in the book. Schmitt discussed Machiavelli, Bodin, Hobbes, and Locke. He discussed Montesquieu's theory of political balance, the French Revolution, and Rousseau's conception of the "volonté génerale." But there is also an examination of Cromwell and the English Revolution as well as Napoleon's later government. It is only after the discussion of the "Sovereign Dictatorship of the National Assembly From 1848" that Schmitt finally turns to Art. 48 of the German Constitution from 1919. Even here, Art. 48 is mentioned after Schmitt's comments about Locke's theory of the legal state and its claim to have authority over life and death. That did not seem to fit with the concept of exception that was found in Art. 48 (Schmitt 1921: 198). As Helmut Quaritsche argued a number of decades ago, Schmitt's interest in Art. 48 was minimal at the time that he was writing *Die Diktatur*. That is why Schmitt devoted only four pages to Art. 48.[3]

3 Quaritsche was certainly right about Schmitt's lack of interest in Art. 48; he may have been correct that Schmitt wrote most of *Die Diktatur* during and shortly after the war (Quaritsch 1996: 2).

Schmitt concludes *Die Diktatur* by pointing out that Art. 48 is not only the latest in the history of dictatorship measures, it is also one of the clearest justifications for the need for such dictatorial measures. He does not reproduce Art. 48 but he does mention its most important points. These include the need to restore "public security and order" ("öffentliche Sicherheit und Ordnung"), the permission to use "*all* necessary measures" ("*alle* erforderlichen Maßnahmen"), and that the article provides almost no limits on the Reichspräsident's power. There are two critical points to make here: the first is to note that Schmitt emphasized "all" ("*alle*") and the second is that he refers to the Reichspräsident's power as "sovereign" power (Schmitt 1921: 198). Later, he observes that Art. 48 allows the Reichspräsident unrestricted use of any and all powers as long as they are employed "to *this purpose*" ("zu *diesem Zwecke*"); that is, to the restoration of "public security and order." But Schmitt suggests that the suspension of basic rights is not unlimited and he complains that this should have been made explicit. He connects this with his observation that the law over life and death is implicit, yet the law over the lifting to freedom of press is explicit.[4] That is the extent of Schmitt's comments on Art. 48; in the final two pages Schmitt returns to his historical investigation of dictatorships throughout the previous two centuries. He ends by noting that in 1850 the Communists claimed that their actions were "just the same 'as in France 1793'" ("dieselbe 'wie in Frankreich 1793'") (Schmitt 1921: 202).

Anschütz's *Kommentar*

The name Gerhard Anschütz will continue to figure in this account. Here his role is as author of the most respected commentary on the Weimar Constitution. First published in 1921 it would go through another 13 editions. It would also grow from 290 pages to 677 in the 1929 edition and to 800 pages in the final edition of 1933. In the "Vorwort (Foreword)" to the first edition Anschütz insisted that he wanted to explain the new constitution, and in order to do that he minimized his reliance on secondary sources and refrained from entering into controversy with other legal scholars. That does not mean that Anschütz did not mention others; indeed, he paid close attention to the previous commentaries on the Weimarer Reichsverfassung that had been published prior to his. In particular, he recognized the importance of those by Friedrich Giese and by Fritz Poetzsch. Giese had published *Die Reichsverfassung vom 11. August 1919* in 1919 and by 1925 it had gone through six editions (Giese 1925). Poetzsch also published his *Handausgabe der Reichsverfassung vom 11. August 1919* in 1919 (Poetzsch 1919). But both Giese's commentary and Poetzsch's work did not meet the scholarly standard that Anschütz was already noted for. He had written an extensive commentary

4 "Das Recht über Leben und Tod wird implicite, das Recht zur Aufhebung der Preßfreiheit wird explicite erteilt" (Schmitt 1921: 200).

on Germany's earlier constitution and that was regarded as a masterpiece—as was his commentary on the Weimarer Reichsverfassung. His commentary is important for a number of additional reasons. Anschütz provided an introduction ("Einleitung") in which he gave a concise and objective account of how the Weimar Constitution grew out of the post-war chaos. Other commentators tended to view that history through their political inclinations and that colored their accounts. The 1921 edition of Anschütz's commentary also contained a 13-page subject index ("Sachregister"). His 1921 edition not only included the typical two-fold division into the structure and tasks of the Reich ("Aufbau und Aufgaben des Reichs") and the basic rights and basic duties of Germans ("Grundrechte und Grundpflichten der Deutschen"), but the two main sections were each subdivided into seven subsections that contained the articles pertaining to the different areas. Finally, and perhaps most importantly, Anschütz's commentary included careful explanations for each of the Weimarer Reichsverfassung's 180 articles. The only one of note for the purposes here is his commentary on Art. 48. The article itself and the explanation covers only two pages in the 1921 edition, which indicated that Art. 48 had not yet achieved its later notoriety. Anschütz's explanation is divided into a brief introductory paragraph and four sections. In the introductory paragraph he maintained that Art. 48 was devoted to two things: Absatz 1 is focused on the failure of the "Land" to execute its duties. Absatz 2, 4, and 5 are concerned with the measures that can, and should be, taken in the struggle against the "extraordinary disturbances of public security and order through the use of a state of exception" ("außergewöhnlicher Störungen der öffentlichen Sicherheit und Ordnung durch Verhänung eines Ausnahmezustandes."). Absatz 3 is linked to both 1 and 2, 4, and 5 (Anschütz 1921: 106).

In 1. of the explanations, Anschütz discussed the execution of the duties that each "Land" has and what actions the Reich is constitutionally entitled to take when a "Land" fails to faithfully execute its duties. He clarified that under the earlier constitution there was a lack of clarity regarding who or what had the authority to determine an outcome if there was a conflict between two "Länder" or between a "Land" and the Kanzler. Anschütz drew attention to Art. 19 of the Weimarer Reichsverfassung, which was the attempt to bring much needed clarity to these types of disputes (Anschütz 1921: 106–107, 66–68). He also noted that the issue of employing "weaponized force" ("bewaffnete Macht") is the strongest means that can be used, but he emphasized that it is not the only means—there can be milder means used to compel the "Land" to comply.

In 2. of the explanation, he clarifies the differences between "Ausnahme" and other exceptional instances. Anschütz suggested that "Ausnahmezustand" is similar to "Belagerungszustand" and that the latter notion of the "state of siege" is mostly identical to the "state of exception" and that both differ from the "Kriegszustand" or the "state of war." The difference lies in that "state of war" describes the destruction of public security and order by a foreign enemy whereas the "Ausnahmezustande" is internal. Anschütz concluded 2.

by noting that only certain parts were carried over from the 1851 constitution (Anschütz 1921: 107).

In 3. of the explanation, Anschütz takes up the issue of how Art. 48 expands the use of power to enforce security and order and how that expansion comes at the cost of basic rights such as personal freedom, freedom of the press, freedom of expression, and freedom of assembly. He questions how any article can dispense with basic rights because basic rights are supposedly not subject to suspension because they are "basic rights" ("Grundrechte").

In 4. of the explanation, he examines the claim that Art. 48 allows the "unlimited" time involved, and again Anschütz argued that there is a contradiction between what Art. 48 allows and what normal laws allow. Even military orders are circumscribed by time and limited in duration; what allows Art. 48 to evade such temporal restrictions? He concludes the section and his explanation by noting that in 1920 extraordinary military tribunals and standing courts were eliminated; thus, the point of the Weimarer Reichsverfassung was to introduce normalcy (Anschütz 1921: 108).

Anschütz's questioning of the provisions detailed in Art. 48 will become more intense and more extensive—not just in the later editions of his commentary but also in numerous writings that he published from 1921 until 1933. Anschütz also became a major figure in the 1932 trial regarding the "Preußenschlag." As will become clear, Gerhard Anschütz was not just one of the leading constitutional scholars of Weimar Germany; he was also a man of conviction and chose democracy and honor over power and convenience.

Richard Grau's Dictator Writings 1922

As with Anschütz, the name Richard Grau will continue to play a major role in this account. The work under consideration here is the book that Grau published in 1922. He will add further writings on dictatorship in 1924, 1925, 1927, and 1932; thus, he should be regarded as the leading authority on Article 48 of the Weimar Constitution.

Grau's title is lengthy and composed of two parts. The main title reads *Die Diktaturgewalt des Reichspräsidenten und der Landesregierungen*. The title is resistant to translation but is something along the lines of "The dictatorship power of the Reich president and the government of the states." In this case, "states" refers to the "states" of Prussia, Bavaria, and the others that made up the Weimar Republic. The second part of the title is in smaller print: *auf Grund des Artikels 48 der Reichsverfassung*. This is more easily rendered as *On the Basis of Article 48 of the Reich Constitution*. It was published by Verlag von Otto Liebmann in Berlin and appeared as the fifth publication in the series Öffentlich-rechtliche Abhandlungen (Public-Law Articles). This series was under the direction of three of Germany's leading legal scholars: Heinrich Triepel, Erich Kaufann, and Rudolf Smend. At the end of his "Vorwort" Grau thanks his teacher Triepel and his brother, the attorney ("Rechtsanwalt") Walter Grau, for their valuable advice and their many important suggestions. The

"Vorwort" also contains Grau's intentions regarding his book. He hoped that it would help Germany return to the notion of law and especially in regards to "Art. 48 RV" ("Artikel 48 Reichsverfassung") (Grau 1922: 5).

Grau's *Die Diktaturgewalt des Reichspräsidenten und der Landesregierungen* has six chapters and a total of 17 "paragraphs" (§). The "Einleitung" ("Introduction") contains § 1; chapter one has §§ 2, 3, and 4; chapter two has § 5; chapter three has §§ 6 through 11; chapter four has §§ 12 and 13; chapter five has §§ 14 and 15; and chapter six has §§ 16 and 17. Most of the chapters are between 15 and 20 pages long, with the exception of the third chapter which is 62 pages long.

The "Einleitung" is only two pages long but contains several important points. The first one is the notion of "Reichsexekution," which is a term that will also reappear in this account. Grau indicated that it meant the fulfillment of the duties of the government. In the case of Art. 48 Absatz 1, the responsibilities of the government(s) are expressively noted: if a Land does not fulfill its duties set out in the Reichsverfassung or in the laws of the Reich, then the Reich president can intercede with the assistance of weaponized power ("Wenn ein Land die ihm nach der Reichsverfassung oder den Reichsgesetzen obliegenden Pflichten nicht erfüllt, kann der Reichspräsident es dazu mit Hilfe der bewaffneten Macht") (Preuß 2015: 598). Grau emphasized the need for clarification of this matter because the time between when the Reichsverfassung was adopted (August 11, 1919) and the time that Grau was writing his book (1921–1922) was exceptionally short. Furthermore, Grau pointed out that while Art. 48 was composed of five paragraphs, it was extremely brief. Grau was partially correct in that last assessment. There were numerous articles which were lengthier: Art. 7 had 26 lines, Art. 18 had 24 lines, Art. 99 had 19 lines, Art. 137 had 23 lines, and Art. 165 also had 23 lines. But there were many more of the 181 articles that were one to four lines. In addition, some of these were as important, if not more so, than Art. 48. To give just two examples: Art. 1 is composed of two lines and two sentences: "The German Reich is a republic. The state force is derived from the people" ("Das Deutsche Reich ist eine Republik. Die Staatsgewalt geht vom Volke aus") and Art. 79 has three lines of which the first is crucial: "The defense of the Reich is a Reich matter" ("Die Verteidigung des Reichs ist Reichssache") (Preuß 2015: 593, 602). Regardless of whether Grau was overemphasizing the length, he was certainly on solid ground to emphasize how new and far-reaching Art. 48 was and that it conferred on one person (the Reich president) enormous powers. Finally, Grau made two further points in the Introduction. One was the issue of how secure the Weimar citizens could be if one person could dismiss so many constitutionally given rights. The other was the friction that is found within the five paragraphs of Art. 48, to say nothing of the friction between that specific article and many of the other 180 articles (Grau 1922: 13–15). Grau intended to provide a compelling account for the need for his examination of Art. 48, and he more than succeeded in providing such a justification.

The first chapter has 15 pages and in it Grau immediately addresses his topic. This is evident in the chapter's title: "The Legal Foundations of the Dictatorship" ("Die rechtlichen Grundlagen der Diktatur"). In addition, § 2 provides the contrast between the dictator on one side and the "Emergency Executive Law" ("Notverordnungsrecht") and the "State of Exception" ("Ausnahmezustand") on the other. Grau begins by insisting that during times of particular danger and internal unrest, the state needs extraordinary tools. This is because the usual instruments that the state has during normal times are insufficient and ineffective to confront extraordinary crises. The Weimarer Reichsverfassung was designed to include specific measures that would ensure that the government would have the necessary instruments to use when needed. Its authors considered Art. 48 as one of the most important measures that could be used. As Grau indicated, it gave the Reich president the powers to restore "public security and order" ("öffentlichen Sicherheit und Ordnung") by any means necessary, including the use of force. This is one of the many points that Grau will later address. Grau also notes that Art. 48 is rather unusual, and he spends much of the first chapter in spelling out how it is unusual. In fact, his entire book can, and should, be read as an account detailing how unusual Art. 48 is. The difference between the "Emergency Executive Law" and the "State of Exception" is that the former is similar to previous legal measures that could be taken during times in which the parliament was not in session. When parliament met again then it could rescind the emergency degree (Grau 1922: 16–17). But Art. 48 confers upon the Reich president the powers to restore "public security and order" regardless of whether parliament is in session. In other words, it takes away from parliament the right to provide laws that would deal with the unrest. Grau emphasizes the enormous power that Art. 48 confers upon the Reich president. He has this power regardless of whether parliament officially approves it (Grau 1922: 18–19). Grau also contrasts the "Ausnahmezustand" with the military powers found in the earlier German constitutions. Grau looked especially to the one in Bavaria and the one in Prussia. Compared to Art. 48, these were rather limited in scope and duration. He contrasts the limits that the military had with the powers conferred by Art. 48. The former could not occupy an apartment or a house without a specific document legitimizing such occupation. In contrast, Art. 48 gives the Reich president that power without any further justification. The right to one's own housing is one of the "basic rights." Grau does not discuss this further but it needs clarification. Art. 115 reads, "The housing of every German is for him a sanctuary and is inviolable. Exceptions are granted only on the grounds of laws" ("Die Wohnung jedes Deutschen ist für ihn eine Freistätte und unverletzlich. Ausnahmen sind nur auf Grund von Gesetzen zulässig") (Preuß 2015: 606). The second sentence is key: only laws can provide exceptions. However, Absatz 5 of Art. 48 includes Art. 115 as one of the seven that can be "wholly or in part" ("ganz oder zum Teil") set aside (Preuß 2015: 598). This lack of constraint will be another major concern that Grau will contend with later (Grau 1922: 21).

Grau stresses that the Reich president has the obligation to counteract what is regularly referred to in the Reichsverfassung as "State of Exception" or something that means the same. But Grau counters that this term is not always employed correctly, and he points to the special use of that term in earlier years and now with respect to areas rather than to the state (Grau 1922: 22–23). Grau concludes § 2 with the claim to simplify the matter: Art. 48 permits the state to possess the continuing effective state force; that is a dictatorship. "The bearer of this force is usually but not always, the Reich president, [that] we call dictator" ("Den Träger dieser Gewalt, der meistens, aber nicht immer der Reichspräsident ist, nennen wir Diktator") (Grau 1922: 23).

Paragraph § 3 continues this discussion with the title "The Immediate Applicability of Art. 48 RV and the Setting Aside of the Earlier Reichs Law" ("Die unmittelbare Anwendbarkeit des Art. 48 RV. und die Beseitung des früheres Reichsrechts"). Grau begins by examining the final Absatz of Art. 48. It is extremely brief but as Grau indicates here as well as later, it is neither very clear nor really helpful. It reads, "A Reich law specifies that which is closer" ("Das Nähere bestimmt ein Reichsgezt") (Preuß 2015: 599). He asks, does Art. 48 regulate the dictator through a law or does it apply for some future law giver to determine? (Grau 1922: 24). After several pages of contrasting Art. 48 with the previous constitution, he concludes this section with the observation that Art. 48 restricts the dictator to a particular time frame—unless there is a change in the Weimarer Reichsverfassung (Grau 1922: 27).

Paragraph § 4 brings the notion of the "Land" into consideration. In particular Grau points to Articles 6 through 12. Articles 6 through 11 spelled out the various ways in which the Reich controlled its citizens' lives. These included Art. 6 on foreign affairs, Art. 7 on general and family law as well as on trade, money, and transportation, and Art. 8 indicating that the Reich had the power to enforce other matters should they arise. Art. 9 claims that the Reich has authority over two other areas: the person who cares for the well-being of another and, most importantly here, "the protection of public security and order" ("den Schutz der öffentliche Sicherheit und Ordnung"). Art. 10 is on religion and schools while Art. 11 is on taxation.

Art. 12 indicates that the lands have jurisdiction over issues not expressed in Articles 7 through 13 but that in these cases the law of the Reich supersedes any law of a "Land." Just to make this clear Art. 13 states, "Reich law breaks Land law" ("Reichsrecht bricht Landrecht") (Preuß 2015: 594–595). Grau calls attention to Art. 9 but he adds that in none of Articles 6 through 11 is there any mention of the Reich as dictatorship. He further adds that the Reichsverfassung grants jurisdiction to the "Land" if it is not expressly claimed by the Reich. So, there is a lack of clarity over who has jurisdiction over matters that are not clearly delineated. In addition, why cannot the "Land" government claim dictatorial powers for itself since that does not appear to be expressly forbidden? Grau admits that such a dictatorial power would be less than the Reich's dictatorial power. But he insists that there is nothing obvious that stops a "Land" from claiming similar powers. In addition, Grau indicates that the Reich cannot initiate a special "Exceptions court" ("Ausnahmegerichts") because that is specifically prohibited by Art. 105: "Exception courts are not permitted" ("Ausnahmegerichte sind unstatthaft") (Preuß 2015: 605). Grau concludes § 4 with the claim that the dictatorship set out in Art. 48 has found its limitation and that there is a contradiction of sorts between the Reich and the "Land" regarding the applicability and the extension of Art. 48 (Grau 1922: 30–31).

The second chapter ("Zweites Kapitel") has the same title as § 5: "The Requirements [or Preconditions] for the Extension of the Dictatorship" ("Die Voraussetzungen für die Ausübung der Diktatur") (Grau 1922: 32). Grau begins by reminding the reader that the "dictatorship force" ("Diktaturgewalt") is legitimized "if in the German Reich the public security and order is gravely disturbed or endangered" ("Wenn im Deutschen Reiche die öffentliche Sicherheit und Ordnung erheblich gestört oder gefährdet wird") (Grau 1922: 32, Preuß 2015: 598). Of course, this clause is only part of the entire sentence but it does make Grau's point accurately. Grau makes the additional point that there is an "or" in that sentence and so it must be clear that security and order can be either "disturbed" *or* "threatened"—meaning that simply being threatened is sufficient to trigger Art. 48 (Grau 1922: 32–33, note 2). He also reminds his readers that the need to maintain order is not new to this constitution but is found in earlier ones as well. But he admits that the notion of threat is one of degrees, and he also allows that "public security" and "private security" are not always the same. Furthermore, the police may be in charge of "private security," but "public security" may involve both the police and the military. But he also allows that there can be overlaps in both cases and suggests that a credible threat against a Prussian minister would not just be a private threat to the minister as a person but also a public threat to the minister as part of the government (Grau 1922: 34–35).

Grau returns to the wording of Art. 48 and insists that it is a threat to public security and order as much as it is an actual disturbance to it. He suggests that this gives the authority the means for not only repression but also prevention. But he also suggests that the degree of danger is a matter of subjective value—what counts as "erheblich" ("serious") is a matter of interpretation (Grau 1922: 36–37). Thus far, Grau has limited his discussion to human threats but now he moves to consider natural threats. What if the threat of disturbance to the public security and order is a storm flood or hunger caused by drought or illness prompted by a plague? Certainly, the police would be allowed to take charge in such cases, but what about the government? Grau insists that Art. 48 would allow the government to intervene in such cases—indeed, it would be a matter of competence if the state government did not try to take charge. Grau then turns to the question of whether there is an abstract danger or a concrete one. Grau's answer is that Art. 48 can be used only when there is a concrete danger to public security and order and not to some abstract or theoretical threat. He further clarifies that the Reichspräsident "kann" ("can") take measures, not that he "must." Yet, Art. 48 also indicates that the Reichspräsident is also obligated to act—because he must use "die nötige Maßnahmen" ("the necessary measures") (Grau 1922: 40–42).

Chapter three is notable for its length at 62 pages, its number § at 6, and its particular focus on the notion of "competences" of the dictator. In the introductory § 6 Grau explains that the Reichspräsident has two different powers: one is the use of weapons and one is the suspension of seven of the "basic rights." The Reichspräsident can use either or both in his attempt at restoring "public security and order." Before addressing these two matters, Grau returns to the phrase "die nötige Maßnahme." He claims that this allows the dictator considerable leeway in his attempts to restore or guarantee "public security and order." But he suggests that this leeway may be too generous because it is decided by a political figure on political grounds when it is a legal issue that should be adjudicated by a judge. Furthermore, a judge is limited by the law; the dictator has no limitations on his powers. The only constraint the dictator has is that he must fulfill his obligation, which is to remove the threats to the "public security and order" (Grau 1922: 44–46). Grau adds that the confusion in Art. 48 continues with the lack of clarity regarding the implementation of these "necessary measures"—are they to be used for a single instance or are they to implemented over a long period of time? Again, the individual who has the power to determine this issue is the dictator and only the dictator. However, Grau also indicates that this issue is not as clearly defined as it might seem to be, and he contrasts it with a military occupation. There, it appears that the military commander has the authority to determine how long military commands will be enforced. Obviously, they will not be extended into eternity so the question is, what is the actual duration of the orders? Grau returns to the question of how long the dictator can employ the measures necessary to restore "public security and order." This is a matter between "one time" ("einstweilge") and "continuing" ("daurend"). This is not just a matter of factual difference but is an issue of legal differentiation. As Grau points out, if the measures are for one time, then they are by definition self-limiting. If they are for a duration, then it is not clear that they are self-limiting. If they are limited, then it is to a much lesser degree than the measures which are limited to one time (Grau 1922: 47). He suggests that one way to determine the measures' length of time is to determine how long it takes for those measures to succeed in reaching their goals. Grau does not continue this line of thinking but instead addresses the critical issue of what type of measures the dictator should choose. Grau suggests that the dictator needs to determine whether the strongest measures are needed or whether weaker measures would be sufficient to restore "public security and order." This question is not a minor one but goes to the heart of the limits of the dictator's powers as well as indicates the dictator's frame of mind. Does the dictator care only about restoring order or does he also care about the appropriate means in securing that goal? Grau points to regulations governing the use of force by the police and that a police officer must act in accordance to the proportionality of the offense. Yet, Art. 48 seems to lack any specific directive regarding proportionality; instead, it says with "nötigen Maßnahmen," which Grau maintains is "an especially strong means, an ultima reason" ("ein besonderes starkes Mittel, ein ultima ratio") (Grau 1922: 48). Grau adds that "armed power" ("bewaffneten Macht") indicates the employment of the military and to use the force that is generally set against external enemies against "inner unrest" ("inneren Unruhe") is to go far beyond normal conditions of a state. Grau emphasizes that "the principle of proportionality" ("Der Grundsatz der Verhältnismäßigkeit") should not be taken to mean that the dictator must begin with the weakest measures and then slowly use increasingly stronger ones until the unrest is put down. Art. 48 only indicates the necessary measures without spelling out what that might mean. Grau points in particular to the history of Art. 48 and the phrase "Bewaffneten Macht." Grau does not detail the history as much as indicates the penultimate reading of Art. 48. But a brief glance at the history shows that the phrase was continually used. It is used in the first draft from January 3, 1919, the second draft from February 10, and the third and fourth drafts of the same month (Feb. 17 and 21), as well as in the fifth draft of June 18.[5] Grau insists that the dictator is not obliged to follow any rules or laws in determining which measures to use. But he does maintain that the dictator has a choice and he offers an illustration: hungry people who are demonstrating can be stopped by shooting them but they can also be stopped by giving them some bread.[6] Grau concludes that it is really up to the dictator's sense of duty and proportionality to determine what types of measures are necessary to restore "public security and order" (Grau 1922: 50).

Much of § 7 is a "short historical review" ("kurzer historischer Rückblick") and concerns the history of changing constitutions. But Grau's point is that the Reichsverfassung can be altered and he points to Art. 76: "The constitution can be altered by way of legislation" ("Die Verfassung kann im Wege der Gesetzgebung geändert werden") (Grau 1922: 55; Preuß 2015: 601). Grau's other point is that § 5 of Art. 48 contains the single sentence "A Reich law specifies that which is closer" ("das Nähere bestimmt ein Reichsgesetz"). As indicated earlier, what that sentence means is very clear, and Grau does little to clarify it.[7]

Grau is far more helpful in clarifying the suspension of basic rights. The title of § 8 is clear: "The Essence of the Basic Right Suspension" ("Das Wesen der Grundrechts-suspension"). This section as well as the following two sections

5 Preuß 2015: 540, 546, 556, 568, 579. In the interest in accuracy, the first draft pertains to Art. 57 and Art. 58; the second to Art. 62 and Art. 63; the third to Art. 65 and Art. 66; the fourth to Art. 67 and Art. 68; and the fifth to Art. 48 and Art. 49. It is not until the actual constitution from August 11 that the two articles are combined into Art. 48. See Grau 1922: 49, footnote 1.

6 "So kann man z.B. hungernde Demostranten durch Schießen zur Ruhe bringen, aber auch dadurch, daß man ihnen Brot gibt" (Grau 1922: 50).

7 (Grau 1922: 56; Preuß 2015: 599). It is noteworthy that Poetzsch and later Giese are silent on Art. 48 § 5, whereas Anschütz maintains that it limits the dictator's power (Poetzsch 1919: 70; Anschütz 1921: 108; Giese 1925: 164–168).

are devoted to the suspension of seven basic rights set out in the second half of the Weimarer Reichsverfassung. These three sections total more than 30 pages and while they are extremely interesting in their own right, the discussion here will be more focused on some of Grau's general observations regarding the suspension of these basic rights (Grau 1922: 58–91). The basic rights are again Articles 114, 115, 117, 118, 123, 124, and 153. Art. 114 guarantees the unrestricted freedom of the individual. Art. 115 guarantees the sanctity of the house. Art. 117 guarantees the right to privacy in communications, regardless of whether it is through the mail, by telegraph, or by telephone. Art. 118 is related to the previous one and it guarantees freedom of speech. This includes by word, by writing, in print, and in picture. It also applies to other unspecified means of communication. It is not, however, unlimited. Unlike 114 and 115, both 117 and 118 can be limited by exceptions as determined by certain authorities. Art. 123 guarantees the right to assemble without obtaining a prior permit with the provision that the assembled people have gathered peacefully and without weapons. Art. 124 guarantees the right to form associations, regardless of whether they are secular or religious. Finally, Art. 153 secures one's property from any limitations on its use and from confiscation. The final sentence of Art. 153, however, does maintain, "its use shall at the same time be in the service of the community's best" ("Sein Gebrauch soll zugleich Dienst sein für das Gemeine Beste") Grau 1922: 58–59; Preuß 2015: 606, 610).

Grau's point in § 8 is that there is a fundamental tension, if not contradiction, between Art. 48 and the notion of basic rights. If the whole intention of the Weimarer Reichsverfassung is to protect basic rights, then how can the same document allow someone to suspend those rights? If they can be suspended, then how can they be regarded as "basic"? (Grau 1922: 60–61, 64). Grau later asks whether the dictator would want to limit his suspension to just these seven basic rights. Why would he not want to suspend others? Indeed, Grau asks whether it is "legitimate" for the dictator to suspend some but not all basic rights (Grau 1922: 71–73). Grau attempts to answer this by appealing to two different grounds for suspension—one appears to be administrative, which would mean the suspension of all basic rights—and the other appears to be the dictator, which means that he is entitled to determine which basic rights need to be suspended and which ones do not (Grau 1922: 73–75). As this stands it does not seem very convincing—which leads Grau to § 9 and "The Individual Basic Rights and Their Suspension" ("Die einzelnen Grundrechte und ihre Suspension") (Grau 1922: 76). Grau specifically focuses on Art. 114, which guarantees an individual's freedom. Yet he notes that what is guaranteed as inviolable in the first paragraph is limited in the longer second paragraph. There, conditions are indicated in which a person's freedom can legally be curtailed. The obvious example is when someone breaks a law, is found guilty, and is sentenced to jail (Grau 1922: 78–80; Preuß 2015: 606). Poetzsch does not address this but Giese does. He explains that the officials holding the individual are legally obligated to explain to him why and under what laws they are entitled to restrict his freedom (Poetzsch 1919: 116–117; Giese 1925: 311). In contrast, Anschütz devotes two full pages to explaining the scope of Art. 114. As often the case with Anschütz's explanations, this is a model of detail and of clarity. But the points that are pertinent to Grau's discussion are (1) Anschütz differentiates between "personal freedom" and "political freedom" where the first can be restricted but the second cannot; (2) "Gesetze" means not just the Reich's laws but also the laws of a "Land"; (3) the police are the ones who have the legal and legitimate basis for arresting and confining someone; and (4) they are enforcing actual laws and not some "program" (Anschütz 1921: 194–196). Grau admits that the police have the power to restrict an individual's freedom, but he insists that the dictator has the power that goes far beyond what the police possess. He points out that the dictator has the power to seize a person's property or bank account. But Grau allows that the dictator would be hard pressed to justify such measures as being necessary to restore "public security and order." Furthermore, Grau points out that there are a few basic rights that explicitly reject any attempts to limit or to hinder as being illegal (Grau 1922: 85–87).[8]

Grau continues his examination of the grounds for suspending basic rights in § 10 but he now turns his attention to the expectation that the dictator should announce the suspension of basic rights. The expectation is based upon the assumption that the announcement not only is a means to inform the citizens but also is a means to help legitimize the suspension. But Grau's attention also returns to that phrase "all or part" ("ganz oder zum Teil"). His point concerns not just "all or part" as it applies to a basic right; instead, it also concerns a time frame. He illustrates this by considering Art. 117 about long-distance communications and suggests that the dictator could allow such communications during the day but prohibit them during the night (Grau 1922: 88–89). The remainder of § 10 is taken up mostly with a very detailed and very complex discussion of various measures that could be taken. But there is a final point about "all or part," and it is Grau's suggestion that it applies to "all" the citizens or only to "some" and that it could be used to safeguard the rights of a minority (Grau 1922: 90).

The final section of the third chapter is focused on the relationship of the dictatorship to the retention of the laws: § 11 "Das Verhältnis der Diktatur zum Vorbehalt des Gesetzes." Rather than discussing the law, Grau spends most of the section criticizing Paul Laband and Hans Kelsen. Grau claims that while Kelsen's theory of law minimizes some of the lack of clarity in Laband's ideas, both Kelsen and Laband suffer because of their positivist approach to law (Grau 1922: 91–95). Much of their problem is their effort to minimize the importance of "power" ("Macht") to law. Grau considers Montesquieu a better

8 Art. 159 governs workers' rights and indicates that it applies to each person in all vocations. The final sentence is explicit: "All restrictions and measures which seek to limit or to hinder this freedom are illegal" ("Alle Abreden und Maßnahmen, welche diese Freiheit einzuschränken oder zu behindern suchen, sind rechtswidrig") (Grau 1922: 86; Preuß 2015: 611).

source because he understood the importance of power but he divided power into three types. But this is not the only part of this section that is a digression; much of the remainder is as well. It appears that Grau has become concerned with obedience and not with power or with law. It is only in the final three pages that he returns to Art. 48, and he repeats his insistence that the dictator is not bound to either parliament or to any administrative office. His final point appears to be that both of those bodies are limited in their authority whereas the authority of the dictator is almost unlimited (Grau 1922: 103–105).

Chapter three was an exceptionally lengthy and complicated chapter; in contrast, the final three are not nearly as long or as difficult. Chapters four through six are, however, important because they help clarify some of the issues covered in chapter three that are somewhat lacking in clarity.

Chapter four is devoted to the organization of the dictatorship and has two sections—the first one (§ 12) is on that topic while the second one (§ 13) is on dictatorship and justice. They are equally important and are about equal length. Previously, Grau questioned whether Art. 48 allowed the Reichspräsident to employ the police or the armed force to restore order. Now, Grau turns his attention to the police and cites Art. 47 that dealt with the Reichspräsident's power to command and Art. 49 that gave him to power to grant clemency. Both Articles 47 and 49 reveal the immense powers that the Weimarer Reichsverfassung conferred upon the Reichspräsident.[9] But Grau points specifically to Art. 48 for giving him the power to create a "type of Reich police force" ("Art von Reichspolizeigewalt"), and he stresses that this force exceeds the power that the normal police force has. He clarifies that when a police force is a normal part of the ordinary administration then it should be referred to as the normal "police" ("Polizei"); however, when it is granted its "extraordinary force" ("außerordentliche Gewalt") then it should be given the particular name of "dictatorship" ("Diktatur"). He explains that the difference is that the normal police is part of a local administration whereas the police "dictatorship is a Reichs force" ("Die Diktatur ist eine Reichsgewalt") (Grau 1922: 106–107). Grau devotes the next several pages to the issue of how limited any local government is in contrast to the massive power given to the dictatorship. The particular example that he suggests is indicative of what actually happened in July 1932. Grau suggests that during the unrest in Berlin the police would be bound by their normal administrative restrictions but that Art. 48 ensures that the Reichspräsident is not limited by any similar restrictions. Indeed, Grau allows that the Reichspräsident can order the Prussian police force to stay out of the way of the security police (Grau 1922: 109–110). Grau maintains that not only does the dictator have the power to keep the police from doing

9 Art. 47 gives the Reichspräsident the highest command over the entire armed forces of the Reich ("Der Reichspräsidenthat den Oberbefehl über die gesamte Wehrmacht des Reichs."). Art. 49 gives him the right to grant clemency, but to grant amnesty requires a law drawn up by parliament ("Der Reichspräsident übt für das Reich das Begnadigungsrecht aus. Reichsamnestien bedürfen eines Reichsgesetzes") (Preuß 2015: 598–599).

something, he also has the power to compel them to act. That is because the dictator has the personal authority but lacks the ability to do everything himself. Thus, the dictator has the authority to order the normal administrative officers to carry out his commands (Grau 1922: 112–113, 116). The problem comes only when there is the question of suspending "basic rights"—does the dictator have that right? It seems that Art. 48 § 2 grants him that power. Grau thinks that Art. 48 grants the Reichspräsident the authority over all administrative offices (Grau 1922: 118–119; Preuß 2015: 596).

Throughout the first 119 pages of his book Grau has maintained an objective if not cold approach to the idea of dictatorship. That shifts immensely in the opening sentence of § 13. It is worth quoting in full with a translation following it:

> Die ungeheure Ansammlung von Macht in einer Hand, wie die Diktatur des Art. 48 RV. mit sich bringt, erzuegt in edem Bürger das Gefühl einer gewissen Rechtlosigkeit.
>
> The monstrous amassment of power that is carried in one hand, as in the dictatorship of Art. 48 of the Reich Verfassung, creates in every citizen the feeling of a certain lawlessness.
>
> Grau 1922: 120

Grau makes it clear that he, like all German citizens, feels a sense of lawlessness that so much power can be legally given to a single individual. That leads to the conviction that the term "law" no longer really means law. Again, this is a prophetic assessment and is an eerily accurate forecast of what will happen a decade later. For now, Grau wonders whether a dictator would seek to minimize that sense of lawlessness by having the justice system assess his powers and determine any limitations. This is what he means by the attempt to assess how the relationship between dictatorship and justice is governed by the Reichsverfassung. Grau indicates that this general problem can be split into the following partial questions: (1) How is the dictatorship related to material law and does justice have the right to subject the dictatorship to legal scrutiny? (2) Does the dictator have the right to insist on an extraordinary court to adjudicate the limits on his power? Which rights does the dictator have in connection with the justice personnel? This last question is critical because, as Grau cites, Art. 102 is explicit about judiciary independence: "Judges are independent and submit only to the law" ("Die Richter sind unabhängig und nur dem Gesetz unterworfen") (Grau 1922: 121; Preuß 2015: 604). But Grau insists that this is no basic right; a stance that appears at odds with the commentary on Art. 102. Poetzsch suggested that 102 was adopted from the earlier constitution and counted as a basic right; Anschütz stressed the judge's autonomy, and Giese insisted that the judge was not only legally instructed to be independent but rather that the judge was unconditionally obligated to be independent ("sondern unbedingt verpflichtet") (Poetzsch 1919: 106; Anschütz 1921: 171–173; Giese 1925: 280–281). Instead, Grau maintains that the originators of the Reichsverfassung were not taking the side of the citizens when designing Art. 102 and that they were not in a position to formulate this judicial independence as a basic right. In effect, Grau implicitly counters the opinions of Poetzsch, Anschütz, and Giese when he maintains that the judge is only bound to the law in the sense that he cannot arbitrarily decide a case. But this, as Grau notes, is nothing extraordinary but is a part of modern law (Grau 1922: 121). More importantly, a judge is bound by the law in determining punishment, but that applies only to normal cases. What makes this difficult to determine is that the case regarding a dictator is not a normal case but is clearly an exceptional case (Grau 1922: 122–124). In addition, while a judge is bound to follow law as it is, the dictator is free to determine which new acts are also punishable.[10] It is also up to the dictator to determine the severity of the punishment. Grau points specifically to the death penalty ("Todesstrafe") and suggests that the dictator could show mercy by reducing a sentence of death to the sentence of hacking off the criminal's right hand (Grau 1922: 124). Grau suggests that the dictator has taken over the function of the state, if even only provisionally. The only real question is what the role of parliament is in such a case. If the dictator is the state, then is there any function left for parliament? Is there any need for parliament to meet in order to pass laws?

Grau also takes up the issue of "extraordinary courts" and he does so because Art. 105 strictly forbids such courts ("Ausnahmegerichte sind unstatthaft") (Grau 1922: 125, Preuß 2015: 605). Poetzsch did not think this article warranted comment; Anschütz maintained that it did nothing more than eliminate military courts; while Giese insisted that it banned all extraordinary courts including military courts, siege courts, honor courts, and anything else that is not a general court (Poetzsch 1919: 107; Anschütz 1921: 176–177; Giese 1925: 286–288). What is interesting is that Grau refers to Anschütz twice in footnotes: where Anschütz noted that Art. 48 § 2 permits the Reichspräsident to suspend seven "basic rights" and in Grau's opinion, that would also mean allowing extraordinary courts (Anschütz 1921: 107; Grau 1922: 126, note 1–2, 127). However, Grau concedes that there is confusion here: while it is clear that Art. 105 is "a genuine basic right in the sense of the Reichsverfassung" ("echtes Grundrecht im Sinn der Reichsverfassung"), he notes that it is not included in the section "Basic Rights and Basic Duties of the Germans" ("Grundrechte und Grundpflichten der Deutschen") (Grau 1922: 127–129).[11] The matter of extraordinary courts is important because of

10 "Der Diktator kann also nicht nur neue Deliktstatbestände, sondern auch neue Straftarten schaffen" (Grau 1922: 124).

11 Art. 105 is included in the first part and in the seventh section governing "The Cultivation of Law" ("Die Rechtspflege"). It is one of seven, starting with Art. 102 as the lead one because of its importance guaranteeing the independence of the judiciary and ending with Art. 108. The second half, which details basic rights and basic responsibilities, does not begin until Art. 109: "All Germans are equal before the law" ("Alle Deutschen sind vor dem Gesetze gleich") (Preuß 2015: 604–605).

two reasons: one is that the dictator acts as a court, if not simply an extraordinary one. Two is that only an extraordinary court would have the authority to curtail the dictator's powers. Indeed, the dictator has authority over all normal courts, their judges and their administrators (Grau 1922: 131–132).

Chapter five is composed of two sections of unequal length. The first one § 14 is three pages while the second §15 is twelve. The first one is relevant and will be treated accordingly while the second one is less relevant. The opening sentence of §14 is crucial because Grau announces that the ordinary person of the dictatorship is the Reichspräsident (Grau 1922: 134). This is justified under Art. 48, but it can pit the Reichspräsident against the Reichskanzler. The Reichspräsident is entitled to employ "all necessary measures" ("alle nötigen Maßnahmen") whereas the Reichskanzler is not at all entitled to all measures—necessary or not necessary. If the Reichskanzler seeks to hinder the Reichspräsident, then as dictator he has the right to overcome the Reichskanzler's resistance through the use of "all necessary measures." The only question is whether the Reichskanzler can attract enough parliamentary votes to limit the dictator's powers, but he and parliament lack the necessary legal means to fully stop the dictator (Grau 1922: 135–136). This shows the lack of balance between the power that the Reichspräsident can legally claim under Art. 48 and the limited power that the Reichskanzler, parliament, and administrators have under the same article.

The concept in § 14 is the ordinary possessor of the power of the dictatorship but the conception in § 15 is the extraordinary possessor. Grau believes that it is the "Land" government ("Landesregierung"), but he does not make much of a compelling case. Art. 48 § 4 does grant the "Landesregierung" the capacity to meet the dictator's powers but it appears rather limited. First, § 4 of Art. 48 indicates that the "Landesregierung" can meet against the Reich's powers "once" ("einstweilig"), but more importantly it appears as if the Reichspräsident or the Reichstag have the power to suspend the countermeasures that the "Landesregierung" has introduced (Grau 1922: 137; Preuß 2015: 599). It is telling that Poetzsch did not mention this in his commentary; Anschütz mentioned that § 2 and § 4 seek to limit that power but not to curtail it; and Giese mostly points to other scholars; including Grau. But he points to Grau's later discussion in chapter six about political control (Poetzsch 1919: 69–70; Anschütz 1921: 108; Giese 1925: 167–169). Grau questions the capacity for the "Landesregierung" to claim any authority under Art. 48. He argues that it does not have the legal authority and if it does make a claim it is not as a "Land" but as an "organ of the Reich" ("Reichsorgan") (Grau 1922: 142–143). To give a sense of how complicated this matter is, Grau has one footnote that covers almost the entirety of two pages. It is in smaller print than the normal printed page and even the text on both pages only contains five lines of which none are complete sentences. The footnote is not even about the Reich but mostly about the Bavarian government (Grau 1922: 144–146). In addition, Grau suggests that if a "Landesregierung" decides to oppose the Reich then it risks losing trust of its own citizens, which could lead to a vote of no confidence and the collapse of that government. Also, the "Landesregierung" has no military support to back its opposition—the military is under the direction of the Reich. Even if the "Landesregierung" could have some support of a military group, it is "severely limited" ("erheblich beschränkter"), unlike that of the Reichspräsident. Furthermore, the "Landesregierung" has command over a far more limited amount of land. As a result, the Reichspräsident has not only more legal authority, but also more military force and a greater geographical power than any "Landesregierung." All this places the "Landesregierung" at a distinct disadvantage should its leaders choose to oppose the dictatorial measures of the Reichspräsident (Grau 1922: 149).

Chapter six is devoted to the concept of "The Control of the Dictatorship" ("Die Kontrolle der Diktatur"), but as Grau notes in the opening paragraph regarding § 16, there is no mention of any kind of control in Art. 48. Instead, the dictator has immense powers and almost no restrictions on what he chooses to do. Rather, Art. 48 gives him almost carte blanche. Moreover, this unlimited power is granted under the legal authority of the Weimarer Reichsverfassung. As Grau puts it, the dictator remains independent from controls (Grau 1922: 150–151). Yet, Grau suggests that under the previous constitution, a judge could impose some constraints on military power and under the present constitution there can also be some judicial review. However, any judge who seeks to limit the powers of the dictator immediately runs into the obstacle that the dictatorship is based upon the Reichsverfassung. That places the judge who intends to restrict or to control the dictatorship in a very precarious position. How can such a judge find any legal grounds to restrict the dictator since the dictator's authority is based upon the most basic and fundamental of all legal documents—the constitution. Grau insists that the wording of Art. 48 gives the dictator massive "flexibility" ("Spielraum"), and he points to the terms "severely" ("erhebliche") and "necessary" ("nötige") as two words that grant the dictator almost unlimited space. He adds that the term "requires" ("erforderlich") and the term "once" ("einstweilige") are also lacking in specificity. So Grau asks how an "administrative judge" ("Verwaltungsrichter") is going to be able to parse this type of language. Furthermore, the "administrative judge" is used to deciding normal cases but Art. 48 is about the exception. But the "administrative judge" cannot rely on extraordinary means in order to determine whether the intended purpose or goal can be reached by the extraordinary measures granted to the dictator. In addition, Grau reminds his reader that the Reichspräsident is not just an "official" ("Beamte") but that he stands at the pinnacle of the entire administrative hierarchy (Grau 1922: 155–157). Grau admits that the upper members of the administration have what is referred to as "staatsrechtliche Verantwortlichkeit"—which means the "legal responsibility of the state." That means the "Reichspräsident," the "Reichskanzler," and the "Reichsminister," but that also means that the decision regarding the question of responsibility is to be determined according to the Reichsverfassung (Grau 1922: 158). But Grau argues that in general the constitution cannot decide about its own issues and in particular it is difficult to conceive how the constitution can provide a clear judgment over the legality of the extension of Art. 48. Nor can any of the three governmental officials since they operate under the constitution and not independently from it. In addition, any "Land" decision is out of the question because the Reichsverfassung makes it abundantly clear with Art. 13 that the Reich has legal precedence over a "Land."[12] What is unclear is why Grau did not make this point. Instead, he discusses penalties for breaking the law and in specific he discusses the application of the death penalty in particular cases. It seems that his point is that in cases of penal law, the court is independent—something that is not the case with a dictator relying on Art. 48 (Grau 1922: 159–160).

In § 17 Grau explains that politics is a more effective control over the dictator than the law, and he points to Absatz 3 of Art. 48. There it is granted to the "Reichstag" to determine whether the Reichspräsident's powers under Art. 48 can be curtailed. Grau also points out that the Reichstag is obligated to scrutinize the president's dictatorial powers and to limit or to halt them when it deems it necessary. Thus, it is neither a legal body nor an administrative body that has the authority and power to put a stop to the president's dictatorship but the political body of the German parliament (Grau 1922: 161–163). However, Grau emphasizes that this is a political decision and not one based upon law. As such, the Reichspräsident is not under *legal* obligation to follow what the parliament has issued but is only under *political* pressure to agree to parliament's demands.[13] Grau concludes his book with a rather pessimistic assessment regarding the control over the dictator. Since a "Land" is subservient to the Reich it lacks power; neither a judge nor an administrator has a right, so that leaves the politicians to minimize or stop the president from pursuing his dictatorial powers. In the end, it appears that the only thing that might prompt the politicians to act is when the costs from not interfering become too high (Grau 1922: 168–169).

12 "Reichsrecht bricht Landsrecht"; that is, the law of the Reich "breaks" or renders any law of a "Land" null and void (Preuß 2015: 595). Giese explained that the Reich had sovereignty whereas the "Land" did not (Giese 1925: 79–80). Poetzsch had argued much the same, that in a situation in which there is a difference of opinion, the higher Reich makes the final decision (Poetzsch 1919: 43–44). In the 1921 edition of his commentary Anschütz spent more time discussing Art. 13—thus suggesting that it was not as clear as Poetzsch and later Giese made it. Nonetheless, Anschütz agreed that historically and now constitutionally the large and greater power has the authority to claim that its decisions trump any smaller and lesser power (Anschütz 1921: 45–48).

13 Grau 1922: 164–166. Grau's footnote 4 on page 166 is not very helpful. He complains that Hans Gmelin's article "Aufnahmezustand" was not very understandable. However, Gmelin was providing a historical account and not so much a legal one. But Gmelin made it clear that parliament had political control (Gmelin 1920: 160).

Richard Grau's *Die Diktaturgewalt des Reichspräsidenten und der Landesregierungen auf Grund des Artikels 48 der Reichsverfassung* may be plodding in some passages and obtuse in a few others, but it is a remarkable commentary on Art. 48 of the Reichsverfassung. Much of it is a masterful rendering of complex ideas, and he mostly succeeds in treating a rather political issue with scholarly restraint. It is little wonder that Grau would continue to be recognized as one of the leading experts on Art. 48—especially as its history grew increasingly contentious.

Grau's dictator book is in marked contrast to Schmitt's dictator book. Although Schmitt was already teaching law when his first book was published, he was politically oriented. As a result, his dictator book is less a scholarly treatise than it is a political work. In contrast, Grau had just finished his law degree and his dictator book was the expected scholarly dissertation. But it is more than just a major dissertation; it is a penetrating analysis of one of Weimar's most perplexing issues—the use and the abuse of Art. 48. In this, Grau's work is much closer to that of Anschütz. Both Anschütz and Grau recognized the legal problems and the political effects of Art. 48 and in their writings during the remaining decade of the Weimar Republic spent much of their efforts in warning how that article could be misused. For Schmitt, Art. 48 would be a political instrument to be used to justify a political result.

Concluding Comments

This chapter began with an account of the situation in Germany during the years 1920 through 1922 and dealt with some of the major problems that Germans faced in that three-year period. Some of these were political (as in the Kapp Putsch) and some economic (as in the rising rate of inflation). The chapter then focused on some passages in Carl Schmitt's writings from 1916 until 1921, and that was followed by a brief reference to Gerhard Anschütz and the 1921 edition of his commentary on the Weimarer Reichsverfassung. The majority of this chapter was devoted to Richard Grau's extensive investigation of Art. 48. As indicated in the beginning of this chapter, Grau was the scholar who devoted the most attention to that article—what it covered and what it implied—and therefore required a lengthy investigation into his account. The next chapter begins with an account of the increasing political and economic problems that Germans faced in 1924, 1925, and even in 1926 before turning to the various discussions of Art. 48 in German scholarly circles and in academic writings.

References

Adair-Toteff, C. (2020) *Carl Schmitt on Law and Liberalism*. London: Palgrave.

Anschütz, G. (1921) *Der Verfassung des Deutschen Reichs von 11. August 1919. Mit Erläuterungen und Sachregister.* Berlin: Verlag von Georg Stilke in Berlin.

Baranowski, S. (2022) "The Centre Party, Conservatives, and the Radical Right." In Rossol and Ziemann. 2022. 363–381.

Bendixen, F. (1917) *Das Inflationsproblem.* Stuttgart: Verlag von Ferdinand Enke.

Bendixen, F. (1918) *Das Wesen des Geldes. Zugleich ein Beitrag zur Reform der Reichsbankgesetzgebung.* Zweite Auflage mit Anmerkungen und Ergänzungen. München und Leipzig: Verlag von Duncker & Humblot.

Berg-Schlosser, D. (1992) "Im Strudel von Inflation und Reparationen. Wirtschaftsordung und Wirtschaftsentwicklung." In Stammens. 1992. 323–342.

Bernecker, W.L. (1992) "Unruhen, Streiks, Fememorde. Die innenpolitische Entwicklung." In Stammens. 1992. 231–240.

Bracher, K.D., Funke, M. and Jacobsen, H.-A., Herausgebern (1987) *Die Weimarer Republik 1918–1933. Politik/Wirtschaft/Gesellschaft.* Bonn: Bundeszentrale für politische Bildung.

Büttner, U. (2008) *Weimar. Die überforderte Republik. 1918–1933.* Stuttgart: J.G. Cotta'sche Buchhandlung Nachfolger.

Dillon, C. (2022) "The German Revolution of 1918/1919." In Rossol and Ziemann. 2022. 27–47.

Erdmann, K.D. (1982) *Die Weimarer Republik.* München: Deutscher Taschenbuch Verlag. 3. Auflage. Handbuch der deutschen Geschichte. Band 19.

Geyer, M. (2022) "The Period of Inflation, 1919–1923." In Rossol and Ziemann. 2022. 48–71.

Giese, F. (1925) *Die Reichsverfassung vom 11. August 1919.* Berlin: Carl Heymanns Verlag. Sechste ergänzte und verbesserte Auflage.

Gietinger, K. (2020) *Kapp-Putsch. 1920. Abwehrkämpfe Rote Ruhrarmee.* Stuttgart: Schmetterling Verlag.

Gmelin, H. (1920) "Ausnahmezustand." In *Handbuch der Politik. Dritter Band. Die politische Erneuerung.* Berlin und Leipzig: Dr. Walther Rothschild. 156–160.

Grau, R. (1922) *Die Diktaturgewalt des Reichspräsidenten und der Landesregierungen. auf Grund des Artikels 48 der Reichsverfassung.* Berlin: Verlag von Otto Liebmann.

Hürten, H. (1987) "Bürgerkrieg in der Republik. Die Kämpfe um die innere Ordnung von Weimar 1918–1920." In Bracker, Funke and Jacobsen. 1987. 81–94.

Kolb, E. (2002) *Die Weimarer Republik.* München: R. Oldenbourg Verlag. 6. überarbeitete und erweiterte Auflage.

Poetzsch, F. (1919) *Handausgabe der Reichsverfassung vom 11. August 1919.* Berlin: Verlag von Otto Liebmann.

Preuß, H. (2015) *Das Verfassungswerk von Weimar.* Herausgegeben, eingeleitet und erläutert von Detlef Lehnert, Christoph Müller und Dian Schefold. Tübingen: Mohr Siebeck. *Gesammelte Schriften.* Dritter Band.

Quaritsch, H. (1996) "Souveränität im Ausnahmezustand. Zum Souveränitätsbegriff im Werk Carl Schmitts." *Der Staat. Zeitschrift für Staatslehre Öffentliches Recht und Verfassungsgeschichte.* 35. Band. 1–30.

Rossol, N. and Ziemann, B., Editors (2022) *The Oxford Handbook of the Weimar Republic.* Oxford: Oxford University Press.

Schabe, K. (1987) "Der Weg der Republik vom Kapp-Putsch 1920 bis zum Scheitern des Kabinettes Müller 1930." In Bracher, Funke and Jacobsen. 1987. 95–133.

Schmitt, C. (1921) *Die Diktatur. Von den Anfängen des modernen Souveränitätsgedankens bis zum proletarischen Klassenkampf.* Berlin: Duncker & Humblot.

Schmitt, C. (1995)[1916] "Diktatur und Belagerungszustand. Eine staatsrechtliche Studie." In *Staat, Großraum, Nomos. Arbeiten aus den Jahren 1916–1969.* Herausgegeben, mit einem Vorwort und mit Anmerkungen versehen von Günter Maschke. Berlin: Duncker & Humblot. 3–23.

Stammen, T. (1992) *Die Weimarer Republik. Das schwere Erbe. Band 1. 1918–23.* München: Bayerische Landeszentrale für politische Bildungsarbeit. 2. Auflage.
Winkler, H.A. (1993) *Weimar 1918–1933. Die Geschichte der ersten Deutschen Demokratie.* München: Verlag C.H. Beck.
Wright, J. (2022) "Foreign Policy: The Dilemmas of a Revisionist State." In Rossol and Ziemann. 2022. 242–263.

4 1923–1926

The Years of Despair and Hope

Introduction

The four-year period of 1923 through 1926 was a complex one. The years 1923 and 1924 were turbulent and marked by economic catastrophes, military occupations, and political violence. In contrast, 1925 and 1926 were both years of relative tranquility. Inflation was finally under control, the French occupation of the Ruhr had ended, and the threat of political violence had at least temporarily subsided. But the issues of what Art. 48 meant, what it covered, and what its possible constitutional and political implications were continued to be debated. These debates were mostly conducted by scholars in papers and in discussions, but that does not mean that they were not heated. After all, Art. 48 was still being referred to by some as the "dictator" article—a claim that was warmly embraced by some and fully rejected by others.

This chapter has three main sections—the first section which sets out three of the main issues that were Weimar's problems during this time frame: economics, foreign policies, and politics. Two sections follow—one section for the years 1923 and 1924 and one for the years 1925 and 1926. The chapter concludes with some final observations. While 1923 and 1924 were plagued by many problems, they will seem minimal compared to those in the years 1932 and 1933. Nonetheless, 1923 and 1924 caused considerable pain and suffering for almost every German citizen. That pain and suffering contributed to the growing recognition that perhaps Weimar's democracy was too ineffective and too lenient to deal with its most difficult and most pressing issues. The use (and abuse) of Art. 48 was regarded as one of the most effective tools that Weimar had to defend itself against public insecurity and disorder.

The Years 1923–1926

Numerous crises plagued Weimar Germany during 1923 and 1924, but the three major ones were inflation, the occupation of the Ruhr region, and widespread political unrest. All three were extremely problematic but as Dirk Berg-Schlosser argued, inflation was the overwhelming problem of the era (Berg-Schlosser 1992: 336). Karl Christian Führer noted that during 1923

DOI: 10.4324/9781003312796-4

inflation made normal everyday living impossible (Führer 2022: 300). Volker Ullrich wrote about a woman who went shopping in Dresden in August of that year and she could not find any butter or eggs and that three pounds of meat cost three million (3,000,000) marks (Ullrich 2023: 72). Ullrich linked the hyperinflation to reparations, but it also had to do with the French occupation of the Ruhr (Geyer 2022: 56). While there had been political unrest, attempted and successful assassinations, and the Kapp-Lüttwitz Putsch during the previous three years, these were mostly precursors to the problems during 1923. Eberhard Kolb has described the years 1919–1923 as years of crises, but he maintained that 1924 through 1929 were years of relative stability (Kolb 2002: 37, 56). That is certainly valid for 1925 through 1929, so this chapter's opening section is largely restricted to the three major issues from 1923.

"Fifty Billion Marks" ("Fünfzig Billionen Mark") is on the copy of a coupon that was reproduced in Berg-Schlosser's article. Berg-Schlosser also produced a table that listed the value of money from January 1913 to January 1920 and then for the years 1921, 1922, and 1923. From January 1913 until January 1922 there was little change. But from July 1923 until mid-November 1923, there was hyperinflation.[1] On November 15, 1923, the German government introduced the "Rentenmark," in which one "Rentenmark" was the equivalent to one trillion "Papermark" (Geyer 2022: 57). Ullrich notes that the German government tried to stop the run-away inflation during the summer but was unsuccessful (Mommsen 2001: 155). Instead, prices that had been rising daily began to rise hourly. The general advice was to spend the money before it lost more value. Later in *Deutschland 1923* Ullrich writes about the height of inflation: October 31, 1923, one U.S. dollar equaled 72 billion and the next day it equaled 130 billion. By November 3 it had jumped to 420 billion where it remained for three days before going to 630 billion and then on November 13 to 840 billion (Ullrich 2023: 79–80, 102, 244). There was no guarantee that the new "Rentenmark" would put a stop to the hyperinflation, but it did.[2]

Some scholars link inflation to reparations, and there is much to be said for that. But the concern here is with the political implications during 1923 and that, of course, includes the problems with the Ruhr region. Martin H. Geyer has suggested that when Wilhelm Cuno became the head of the government in 1922 he was determined to introduce conservative values. That included filibustering reparations, and those actions were accompanied by the slogan "First bread, then reparations." That meant that Germany was no longer in accordance with the agreement. In response, the Allied Reparation Committee

1 January 1913 was 1.0; January 1920 was 15.4; July 1920 was 9.4; January 1921 was 15.4; July 1921 was 18.3; January 1922 was 45.7; and July 1922 was 117.0. In contrast, January 1923 was 4279.0; July 1923 was 84,150.0; August 1923 was 1,110,100.0; September 1923 was 23,540,000.0; October 1923 was 6,014,300,000.0; and November 15, 1923, was 1,000,000,000,000.0 (Berg-Schlosser 1992: 336–337).

2 Mommsen 2001: 187. Winkler noted that it was referred to as the "Wunder der Rentenmark" ("Miracle of the Rentenmark") (Winkler 1998: 237).

determined that since Germany had breached the agreement, then France and Belgium would carry out their threat to occupy the Ruhr area (Geyer 2022: 56). There, workers engaged in "passive resistance," but there were also strikes in different parts of northern Germany. Heinrich August Winkler referred to some of these as "Cuno-strikes" (Winkler 1998: 202–203). Ullrich details Cuno's political failures and points in particular to the strikes by the book pressmen in August 1923. The strikes began on the tenth and only days later Cuno was gone from the government (Ullrich 2023: 57–70).

Of the many instances of political unrest in Germany during 1922 and 1923 there are two that stand out: the assassination of Walther Rathenau and the Hitler-Ludendorff Putsch. Although Rathenau died in 1922, his assassination had major repercussions into the following year. Rathenau was an unusual figure; he was the son of the founder of the German firm AEG and became a successful industrialist. He was an intellectual, scholar, and writer. He was fairly religious and one of the few Jewish intellectuals who publicly professed his faith. Finally, he was a statesman and one who was active during the war and then again in the Weimar government (Hesse and Marx 2022: 430; Berg-Schlosser 1992: 327). One way to approach the multi-talented Rathenau is through the book review that Gustav Schmoller had done in 1917—before Rathenau's death. Schmoller had been a leading intellectual figure in Germany for decades and his opinion was among the most valued. He was reviewing three of Rathenau's books but he focused mainly on *Von kommenden Dingen*. He characterized Rathenau's book as a combination of historical accounts and confessions of personal belief. Schmoller pointed out that Rathenau's hope for a more just and fair economy was laudable but not very realistic. But Schmoller insisted that Rathenau was among the best that Germany had and that his service to the state should be more recognized than it was (Schmoller 1922: 3, 11, 26). Of course, such an individual as Walther Rathenau was bound to draw criticism. According to Hans Mommsen, in the early years of the Weimar Republic, Rathenau was already despised by the Right (Mommsen 2001: 156). Winkler noted that the radical Right hated Rathenau because he was Jewish and an intellectual (Winkler 1998: 173). Rathenau was assassinated on his way to his office as the foreign minister on June 24, 1922. The effects of this cold-blooded murder were immediate but also lasting (Winkler 1998: 177, 180–185). Nadine Rossol suggests that many Germans regarded the murder of Rathenau to be an attack on the Weimar Republic itself (Rossol 2022: 272).

The other major political catastrophe was the "Beer Hall Putsch." It is mostly known as Hitler's Putsch yet at the time, the dominant individual was not Adolf Hitler but Erich Ludendorff. The November Putsch at the Bürgerbräukeller in Munich is well documented, so it does not need to be discussed here.[3] The same, if not more, could be said about Hitler. But Ludendorff is

3 For some accounts see Ullrich 2023: 199–211; Mommsen 2001: 210–215.

slightly different given that he is not well known, his participation in the Beer Hall Putsch is often minimized, and his inclination towards dictatorship is important in the history of Art. 48.[4]

By most accounts, Erich Ludendorff was a difficult man and his life was filled with both successes and failures. One of the best biographies of Ludendorff is the one by Wolfgang Venohr. Venohr noted that during some of his life, Ludendorff was honored and respected for his military victory at Tannenberg in 1914, but that he died lonely and outcast. Venohr's assessment that Ludendorff's name is almost forgotten is as true today as it was in 1993 (Venohr 1993: 9, 14). Venohr described Ludendorff's relation to Hitler as complex. In 1923, he regarded Hitler as one who could command the people, but after the Putsch his assessment changed. As the 1920s continued, Ludendorff began to warn his old friend and fellow officer Paul von Hindenburg that Hitler was an increasing threat to Germany (Venohr 1993: 16–19). As much as Venohr's biography is highly recommended, it focused on Ludendorff's military life during the war. As such, Venohr was largely silent about Ludendorff's dictatorship during 1916 and 1917. Ludendorff along with Hindenburg demanded that production of weapons took precedence over almost everything else. Despite widespread shortages of food, Ludendorff insisted on the "Hindenburg-Programm" because it was demanded by the "spirit of the total war" ("Geist des totalen Kriegs") (Nipperdey 1998: 794–796). Ludendorff's belief that everything was justified in the defense of Germany may have been appropriate during the war, but it was less convincing as the grounds for the "Beer Hall Putsch."

All three of these crises prompted government interventions, but the political problems arising from the occupation of the Ruhr and the unrest caused by the "Beer Hall Putsch" compelled Ebert to invoke Art. 48. Ebert had used it in 1919 and 1920 but it was mostly limited, but during 1923, Ebert invoked it not only because of the Ruhr crisis and the Munich Putsch, but also to dissolve the regional government in Sachsen (Winkler 1998: 227; Wirsching 2000: 11; Caldwell 2022: 125). With this historical background in mind, it is time to turn to the arguments surrounding the use of Art. 48 in the years between 1923 and 1926.

Art. 48 in 1923 and 1924

The first important discussion regarding Art. 48 came in April 1924. It was at the third conference of the Vereinigung der Deutschen Staatsrechtslehre

4 For example, the "Proklamation" that is reproduced in Stammen claiming that the Berlin regime has been replaced by the provisional German national regime is signed by the following: "Gen. Ludendorff, Ad. Hitler, Gen. v. Lossow, Obst. V. Seisser." The photograph shown two pages later shows Hitler in a suit and tie standing next to Ludendorff in his military uniform (Bernecker 1992: 237, 239). Kolb emphasized that it was Ludendorff's reputation that gave him the power of leadership in late fall 1923 (Kolb 2002: 54–55).

that it was discussed. The Vereinigung der Deutschen Staasrechtslehrer was founded in 1922 in Berlin. It was composed of more than 80 of the leading jurists in Germany at the time: Hugo Preuß, Rudolf Smend, and Heinrich Triepel were the ones representing Berlin. Erich Kaufmann and Carl Schmitt came from Bonn and Gerhard Anschütz and Richard Thoma represented Heidelberg. Hermann Heller and Walter Jellinek came from Kiel and Hans Nawiasky arrived from Munich. Triepel was voted chairman with Anschütz and Fritz Stier-Somlo as the other two members of the executive committee. The conference in 1922 is not pertinent to this account and one was not held the following year. So, the second conference of the group took place in Jena on the April 14th and 15th of 1924. It is relevant because all four of the major papers delivered there were related to Art. 48. The first two by Gerhard Anschütz and Karl Bilfinger may not seem so relevant but they are. The second two by Carl Schmitt and Erwin Jacobi go straight to the heart of the matter of Art. 48. The first topic was German federalism in the past, present, and the future, and it is relevant to this study because the issue is how much central power is desired or warranted. In the first two speeches this is mostly an abstract discussion but it becomes more concrete in the second two papers.

Gerhard Anschütz was the first to speak. He insisted that any discussion about federalism would be useless unless the discussion also included an examination about its opposite—unitarianism. He further insisted that only by making that concept clear would the concept of federalism also become clear. He further clarifies that federalism and unitarianism are not totally exclusive and that there can be degrees of each in both. The more power that is concentrated in one single entity the more unitarian that government is. The less power that is concentrated and the more it is diffused, the more federalist the government is. Anschütz then briefly discussed the composition of the German Reich under Bismarck and referred to the outstanding studies by Triepel and by Smend (Anschütz 1924: 11–15). Before turning to the present, he called attention to the fact that the Weimar Constitution was not just disliked, it was also despised. Anschütz maintained, "The Weimar Constitution has many opponents, indeed enemies" ("Die Weimarer Verfassung hat viele Gegner, ja Feinde") (Anschütz 1924: 16). In fact, many members of the national assembly wanted not just unitarianism; they wanted a single state ("Einheitstaat"). That did not occur—and Anschütz clarified that the German Federation was not composed of "Länder" (that is, many states), but was a federation of the German "Volk" (Anschütz 1924: 17–18). However, he drew attention to the imposition of taxes during 1923 and suggested that the government's actions rendered it more unitarian and less federalist. He drew attention to Art. 18—which is a very lengthy and somewhat convoluted article—and it purports to set out the contrast between the central state and its member states. It attempts to balance the need for centralized power with decentralized peoples' needs. It spoke specifically about the "Will of the population" ("Wille der Bewölkerung") (Preuß 2015: 595–596; Anschütz 1924: 18–19). Anschütz's position is on the side of federalism, and he repeatedly warned against the Prussian hegemony. It was not just in taxation that Berlin was seeking to impose its will; it was also in the military. Yet, Anschütz allowed that it was misleading to think that the army could be regarded as a composite. He admitted that the army was neither federalist nor decentralized, but it must be unitary out of technical and political grounds. He further conceded that the military was the only genuine "means of power" ("Machtmittel") and that it was needed not only to repel external enemies but also to quell internal rebellions. Having said this, Anschütz suggested that the Weimar government needed to be "oiled" with more than a drop of federalism; he then turned to the notion of Germany's federalism in the future (Anschütz 1924: 20–21).

Before turning to this topic, Anschütz maintained that talking about the future is more than making claims about what *will be*; it is also a matter of what *should be*; that is, it is a matter of what we wish the future should be like. It is a combination of is and ought—"das Seinsollende"—and that means a value judgment ("Werturteil") (Anschütz 1924: 21–22). He suggested that the wish depended largely on what part of Germany the person was from: the Prussian wants unitarianism but a person from Bavaria wants more federalism. Anschütz noted that regardless of what Bavaria would want, it was too small to take on the leadership of Germany (Anschütz 1924: 22–24). Looking at a map of Germany today, one might be confused by his claim. Bavaria is one of the largest "Länder"; but in 1924 Prussia was far larger. Anschütz indicated that the issue was two-fold: "more freedom *from* the Reich and more freedom *within* the Reich" ("mehr Freiheit *vom* Reich und mehr Freiheit *im* Reich") (Anschütz 1924: 24–25). The first means more autonomy for the governments that make up Weimar. In turn, that means more self-determination. The second means more power and influence within the central government. This leads to Anschütz's final point regarding vetoes. The details do not matter here, but the central question was about Prussia's dominance over the other areas. Should Prussia be dissolved? Anschütz mentions a slogan that was popular: "*Prussia* must *die*, so that the *Reich* can *live*" ("*Preußen sterben* muß, damit das *Reich leben* kann") (Anschütz 1924: 31). Anschütz did not fully endorse this sentiment but he concluded his paper by insisting that Germany needed counterweights to the centralized power in Prussia.

Anschütz was a highly respected full professor of constitutional law. He had taught at Heidelberg and then Berlin but returned to Heidelberg where he felt more comfortable. He was also well regarded as the author of the famous commentary on the Weimar Constitution. In contrast, Karl Bilfinger was still a "Privatdozent," meaning that he was licensed to teach but not at the professorial level. He was paid with student fees rather than directly by the state.[5] Bilfinger would go on to make a name for himself, but here he was at a disadvantage compared to the previous speaker.

5 Professors received a state salary as well as fees from students; "Privatdozenten" were dependent solely on students who paid for attending their lectures.

Karl Bilfinger began his lecture by appealing to Germans who write about the federalism from the previous century. He maintained that federalism in the early 1800s was dynamic and political (as opposed to static and legal). But he insisted that it should be approached historically, so he mentioned the federation from 1871 and that from 1919. Bilfinger noted that the one from 1871 was rooted in German history, but that the later one was more forward-looking. But his concern was with the present state, and he insisted that it could be considered from two points of view: first, it could be viewed as an individual state; that is, for itself but among other individual states. Second, it could be viewed as a state in connection with the whole; that is, connected to the Reich. The first he referred to as "individualism," but he does not appear to have offered a clear label for the second. This is not the only frustrating point about Bilfinger's paper. But he did indicate that individualism is the negative side of federalism. The active and dynamic side is, in Bilfinger's account, the more interesting one, and he devoted several pages to its discussion. It is the force that binds the different parts of the state, and he noted that there is a scale from weakest to strongest. In addition, active federalism serves to balance the interests of the member states. He then turned to the question about hegemony: does hegemony belong to the essence of federalism? Here, Bilfinger's answer shows the clear difference to the answer given by Anschütz. Bilfinger's gave a "fundamental yes" and he insisted that his answer was not just an abstract one, but was crucial for the federalism of the German Reich (Bilfinger 1924: 37–38). He based much of this on the history of Prussian hegemony, and he cited Bismarck as the last and perhaps best representative of Prussian dominance. Bilfinger argued that Bismarck was more than justified to dominate parliament and that the Reich and hegemony took precedence over the Reichstag. Indeed, Bilfinger maintained that the policy of "individualism" was bound to fail because it lacked unity. He insisted that the German state needed a "strong, unified will" ("starke, einheitliche Wille") (Bilfinger 1924: 39, 41–44). Bilfinger would not speak about the present crises between Reich and the individual states, but he suggested that these conflicts were leading to anarchy. Weimar's constitution placed too much power in the hands of the individual states when what is needed is a type of "hegemonic" German federalism that would allow the leader of the Reich to confront these problems (Bilfinger 1924: 47).

Bilfinger moved to the question about German federalism in the future and he replaced that with the question regarding whether German federalism even has a future.[6] Bilfinger was reluctant to offer a definitive answer, but he cast doubt about federalism's future in Germany. Instead, he hinted that what was needed to secure Germany's future was not Weimar's federalism. Instead, he suggested that it needed something that was similar to Bismarck's "federalism"

6 "Nun zum *deutschen Föderalismus in Zukunft.* Hat der deutsche Föderalismus noch eine Zukunft?" (Bilfinger 1924: 47).

(Bilfinger 1924: 49–51). It is necessary because of the increasing claims from the individual states, and he pointed to the differing responses to these claims. Sometimes it is an inclination to the Right and sometimes to the Left. But this lack of direction is dangerous, and Bilfinger mentioned the importance of Art. 48. He conceded that this debate over Art. 48 is a controversial one but he insisted that this is one of the most important political questions. The answer must be to concede that it is the Reichskanzler who has ultimate responsibility—more so than the "*Bundesrat und Reichstag*" (Bilfinger 1924: 53–54).

Bilfinger began to conclude by noting that his theme brought them back to the "Prussian question." He noted that it is frequently heard but suggested that it should disappear. For many, the "Prussian question" is a question about Prussian power; but it is clear from what Bilfinger had said that he believes that that is a very good thing. What is needed is a unified state and that is what Prussia has and what it offers. He indicated that the idea of a federalism within a unified state is a contradiction in itself, both legally and politically.[7] Bilfinger concluded by urging that there be a unified state under the direction of one person. This is necessary for Germany to confront the pressures from the perpetual external emergencies as well as to help overcome the ongoing inner ones (Bilfinger 1924: 57).

The discussion regarding Anschütz's and Bilfinger's lectures was considerable and heated. Fifteen people spoke, including Hans Kelsen, Heinrich Triepel, Fritz Stier-Somlo, and Hans Nawiasky. There was an overwhelming agreement with Anschütz's defense of federalism, and less agreement about the organization of the state. But the biggest debate concerned the "Prussian-German problem"—some speakers regarded the restoration of the past Prussian hegemony to be impossible while others insisted that that is exactly what was needed (Verhandlungen 1924: 60–61). It is the emphasis on the need for strong leadership that was the topic of the next two papers.

The actual topic for the second two papers was "Die Diktatur des Reichspräsidenten," which can be translated as "The Dictatorship of the Reich President." Note that it does not say "Dictator" but "Dictatorship" and that it does not say "Presidents" but "President." Neither Carl Schmitt nor Erwin Jacobi address either of these points; one might assume that they wanted to make this topic abstract so they chose "Dictatorship" and made it singular regarding a specific president. The problem with the first assumption is that Schmitt's book was *Diktatur* rather that *Diktator* and that he intended that book to be an abstract account. It is not clear why Jacobi would be content with either of these issues, but he evidently was. One more important point to mention is that Schmitt reproduced his 1924 paper in the second edition of *Die Diktatur*.

7 "Der gedanke eines Föderalismus innerhalb eines Einheitsstaats ist juristiche ebenso wie politische ein Widerspruch in sich" (Bilfinger 1924: 56).

However, that "Anhang" differs from Schmitt's 1924 paper in many ways. The most significant change is the addition of a lengthy final section. For historical consistency, only the 1924 paper will be cited.[8]

Both Schmitt's and Jacobi's papers carry the title "Die Diktatur des Reichspräsidenten nach Art. 48 der Reichsverfassung" and both are rather lengthy and exceedingly complex explorations of Absatz 2 of Art. 48. Both papers warrant detailed examinations, but that cannot be done here. What can be done is to provide an account that sufficiently explains Schmitt's and Jacobi's most important and relevant points.

It is clear from his opening paragraph that Carl Schmitt is taking exception to the tendency to interpret Art. 48 as having limitations on the executive power of the Reich president. This is made clear by Schmitt's rejection of the conventional reading of Art. 48 and by his insistence that those who are inclined to interpret Art. 48 that way are willfully misinterpreting it. These are strong statements, but Schmitt typically began his writings with provocative opening statements (Schmitt 1924: 63). Schmitt objects that scholars have been too eager to claim that Art. 48 Abs. 2 constrains the Reichspräsident when it does not do that. (Schmitt 1924: 63–64). Schmitt emphasizes that the listing of the seven basic rights as being set aside during the state of exception shows that this proves that the powers that the Reichspräsident has are not, and cannot, be restricted. Schmitt further contends that Art. 48 Abs. § 2 supersedes Art. 105. It is not a problem that Art. 105 states that there cannot be "courts of exception,"[9] because Schmitt insists that Art. 48 Abs. 2 states that there can, and must, be "courts of exception." Schmitt then spends several pages outlining all of the flaws in the interpretations of Art. 48 Abs. 2, and he suggests that these misunderstandings might have been avoidable. Schmitt notes that it would have been helpful if the Reich's government had taken the time to clarify Art. 48 Abs. 2, but unfortunately, it did not (Schmitt 1924: 69). Schmitt points to further difficulties with the standard interpretation of Art. 48 Abs. 2 and maintains that there needs to be a fundamental (re)examination of what Art. 48 Abs. 2 says, what it means, and what it actually does. It needs this clarification because Art. 48 is not just an article in the Weimar Constitution; it can determine life or death. This clarification of Art. 48 and in particular Abs. 2 is the main task of Schmitt's paper (Schmitt 1924: 70).

Schmitt begins with a discussion of what "außer Kraft setzen" means. As indicated in the second chapter, this phrase is not easy to translate. Literally

8 The other reason why some readers may prefer the version in *Die Diktatur* is that Schmitt provides a detailed table of contents. He divides his essay into four main groups. Heading I has eight sections, II has seven, and III has three (with the first one having three subsections). The later addition to the 1928 edition has the main section IV, which has three subsections (Schmitt 2015: 216). The pagination in the second edition varies slightly from the later editions (see Schmitt 1928). The other major difference is that in the 1928 edition the footnotes begin on each page with 1, whereas in the eighth edition they are sequential.

9 ("Ausnahmegerichte sind unstatthaft") (Schmitt 1924: 64, 2015: 218; Preuß 2015: 605).

it means "to set out of power," but what it means is that the rule or law is "no longer applicable." Schmitt focuses on how the norm is set aside: "Out of power means suspending and setting aside" ("Außer Kraft setzen heißt aufheben und beseitigen") (Schmitt 1924: 74). In normal times, the need to suspend rules or norms is neither difficult nor usual. But during a "state of exception" ("Ausnahmezustand") it is both necessary and imperative. It is even more necessary and imperative when the "state of exception" requires suspending some basic rights ("Grundrechte"). Art. 48 Abs. 2 states that not just one or two but seven basic rights must be suspended. In other words, the seven basic rights are no longer applicable. Of course, that is the problem that was also discussed in Chapter 2: how can a basic right be set aside? Is not a basic right a right that is so fundamental that it cannot be set aside? Schmitt addresses that by pointing out that the Reichspräsident has the power to suspend certain basic rights but not all of them. That is why Art. 48 Abs. 2 specifically lists the seven basic rights that can, and must, be suspended when the Reich is threatened (Schmitt 1924: 76–77).

Schmitt devotes almost five pages to his reconstruction of the historical development of Art. 48. It is a difficult five pages to read through and he is not totally convincing. As such, it can be ignored, but what is important is Schmitt's observation regarding the claim that the regulation governing Art. 48 Abs. 2 is "a Provisorium" (Schmitt 1924: 82). It is not clear at the outset what he means by this term since it is not a typical German word. What it apparently means is that it is a "temporary measure." As such, it is something with which Schmitt takes issue. He points out that in the initial discussions about this Absatz that there was no mention of it being temporary. If anyone had thought it important to spell out that this was a time-limited option, someone would have done so.

Instead, Schmitt argues that he was not the first to notice that there was a "gap" ("Lücke") in this article and that was Graf zu Dohna. However, Graf zu Dohna was discussing what Schmitt refers to as "state emergency law" ("Staatsnotrechts"), but he insisted that that is not the same as an "Ausnahmezustand" constitutional article. One is simply a law that applies in particular cases; the other is a fundamental part of the constitution that is applicable if and when the Reichspräsident determines that it is necessary (Schmitt 1924: 83–84). Schmitt points to the need for states to introduce such "states of emergency laws" during wars and reminds his audience that that is not exactly the same situation as with the "state of exception." Schmitt apparently believed it was not necessary to point out that war is an all-too-frequent occurrence whereas a "state of exception" is exactly that—an abnormal situation. It is an abnormal situation because states are frequently threatened by foreign enemies, but it is an internal threat to the very existence of the state that makes the "state of exception" so exceptional (Schmitt 1924: 83–84).

Schmitt seeks to minimize the sense that the Reichspräsident has the same unbridled power as a sovereign prince. While the medieval prince had unlimited power that was based upon divine authority, the Reichspräsident has the power which has been delegated by the constitution.[10] To underscore his point, Schmitt reminded his listeners that others had emphasized the difference between a medieval monarch and the Weimar President: a General Maercker and the member of parliament. Dr. Cohn had both done this. Their point, which is emphasized by Schmitt, is that Art. 48 Abs. 2 is part of a *democratic* constitution (Schmitt 1924: 85–86). But Schmitt seems to make this confusing: on one hand, he insists, "The monarch is therefore sovereign, not [a] dictator" ("Der Monarch ist dann Souverän, nicht Diktator"), but on the following page he writes, "Either sovereign dictatorship or constitution; the one excludes the other" ("Entweder souveräne Diktatur oder Verfassung; das eine schließt das andere aus") (Schmitt 1924: 86–87). Schmitt invokes some historical examples but none of them appears to clarify the point that he is attempting to make.

The point that Schmitt moves to make next revolves around the first sentence of Abs. 2 of Art. 48. He does not bother to cite it, but it does not present a difficulty in relation to Abs. 5; that is, the paragraph that refers to a general law. But here, Schmitt appears to give way to his true intentions regarding the powers of the Reichspräsident: that he has virtually unlimited power as president as indicated by Schmitt's comment that this exceptional power can be characterized as "The dictatorship of the Reichspräsident" ("Die Diktatur des Reichspräsidenten") (Schmitt 1924: 89).

Schmitt turns his attention to differentiating Art. 48 Abs. 2 from other legal and constitutional provisions and rules. He acknowledges that this paragraph in the "republican-democratic constitution" ("republikanisch-demokratischen Verfassung") provides broad powers. It should be clear that he is using the terms "republican" and democratic" is their general sense and certainly not in reference to the two American political parties. What he is stressing is the bona fides of the Weimar Constitution and how that gives authority to Art. 48 Abs. 2. A dictator would just use the power that he has to try to nullify the constitution; the Reichspräsident must use that article in order to save the entire constitution. It is, he claims, not just the purpose of that article, but also the foundation for the entire constitution—namely to determine what the order is. It is telling that just after this, Schmitt talks of "basic rights and quasi basic rights" ("Grundrechte und Quasi-Grundrechte") (Schmitt 1924: 91–92). But he makes it clear that he believes that "public security and order" is a basic right that cannot be curtailed under any circumstances. Schmitt claims that it is not just a matter of "legal police" ("polizeirechtlich") but also, and more importantly, "a category of the constitutional law" ("eine Kategorie des Verfassungsrechts"). In a telling phrase, Schmitt says, "It would be politically naïve and juridically wrong" ("Es wäre politisch naiv und juristische falsch") to try to use "an idyllic and pre-March [1848] concept of peace and security"

10 It may be noteworthy that in these pages Schmitt cites a number of different authorities, including Richard Grau, but it is even more interesting that he cites both *Die Diktatur* and *Politische Theologie*. See Schmitt 1924: 84, note 2; 85, notes 1 and 3; 85, note 1.

("eine idyllischen und vormärzlichen Begriff von Ruhe und Sicherheit") to apply to the current crises. Instead, abnormal measures are required during abnormal times, and Art. 48 Abs. 2 provides the authorization for such abnormal measures in such abnormal times. He clarifies that such exceptional powers are needed in order to restore normality. As such, Art. 48 Abs. 2 is not only legally sound but also absolutely necessary (Schmitt 1924: 92). Furthermore, that article and that paragraph allow for an immense amount of "flexibility" ("Spielraum") so as to decide what measures should be taken to restore "public security and order." But Schmitt insists that the final authority does not rest with that article but rather with the legally elected "Reichspräsident" (Schmitt 1924: 93).

Schmitt turns his attention to the word "measures" ("Maßnahmen") and he observes that it was "perhaps not [an] unintentionally chosen" ("vielleicht nicht unabsichtlich gewählt") term and that Preuß had not used it in the earlier version (§ 63) of that article. He seems to imply that the Reichspräsident is not bound by legal constraints in deciding what "measures" are needed. He repeats his claim that legal constraints are applicable only during normal times, but do not, and cannot, be applied during "states of exception" (Schmitt 1924: 96–98). To emphasize his point, Schmitt insists, "The Reichspräsident is no law giver" ("Der Reichspräsident ist kein Gesetzgeber") (Schmitt 1924: 99). Art. 48 is a legal article and part of the constitution, but its application cannot be evaluated or judged according to legal criteria because it lies beyond legal norms. "The awareness of this difference at least should not be lost in the science of law" ("Das Bewußtsein dieses Unterschiedes sollte wenigstens die Rechtswissenschaft nicht verlieren") (Schmitt 1924: 100–101). Schmitt concludes that limits apply to normal laws and there are legal means to decide what these limits should be. But a "state of exception" is not normal and normal laws cannot apply; therefore, there are no legal means to determine what any limits should be. It must have been the intention to write Art. 48 Abs. 2 in such a way that there is no control over how it is to be applied; it is left up to the person in charge: the Reichspräsident (Schmitt 1924: 103).

Erwin Jacobi's lecture has the same title as Schmitt's has and like the previous speaker Jacobi notes the complexity of Art. 48 Abs. 2. Jacobi agrees with Schmitt that the received view of that article is problematic and so, like Schmitt, he will offer a different interpretation. Like Schmitt, Jacobi sees no contradiction between Art. 48 Abs. 2 and other articles of the Weimarer Reichsverfassung. Specifically, Jacobi quotes from the report of the national assembly from March 3, 1920, in which it states that there is no limitation on any measures; the only possible difficulty is if the Reichspräsident tried to set aside the entire constitution. But Art. 48 Abs. 2 does not indicate that that is what the Reichspräsident should do. What it does say is that he should take the necessary measures to restore "public security and order." Jacobi refers to Richard Grau's monograph and specifically to the part about the inapplicability of Art. 48. However, Jacobi suggests that this is a misreading of the article. In Jacobi's opinion it is problematic that Grau's interpretation has been accepted, and Jacobi points particularly to Hugo Preuß's three-fold reliance on it[11] (Jacobi 1924: 105–108). In contrast to Schmitt, Jacobi spends several pages on the meaning of the phrase "*to set aside a constitutional article*" ("*Außerkraftsetzung eines Verfassungsartikels*"). That he emphasized it is an indication of the importance he gave to it. Moreover, it is not merely an issue of setting it aside; it is also a matter of bringing it back into force ("Wiederinkraftsetzen") (Jacobi 1924: 109). He maintains that a law is insufficient to set an article aside and a law is also insufficient to reintroduce it (Jacobi 1924: 110–111). Jacobi does not dwell on this but spends several pages on the history of exceptions in German constitutions (Jacobi 1924: 111–115).

When Jacobi returns to his main theme he points out that Art. 48 does not include a general dismissal of basic rights but specifically lists seven. He emphasizes the point that the other basic rights are not suspended but continue to be in force. Thus, those critics of Art. 48 Abs. 2 who insist that that article gives too much power to the Reichspräsident are wrong. This leads to Jacobi's more detailed investigation into the powers and limits that Art. 48 gives to the Reichspräsident. Jacobi opines that far from giving the Reichspräsident unlimited powers, the article specifically restricts him to apply Art. 48 only when "public security and order" is threatened or disrupted (Jacobi 1924: 117–118). While Schmitt had focused almost exclusively on Abs. 2, Jacobi briefly discusses Abs. 4. He does so because that paragraph dealt with the issue of how Abs. 2 applies to the "Land" governments (Preuß 2015: 599). He does so because of the Reich's temporary suspension of the Sächsist government in October of the previous year (Jacobi 1924: 121–122). But as Jacobi points out, the involvement of the federal government in a state's affairs is not just a legal issue but also a political judgment. In this sense, a judge is not the best person to decide whether that involvement was warranted. He points in particular to two phrases which cannot be determined by legal means: "temporary" ("vorübergehend") in Abs. 2 and "in the interim" ("einstweilig") in Abs. 4. The length of time in both terms is not a matter of law but a matter of interpretation. In addition, the determination that "public security and order" has been restored is not a legal determination that can be made by a judge; it is a practical decision that is rendered by the person in charge—the Reichspräsident (Jacobi 1924: 123–124, 126–127). What Jacobi is willing to admit is that there can be a dispute between the Reichspräsident and parliament over how long the "state of exception" is in force. But, that is also a political problem

11 The article Jacobi was referring to was one that Preuß published in 1923. It is entitled "Reichsverfassungsmäßige Diktatur" and in it he argued that the Weimarer Reichsverfassung does not authorize a dictatorship. Preuß did suggest that it needed to be addressed and clarified. It is noteworthy that Jacobi did not acknowledge that Preuß cited Schmitt's *Die Diktatur*. It is even more noteworthy that Jacobi indicated that Preuß relied on Grau three times when the actual count is closer to ten (Preuß 2008: 528–531, 533, 535). There are pages in which Grau is cited or mentioned more than once. Jacobi cites Grau almost a dozen times (Jacobi 1924: 107, 110, note 1; 117, note 1; 123, notes 1–2; 127, note 2; 128, notes 2–3; 129, note 1; 130, note 1).

that can be solved only by the political players. It cannot be externally ordered by a judge. As Jacobi emphasizes, this is a matter of the "will of parliament" ("Wille des Parlaments") (Jacobi 1924: 128). Yet, even here the position of the Reichspräsident is superior to the parliament; the former executes and the latter legislates. It is the Reichspräsident who invokes the "state of exception" and it is he who declares when the danger has passed (Jacobi 1924: 129–130).

In the fourth and final section Jacobi concentrates on the issue of the means used to restore "public security and order." This includes the utilization of the full force of the Reich as well as the suspension of basic rights. But it also includes what suffices as the declaration of the "Ausnahmezustand"—is it a red flag or the sound of a drum? These are complex questions and Art. 48 does not address them. It is left up to the judgment of the Reichspräsident. Jacobi adds another difficulty: what is more important: the "*unity of law*" ("*Rechtseinheit*") or the "*unity of the Reich*" ("*Reichseinheit*")? Jacobi does not offer his answer to these questions. What he does offer is that these are important matters that need to be clarified. Jacobi concludes by suggesting that each revolutionary period is followed by the need to make adjustments and changes—with the implication that 1924 is a year in which these should be made (Jacobi 1924: 134–136).

Before turning to the relevant contributions to the debate in 1925 and 1926, it is helpful to reflect on these four papers presented at the 1924 conference. Although Bilfinger was not yet a professor, he would be soon.[12] More important, Bilfinger would join Schmitt and Jacobi in the court case resulting from the 1932 "Preußenschlag." These three would be on the side of the Reich and Anschütz would be speaking for Prussia. Anschütz spent the years between 1919 and 1932 defending the Weimar Constitution and arguing for pluralism and tolerance; Schmitt, as well as Jacobi and Bilfinger, spent much of those years criticizing the Weimar Constitution and arguing for a single, unified authority.

Art. 48 in 1925 and 1926

There are two contributions to the Art. 48 debate during 1925 and one in 1926. Grau had made one in 1925 and another the following year; Hans Nawiasky published one relevant article in 1925. The first one by Grau is rather brief—it is an article in the journal *Juristische Rundschau*—however, it is a continuation of his exploration of the basis and limits of Art. 48. It has a lengthy and rather unwieldly title: "Die Verordnung des Reichspräsidenten zur einstweiligen Regelung der Aufwertung und ihre zivilrechtlichen Wirkungen." If one reads the first sentence one might get the sense that Grau's essay

12 Later in 1924 Bilfinger would become a professor at Halle. He would then go to Heidelberg during the 1930s. It was during the 1930s that he joined the Nazi Party and was imprisoned after the Second World War. He was "denazified" and returned to teaching in the later 1940s and 1950s.

is focused mostly on the issue of taxation and has little relation to the debate about Art. 48. However, within a span of eight pages, Grau mentions the article 38 times. The details of the actual case are irrelevant to this investigation; the comments that Grau makes on Art. 48 are relevant and important. They are because the issue is the same as the one that has been the continuing topic of this book—what are the powers and the limitations of Art. 48? In this specific journal article Grau's question revolves around the notion of legal authority. If the Reichspräsident can simply declare that a law or ruling is not valid, then is that not an "not admissible intrusion on judicial independence" ("unzulässiger Eingriff in die richterliche Unabhändigkeit") (Grau 1925: 84)? Grau suggests that there are two aspects here: the facts and the law. But as Grau points out, any judicial decision is based upon positive law. It is not founded on some ethical principle but on political facts: does it seriously threaten or destroy "public security and order"? If it does, then Art. 48 comes into force. This is not a matter for the courts to decide; this is left solely up to the Reichspräsident. Furthermore, it is in the best interest of the Reich if the Reichspräsident does not announce what he is going to do. Instead, his measures are more likely to succeed if he keeps his intentions secret until the right moment (Grau 1925: 85–86). Grau stresses again that this is not a legal issue but a political matter. A judge is bound by the law and must make decisions based upon legal precedence; he cannot appeal to political matters in helping to arrive at the correct legal decision. In contrast, the Reichspräsident should have the correct political assessment of the actual situation; it is a faulty decision if it is based upon faulty or incomplete information. Grau again emphasizes that this is not at all a legal matter but a political one. If it were ultimately left up to a judge to determine whether the introduction of measures restores "public security and order," then the "true holder of power" ("wahre Machthaber") would not be the Reichspräsident, but would be the highest court (Grau 1925: 86). It cannot be the case that a court can review what the Reichspräsident has decreed in such a case. The only judicial intrusion which can be allowed is when a court wants to determine whether the measures that the Reichspräsident invoke are based on "bare arbitrariness" ("barer Willkür") or if such measures appear to be a total misuse and are completely inappropriate to the situation. But these are matters that can be determined only after the Reichspräsident has ordered such measures (Grau 1925: 87). Grau suggests that this is not a matter of "due process of law" (Grau 1925: 90. He gives this in English). Indeed, Grau maintains that the "Reichs finance court" ("Reichsfinanzhof") erred in maintaining that the Reichspräsident overstepped his authority with his intrusion into financial matters. However, Grau insists that he was well within his rights to do so; in fact, he was obligated to intervene because the situation was threatening "public security and order." Art. 48 gives him the authority and indeed obligates him to intervene any time he has legitimate reasons to believe that "public security and order" is under threat (Grau 1925: 90). The problem that Grau sees is that the "Reichsfinanzhof" mixed legal and political reasoning; thereby, overstepping its authority. It is clear to Grau that the court seriously erred in its intervention and that its error was magnified because it was intruding not just upon any law, but upon a constitutional law—Art. 48 (Grau 1925: 92).

Grau adds another complaint against the finance court: Art. 48 is limited to *temporary* measures while the court's decision is *permanent.* Grau concludes that such "legal-political" grounds are dangerous; not just now, but for the future. He suggests that he may return to this theme sometime later (Grau 1925: 93, 95–96). He does return to the discussion of Art. 48 in 1926, but that essay has little resemblance to the theme set out in his 1925 article.

Nawiasky 1925

Unlike Richard Grau's 1925 article, which was quite short and had a long title, Hans Nawiasky's article is quite long and has a short title. Like Grau's article, Nawiasky's is focused on Art. 48. This is indicated by the title: "The Interpretation of Art. 48 of the Reich Constitution" ("Die Auslegung des Art. 48 der Reichsverfassung"). His article is 55 pages in length and composed of six sections. The first three total just 11 pages and all are concentrated on the "new theory." In the final three sections Nawiasky is highly critical of what he refers to as the "Schmitt-Jacobi Theory," offers a possible defense, and then offers his own theory in the final section.

In the first three sections Nawiasky notes that the received view regarding Art. 48 was that it was clear from the history of its development that it was intended to have wide-ranging powers and would have few limitations. The interpretation was criticized by both Carl Schmitt and Erwin Jacobi at the 1924 Conference of the German "Staatsrechtslehrer." In Nawiasky's opinion, the "Schmitt-Jacobi Theory" was not subjected to much criticism during the conference and that he was going to provide such a critique. Nawiasky suggested that he would offer a possible counter-criticism before turning to his own theory regarding Art. 48.

Nawiasky provides three main points which are based upon the "Schmitt-Jacobi Theory"—that there is really no limitation on the Reichspräsident; that it basically allows him to install a "sovereign dictatorship" ("souveräne Diktatur"); and that there is a sharp opposition between the measures allowed and the normal functions of law (Nawiasky 1925: 1–7). Nawiasky suggests that there are a number of consequences that follow from the "Schmitt-Jacobi Theory" and these include the minimum of organization and the maximum of power. He suggests that their theory amounts to making the Reichspräsident into something like "an absolute king" ("ein absoluter König"). With little or no hindrances, the Reichspräsident is a "Reichsdiktator." He suggests that such a wild Reichspräsident could become like "an apocalyptic rider" ("ein apokalyptischer Reiter") running roughshod over defenseless governmental bodies. In addition, the Reichsdiktator has weapons on his side and has withdrawn seven of the basic rights (Nawiasky 1925: 7–8). In addition, there is the lack of clarity regarding the phrase "necessary measures" ("nötigen Maßnahmen") as well as the lack of judicial review. This is tantamount to having no legal or political responsibility (Nawiasky 1925: 10).

Section IV is Nawiasky's "Critique of the New Theory" ("Kritik der neuen Theorie"). He suggests that this theory is not without contradictions, and he notes that there is one between the lack of organization and the need for more in order to carry out these necessary measures. He points out that Schmitt himself alludes to the need to delegate power. Nawiasky suggests that one has a choice: either to maintain the minimum organization or to give up the necessary dividing of power. In any case, this is a problem for "a scarcely limited dictatorial absolutism" ("ein kaum beschränkten Diktaturabsolutismus") (Nawiasky 1925: 11–13). But he points out that Schmitt also claims that the Reichs dictatorship rests on legal grounds, so how can Art. 48 be both extra-legal and legally based?

Nawiasky repeats his assertion that the "Schmitt-Jacobi Theory" is apocalyptic and that he contends that it is nothing less than dictatorial. Furthermore, he maintains that their interpretation eliminates all restrictions and basically allows the Reichspräsident to do whatever he wants. In Nawiasky's opinion, this makes Art. 48 a "special ruling" ("Sonderregelung") that departs from the constitution rather than a normal constitutional article (Nawiasky 1925: 14–16). Yet, this interpretation actually changes what Art. 48 says, and he argues that that approach is not the type of change that the Weimar Constitution authorizes. He cites some writings by Heinrich Triepel and Graf zu Dohna who had argued at the Heidelberg conference of the German jurists that any change to the content of an article is already contradictory. As a result, the "Schmitt-Jacobi Doctrine" ("Schmitt-Jacobische Lehre") is self-repudiating (Nawiasky 1925: 17–18). Any attempt to justify their interpretation fails on legal grounds and can only be regarded as an act done by a dictatorship (Nawiasky 1925: 19).

Nawiasky argues further that one cannot use the single Art. 48 to set aside the entire constitution. Why would such a dictator limit himself to setting aside just those seven basic rights when he is allowed, and even encouraged, to take any and all measures that he sees fit to restore "public security and order"? Yes, the constitution governs the normal order and Art. 48 is designed specifically to deal with an abnormal order. But that does not mean that Art. 48 is in opposition to the normal but is an addition to it. He states, "*Art. 48 is a special norm, that requires a strict interpretation*" (emphasis is original) ("*Art. 48 ist eine Sondernorm, die strenge Auslegung erfordert*"), but that does not imply the negation of the constitution; rather it indicates that there are limits to that article (Nawiasky 1925: 21–22).

The next point that Nawiasky raises focuses explicitly on the alterations of the "dictatorial article" ("Diktaturartikel") in comparison to the other articles. He points particularly at Jacobi's claim that there is no conceptual problem with the idea that there can be a "deviation [or a departure] from the regular law" ("Abweichung von dem Regelrecht"). Yet Art. 48 does not specifically allow for that deviation. Any attempt to suggest a way around this is not only bound to fail, but does not even need additional proof (Nawiasky 1925: 23–25).

Schmitt and, less so, Jacobi have claimed that Absatz 2 of Art. 48 indicates that that article differs from all the others. Certainly, Schmitt and even Jacobi have insisted that that paragraph confers dictatorial powers—powers that allow the dictator to suspend all other articles. Nawiasky suggests that he grant that that is the case and then proceeds to draw consequences from that (temporary) concession. The main one is that the lack of positive information given in Art. 48 allows other scholars to draw their own conclusions without much regard for the accuracy of those claims. Therefore, it is necessary to examine the sentences that make up Art. 48 Abs. 2. For example, the first sentence has an implicit rule regarding the reestablishment of "public security and order" and that actually limits the dictatorial powers. This leads to a further consequence; namely, that there are no grounds for altering the constitution. This leads him to his next point and that concerns the claim regarding "necessary measures." Nawiasky suggests that sentence 1 and sentence 2 are at odds; while the first one says that "necessary measures" can be taken, the second one states that seven basic rights can be partially or fully suspended—at least temporarily (Preuß 2015: 598; Nawiasky 1925: 26–27). While these two sentences may not be at odds after all, Nawiasky insists that sentence 2 is not necessary to state because it is more than implicit in the phrase "necessary measures." But what he does object to is the reading by Schmitt which basically gives up protecting the constitution which is a "protecting good [thing]" ("schützende Gut"). Implicit in Nawiasky's comments is the doubt that something that protects can be left without protection.

Nawiasky then turns to the concept "measures" ("Maßnahmen"). Both Schmitt and Jacobi are content to leave this concept alone, but Nawiasky contends that it is not at all clear what it means. First, it seems to be a simple matter of facts; but second, it appears to be a legal finding. It is with the second example that Nawiasky insists that the lack of real clarity begins. He asks, how can this be regarded as a judgment, because a judgment does not come at the beginning of a legal case but only at the very end? It is a "result" ("Ergebnis"). This seems to be no longer a matter for a "legal form" ("Rechtsform") but a matter of "legal content" ("Rechtsinhalt"). But he asks, where are the boundaries between an appropriate and an inappropriate content? He dismisses the notion that that boundary or those boundaries can be determined by considering its purpose. However, it is not "measures" that is the crux of the issue; it is the claim regarding "necessary." Indeed, "necessary" is even less clear than "measures" (Nawiasky 1925: 28).

Nawiasky next discusses the notion of "temporary" and how that term is also not specified in Art. 48 Abs. 2. But he draws attention in particular to the "temporary" suspension of the seven basic rights. Schmitt wants to assert that the term "temporary" can mean almost any length of time and that it is the dictator who is the one to determine when that time ends. Nawiasky argues that Schmitt's claim cannot be correct because Art. 102 spells out the fact that judges are independent and submit only to the law ("Die Richter sind unabhängig und nur dem Gesetz unterworfen") (Preuß 2015: 604). The law is not the dictator and the dictator is not the law. In contrast to Schmitt, Nawiasky maintains that the law is above the dictator and that the dictator must follow the law. This is especially critical when it comes to the matter of "measures" ("Maßnahmen") and that they must be limited. This is further underscored when there are clear boundaries, which he insisted is applicable to Art. 48. The boundaries are set with the basic rights and that measures cannot be employed which violate those. Any violation of basic rights is a violation of the constitution's duty to protect. One of the most basic rights is the right to assemble, and any restriction of the right to assemble or to join a group is unconstitutional; just as any censorship is a violation of the basic right to one's expression. Nawiasky concludes section 4 with the claim, "Our analysis has shown that the apparent concentration of power is really only a simmering soap bubble that is rapidly dirtied" ("Unsere Analyse hat dann aber gezeigt, daß diese scheinbare Machtkonzentration doch nur eine schillernde Seifenblase ist, die rasch zerstäubt") (Nawiasky 1925: 31–32, 36).

Nawiasky reminds his readers that section 3 was a setting out of the prevailing theory and section 4 was his criticism of that theory. Section 5 is an attempt at an "anti-critic" ("Antikritik"). Nawiasky suggests that Schmitt has three grounds for his interpretation of Art. 48. The first one is the claim that the necessary measures are legitimized by Art. 48 to restore "public security and order" ("öffentliche Sicherheit und Ordnung"). And, presumably with the addition of "armed power" ("bewaffnenten Macht"), these measures can and will be carried out. But as Nawiasky points out, these are "extraordinary measures" ("außerordentliche Maßnahmen") and so they lie outside of the law. He argues that it is contradictory to use abnormal means to restore normal order (Nawiasky 1925: 38–39). Nawiasky argued that Schmitt's contention was not convincing largely because he predicated his thesis on a debated interpretation. He pointed in particular to the difference between the temporary suspension of a law but still in accordance with a norm and the suspension of the norm itself. Art. 48 Abs. 2 allows for the temporary suspension of a law, but not of the norm. In addition, Nawiasky contended that Schmitt's reasoning did not appear to differentiate among three things: the altering of the constitution, the suspension of the constitution, and the interruption of the constitution ("Verfassungsänderung. Verfassungssuspension und Verfassungsdurch-brechnung") (Nawiasky 1925: 39). To clarify this, Nawiasky appealed to constitutional history beginning with 1850/1851 and 1871 and even the Weimar Constitution. In each case, the constitution allowed only for the temporary suspension of certain rights and only for a certain amount of time. In each of these cases, it was the military that decreed these measures and only during war time (Nawiasky 1925: 40–41). Moreover, Schmitt's argument does not withstand further scrutiny. While Schmitt insisted that the power lies in the Reich, Nawiasky maintains that power mostly is given to the "Land." His larger point is one that he made slightly earlier and repeats again: the suspension of the law is through the "dictatorship article" ("Diktaturartikel") and not through the "dictatorship organ" ("Diktaturorgan") (Nawiasky 1925: 42–43). The distinction appears to be that the first is a piece of paper while the second is an actual entity. Furthermore, Schmitt wants to maintain that the exception has more importance than the norm, but that cannot be true. The constitution is the law; the exception is not. This is clearly in evidence given that "contract- and economic freedom" ("Vertrags- und Wirtschaftsfreiheit") are based upon the law and not upon the exception (Nawiasky 1925: 45–46).

Nawiasky concludes section 5 with the observation that he had considered what Schmitt and others could have replied; however, what he claims is that this "Antikritk" section substantiated what he had argued earlier in his "Kritik" section. This should not be taken to mean that Schmitt's "new thesis" was worthless because it was wrong. Rather, it had value because it made Nawiasky rethink the parameters of Art. 48 and offer the best rebuttal to Schmitt (Nawiasky 1925: 46–47).

In section 6 Nawiasky provides his own theory. He begins by noting that Art. 48 is not a normal law but is a "special law" ("Sonderrecht"). He adds that it departs from normal law in two ways: (1) in terms of altering its organization and (2) in terms of altering the limits on power. Regarding (1), it alters the organization by vesting the Reichspräsident with more than his normal executive powers; it grants him even more power than as head of the army in that he is given authority over any and all "weaponized forces." Regarding (2), there is a reduction of limits on the Reichspräsident's powers. Nawiasky questions the validity of this and he indicates the problems with suspending the seven basic rights. How is it, he asks, that it is permissible to suspend these particular seven and not any of the others? What makes the others sacrosanct while the seven are not? Given the extraordinary powers, why should normal governmental officials work to aid the Reichspräsident? Could not the Reichspräsident simply declare that all rights are suspended and insist that all officials work just for him? Does the placement of all power in the hands of the Reichspräsident mean that the "Land" governments are rendered obsolete? These are issues that Nawiasky brings up. Not only does he not answer them, but also he does not really provide much of the positive account that he had promised (Nawiasky 1925: 48–54).

Grau 1926

The final article to be discussed in this chapter is a lengthy one published by Richard Grau. His 47-page essay appeared in the 1926 edition of the *Archiv des öffentlichen Rechts.* What makes Grau's article somewhat unusual is not its length, but that it was not listed in the main section of essays. Instead, it was listed as one of only four essays in the section "From the Practice of State Law" ("Aus der Praxis des Staatsrecht"). Yet, as Grau's article shows, his preoccupation was with the theoretical aspects of Art. 48, and less so with any practical applications. As with many of Grau's earlier publications, this one also comes with a lengthy and translation-resistant title. An attempt would be: "Towards a Legal Formulation Regarding the Examination of the Constitutional Agreement of the Reich Laws and the Reich Decrees" ("Zum Gesetzentwurf über die Prüfung der Verfassungsmäßigkeit von Reichsgesetzen und Reichsverordungen"). The title would suggest that Grau's article had little to do with Art. 48; yet almost everything he wrote between 1922 and 1932 revolved around either Art. 48 itself or issues which were directly related to it. In the case of this article, Grau's concern is with the disagreements regarding a law and who is entitled to resolve such disagreements. Of course, Grau would have no way of knowing how this would become *the* issue between Schmitt and Kelsen as to who is the legitimate guardian of the constitution nor would he have known that it would explode in the court case regarding the "Preußenschlag." What he did know, based upon his previous studies, was that the law was not as straightforward as some people had believed and that there were more arguments about what laws meant and how they should be adjudicated. Part of this is because Grau recognized that law was not a strictly legal matter but involved politics. Thus, there is a tension between a judge's vow of independence and his political inclinations (Grau 1926: 290–292). This tension is especially prominent in disagreements between a majority and a minority and involves the question regarding what tactics are appropriate for the minority party to use in the conflict with the more powerful majority party. Grau does not suggest this but he hints that part of the difficulty in dealing with legal conflicts is that Germany is a federalist state and not a unified one. Accordingly, there are going to be discrepancies between one "Land" and another or between a "Land" and the state government. Regarding the second instance, Grau specifically invokes Art. 48 Abs. 2 and how the Reichspräsident has the dictatorial power to decide what measures are necessary to take to ensure "public security and order" (Grau 1926: 299–303). Grau indicates that dictatorial power is not legal power but is political force and as such undermines the "unity of constitutional law" ("Einheit des Verfassungsrecht") (Grau 1926: 394, 309, 321, 329). The notions of unity and stability are two key themes in this essay by Grau. On the one hand, he admits that there are some constitutions that are too rigid and resistant to change and, on the other hand, there are some other constitutions in which changes are too easily and too quickly made. What Grau is implicitly promoting is a constitution that changes if and when changes are genuinely required (Grau 1926: 304–307).

Grau then takes up the issue of the constitutional court. He does not begin that discussion with an explicit reference to that court; rather, he writes in terms of courts which judge laws—what he calls "Prüfungshofe." The types of courts that he has in mind are foreign courts—the Austrian constitutional court and the American Supreme Court. However, he allows that the Weimar Constitution appears to place most authority in the hands of the Reichspräsident and he is the one to provide an analysis of the validity of laws. It is here that Grau offers one of the first expressions of the phrase "guardian of the constitutional law" ("Hüter des Verfassungsrechtes") (Grau 1926: 310–313). The debate regarding who should be the "guardian of the constitution" ("Hüter der Verfassung") would soon become hotly contested, but here the emphasis remains on Grau's comments. One of Grau's biggest concerns is when there is a discrepancy between old and new laws and while one may be inclined to accord greater weight to the newer law, there may be reasons for believing that the older one is more appropriate. This is sometimes the task of the judge, and yet the judge must rely on the interpretations provided by other officials. Much of this is dependent on the knowledge of the judge; the more knowledgeable the judge is in this instance, the less he needs to rely on the information provided by others (Grau 1926: 322–323). After briefly discussing foreign courts as well as the disputes between a "Land" and the Reich, Grau concludes with some positive comments. These are basically ideas that he has laid out earlier in his essay, but he believes it important to emphasize them. Foremost is the idea (and ideal) of the "unity of the constitution" ("Einheit der Verfassung") and secondarily, the notion that legal decisions are not simply a matter of law but include political considerations (Grau 1926: 329–330). That this second point carries undertones of Carl Schmitt's thinking is made clear when Grau invokes the idea of the "dominance of the judge" ("Herrschaft der Richter"), and he specifically cites Schmitt's *Politische Theologie* (Grau 1926: 332, note 39). However, Grau also mentions the importance of Art. 109 which states that all Germans are equal under the law ("Alle Deutschen sind vor dem Gesetze gleich") (Preuß 2015: 605), and he concludes with the advice from Rudolf Gneist that the Weimar Constitution stands more firmly if it is founded on the legal convictions of a majority of German lawyers and advocates (Grau 1926: 334). Grau may not have been a committed democrat, like Nawiasky and some others, but unlike Schmitt he was committed to the stable existence of the Weimar Constitution.

Concluding Comments

This chapter began with a historical overview and while it covered the four-year period of 1923 through 1926, it focused mostly on 1923. As indicated, that year was particularly fraught with crises: economic, social, and political. That is why it was emphasized and why it was the year that contributed to so many essays on the meaning and limits of Art. 48. The years 1927 through 1930 will be filled with their own problems and crises, but they will be more like the ones of 1925 and 1926 than like 1923. It will be with the economic collapse in 1929 that the crises in Weimar will reach a fevered pitch resulting in the "Preußenschlag" of July 1932, the takeover of Prussia, and the elevation of Adolf Hitler. The other two main sections were discussions of some of the most relevant lectures and writings on Art. 48. The second section began with brief discussions of conference papers given by Anschütz and by Bilfinger. Although they were not directly connected to the debate about Art. 48, their relevance lay in their discussions regarding the dominance of the state or the rule of federalism. The two papers given by Schmitt and Jacobi sided more with Bilfinger in that both later speakers insisted on the necessity of a single state authority. Jacobi may not have been as enthusiastic about the need for dictatorship as Schmitt, but it was obvious enough that he shared much of the same conviction. The third and final section of this chapter analyzed Hans Nawiasky's contribution. Although he was less than complete in offering a positive doctrine, his criticisms of the "Schmitt-Jacobi Theory" are trenchant and compelling. This section also investigated two articles by Richard Grau. The first one had direct connections to the debate about Art. 48; the second one was less so. However, there has been the contention throughout this book that Grau was one of the most prolific and one of the most scholarly writers to have addressed the meanings and limitations of Art. 48. As with Schmitt, Jacobi, and others, Grau will continue to play a crucial role in the debates surrounding the controversial Art. 48.

References

Anschütz, G. (1924) "Der deutsche Föderalimus in Vergangenheit, Gegenwart und Zukunft." In *Der deutsche Föderalismus/Die Diktatur des Reichspräsidenten.* Verhandlungen der Tagung der deutschen Staatsrechtslehrer zu Jena am 14. und 15. April 1924. Berlin und Leipzig: Walter de Gruyter.

Berg-Schlosser, D. (1992) "Im Strudel von Inflation und Reparationen. Wirtschaftsordnung und Wirtschaftsentwicklung." In Stammen. 1992. 323–345.

Bernecker, W.L. (1992) "Unruhen, Streiks, Fememorde. Die innenpolitische Entwicklung." In Stammen. 1992. 231–248.

Bilfinger, K. (1924) "Der deutsche Föderalimus in Vergangenheit, Gegenwart und Zukunft." In *Der deutsche Föderalismus/Die Diktatur des Reichspräsidenten.* Verhandlungen der Tagung der deutschen Staatsrechtslehrer zu Jena am 14. und 15. April 1924. Berlin und Leipzig: Walter de Gruyter.

Caldwell, P.C. (2022) "The Weimar Constitution." In Rossol and Ziemann. 2022. 119–140.

Erdmann, K.D. (1982) *Die Weimarer Republik.* München: Deutscher Taschenbuch Verlag.

Führer, K.C. (2022) "Social Policy in the Weimar Republic." In Rossol and Ziemann. 2022. 291–313.

Geyer, M.H. (2022) "The Period of Inflation, 1919–1923." In Rossol and Ziemann. 2022. 48–71.

Grau, R. (1925) "Die Verordnung des Reichspräsidenten zur einstweiligen Regelung der Aufwertung und ihre zivilrechtlichen Wirkungen." *Juristische Rundschau.* 1. Jahrgang. Nr. 2. 84–96.

Grau, R. (1926) "Zum Gesetzentwurf über die Prüfung der Verfassungsmäßigkeit von Reichsgesetzen und Reichsverordungen." *Archiv des öffentlichen Rechts.* Neue Folge 11. Band. Der ganzen Folge. 50. Band. 287–334.

Hesse, J.-O. and Marx, C. (2022) "The Overstretched Economy: Industry and Financial Services." In Rossol and Ziemann. 2022. 429–453.

Jacobi, E. (1924) "Der deutsche Föderalimus in Vergangenheit, Gegenwart und Zukunft." In *Der deutsche Föderalismus/Die Diktatur des Reichspräsidenten.* Verhandlungen der Tagung der deutschen Staatsrechtslehrer zu Jena am 14. und 15. April 1924. Berlin und Leipzig: Walter de Gruyter.

Kolb, E. (2002) *Die Weimarer Republik.* München: R. Oldenbourg Verlag. 6. überarbeitete und erweiterte Auflage.

Mommsen, H. (2001) *Aufstieg und Untergang der Republik von Weimar. 1918–1933.* München: Econ Ullstein List Verlag. 2. Ausgabe.
Nawiasky, H. (1925) "Die Auslegung des Art. 48 der Reichsverfassung." *Archiv des öffentlichen Rechts.* Neue Folge 9. Band. 1–55.
Nipperdey, T. (1998) *Deutsche Geschichte 1866–1918. Band II. Machtstaat vor der Demokratie.* München: Verlag C.H. Beck.
Preuß, H. (2008) *Politik und Verfassung in der Weimarer Republik.* Herausgegeben und eingeleitet von Detlef Lehnert. Tübingen: Mohr Siebeck. *Gesammelte Schriften.* Vierter Band.
Preuß, H. (2015) *Das Verfassungswerk von Weimar.* Herausgegeben, eingeleitet und erläutert von Detlef Lehnert, Christoph Müller und Dian Schefold. Tübingen: Mohr Siebeck. *Gesammelte Schriften.* Dritter Band.
Rossol, N. (2022) "Republican Groups, Ideas, and Identities." In Rossol and Ziemann. 2022. 265–290.
Rossol, Nadine and Ziemann, Benjamin, Editors (2022) *The Oxford Handbook of the Weimar Republic.* Oxford: Oxford University Press.
Schmitt, C. (1924) "Der deutsche Föderalimus in Vergangenheit, Gegenwart und Zukunft." In *Der deutsche Föderalismus/Die Diktatur des Reichspräsidenten.* Verhandlungen der Tagung der deutschen Staatsrechtslehrer zu Jena am 14. und 15. April 1924. Berlin und Leipzig.
Schmitt, C. (1928) *Die Diktatur.* München and Leipzig: Duncker & Humblot. Zweite Auflage.
Schmitt, C. (2015) *Die Diktatur.* Berlin: Duncker & Humblot. Achte, korrigierte Auflage.
Schmoller, G. (1922) *Walther Rathenau und Hugo Preuß. Die Staatsmänner des Neuen Deustschlan.* München und Leipzig: Verlag von Duncker & Humblot.
Stammen, T., Herausgebern (1992) *Die Weimarer Republik. Das schwere Erbe. Band 1 1918–1923.* München: Bayerische Landeszentrale für Politische Bildungsarbeit. 2. Auflage.
Stürmer, M., Herausgebern (1993) *Die Weimarer Republik.* Meisenheim: Verlag Anton Hain.
Ullrich, V. (2023) *Deutschland 1923. Das Jahr am Abgrund.* München: C.H. Beck.
Venohr, W. (1993) *Ludendorff. Legende und Wirklichkeit.* Berlin and Frankfurt am Main: Verlag Ullstein.
Verhandlungen (1924) *Der deutsche Föderalismus/Die Diktatur des Reichspräsidenten.* Verhandlungen der Tagung der deutschen Staatsrechtslehrer zu Jena am 14. und 15. April 1924. Berlin und Leipzig. 5–10, 60–62, 137–139.
Winkler, H.A. (1998) *Weimar 1918–1933. Die Geschichte der ersten deutschen Demokratie.* München: Verlag C.H. Beck.
Wirsching, A. (2000) *Die Weimarer Republik. Politik und Gesellschaft.* München: Oldenbourg Wissenschaftsverlag.

5 1927–1929

The Years of Peace and Panic

Introduction

The three years 1927–1929 may have lacked some of the turmoil of the preceding years but they still contained moments of stress and panic. Although the focus of this chapter is primarily on these three years, it also treats some points before and after that time. In essence, it begins in 1925 with the death of Friedrich Ebert and it ends in 1931 with Hans Kelsen's response to Carl Schmitt. It encompasses the election of Paul Hindenburg as president and it ends in 1929 with the collapse of much of Germany's economy as a result of the Wall Street crash. It was during these four plus years that some of Germany's leading constitutional scholars continued or joined the debate over the function of the president, the role of parliament, and the position of the "Land" in determining what Art. 48 of the Weimarer Reichsverfassung meant, how much it covered, and how it should be applied. There were three major figures in this debate: Carl Schmitt and Richard Grau, who were joined by Hans Kelsen.

This chapter has six main parts. The first one provides a historical sketch of the years 1927 to 1929. The second part is an investigation into another of Richard Grau's contributions to the debate about Art. 48, and it can be considered as a reply to Carl Schmitt. The third part is a discussion of two writings on the execution of the laws of the Reich. Kelsen wrote an essay, and a rather unknown scholar by the name of Wolfgang Flad wrote a small book on the topic. Flad's monograph can be read partially as a response to Kelsen's essay. The fourth part is a discussion of Anschütz's 1929 edition of his commentary on the Weimarer Reichsverfassung. As before, the concentration here is on his comments on Art. 48, and while they are not as exhaustive as in the 14th and final edition, they are much more extensive than what he had written in 1921. The fifth part is an examination of Schmitt's "Hüter der Verfassung," while the sixth part is Kelsen's second contribution in this chapter. "Wer soll der Hüter der Verfassung sein?" is Kelsen's reply to Schmitt. The chapter ends with some brief concluding comments.

1927–1929: The Historical Context

When Friedrich Ebert died on February 28, 1925, many people mourned his passing but many others were heartened. Ebert was a well-respected member of

DOI: 10.4324/9781003312796-5

the SPD and a committed democrat. With Ebert's death, Weimar's opponents believed that they were becoming more successful in undermining the government. One of the more helpful indications of this success was the election of Paul Hindenburg in 1925. He was, as Friedrich Freiherr Hiller von Gaetringen noted, the "Monarchist." Hindenburg was an indication of the strength of the monarchists and a sign of the weakness of the Republic (Hiller von Gaetringen 1993: 254). Hindenburg's decisions and actions in the last days of the Weimar Republic tarnished his reputation, so it is difficult to understand his position and importance during the First World War. One of Hindenburg's most recent biographers reminds us that Hindenburg was the "incarnation of national unity," and that reputation was reinforced with his victory at Tannenberg. In addition, Wolfram Pyta suggested that Hindenburg embodied what Max Weber had referred to as "charismatischen Herrschaft." This Weberian concept was about the type of authority that was based neither upon tradition nor upon laws, but was founded solely on the devotion to the leader's personal charisma (Pyta 2009: 91, 93, 289–293). Pyta argued that while Hindenburg was beloved by many, his election to the presidency was not at all assured. This doubt was caused in part by the attacks on Hindenburg from his opponents and their allies. But it was also caused in part because Hindenburg himself was reluctant to campaign (Stibbe 2022: 82–83). But Hindenburg was elected in April of 1925 (Pyta 2009: 469–473; Kolb 2002: 84–85). Much of Hindenburg's attraction was the "longing for the good old time" ("Sehnsucht nach guten alten Zeit") (Büttner 2008: 346). The "longing for the good old time" was also partially responsible for the initial acceptance of the Nazi Party from 1925. The party continued to attract more members in the following years, and 1926 saw the introduction of the obligatory "Hitler salute" ("Hitler Gruß") (Mommsen 2001: 392–393, 399, Megerle 1994: 31–33). But the years 1927 through the fall of 1929 were largely years of relative peace, if not prosperity. Theo Stammen referred to them as "golden twenties" (Stammen 1994: 359–360). Whether that is an accurate assessment is questionable; what is not is that compared to the previous three years and to the later three years, 1927 and 1928 were considerably more peaceful. The year 1929 is a slightly different matter. While most of that year saw political and economic stability, the effects of the U.S. stock market had far-reaching repercussions, especially in November and December of that year (Ruck 1995: 132, 135–136). But the concern here is not with economic crises but with the legal debates regarding Art. 48 of the Weimarer Reichsverfassung.

Grau's 1927 Art. 48

Chapter 4 ended with a discussion of Richard Grau's 1926 article, so it seems somehow fitting that this chapter begins with an investigation of another of Grau's essays. It is even more appropriate given its title "Diktaturgewalt und Reichsverfassung" ("Dictatorial Power and the Reich's Constitution"). Before turning to this essay, it is noteworthy to comment briefly on the volume in which it is found. It was a "Festschrift" for Emil Seckel. Seckel (1864–1924) was trained in law at Tübingen and taught at the University in Berlin. He was rector in 1920 and was influential in his capacity as professor and as rector. Normally, a "Festschrift" is in honor of some scholar's birthday, but since Seckel had died in 1924, the volume was a "Gedächtnis" ("remembrance"). Another noteworthy point was that it was a relatively minor contribution in that there were only seven contributors. Of these, three were professors, one was a "Privatdozent," and three were attorneys. All three of the attorneys resided in Berlin—including Richard Grau and his brother Walter.

"Diktaturgewalt und Reichsverfassung" is lengthy (64 pages) and divided into four parts plus an introduction. The introduction, Part I, and Part IV are brief. In contrast, Parts II and II are lengthy at roughly 20 pages each. Grau was never noted for clarity and this essay is even less clear than his previous writings. At least he was relatively clear and concise in setting out the problem and its significance ("Das Problem und seine Bedeutung") in his introduction.

Richard Grau begins by observing that people had become accustomed to speak about a dictatorship when discussing the Reichspräsident and the government of a "Land." But he reminds his readers that the concept of dictatorship has historically referred to a "formal illegal extraordinary force of a single holder of power" ("formell unrechtmäßigen außerordentlichen Gewalt eines einzelnen Machthabers"). In this sense, the concept of a dictatorship in the Weimar Constitution is partially based upon Roman law (Grau 1927: 430–431). But the notion of a dictatorship in Roman law was not negative or at least neutral. In contrast, the concept of a dictatorship in Weimar is not regarded as neutral but is considered suspect. Grau pointed specifically to Hans Gmelin's article "Der Ausnahmezustand" in the *Handbuch der Politik* and to the reaction to the Bavarian authorities' insistence on the immunization of Bavarian soldiers (Grau 1927: 432–433; Gmelin 1921: 159–160). Grau suggested that the difference in attitude between the Romans and today's Germans towards dictatorship rests on the fact that the former was based upon tradition and moral worth. For the latter, tradition and moral worth are almost entirely missing. As a result, in the middle of the 1920s Germans regard it as simply an instrument that ministerial bureaucrats use (or misuse). Grau explains that what is needed is a clarification of the relationship between dictatorship and the Reichsverfassung, and he will show that there are constitutional limits to the dictatorship and especially to Art. 48. He notes further that Schmitt and Jacobi had argued in their papers at the 1924 conference that there were no limits on the dictatorship's powers (Grau 1927: 433–434).

Part I is Grau's discussion regarding the boundaries of the question ("Abgrenzung der Streitfrage"). It is slightly more than two pages but he makes some important points. First, he insists that people need to regard the question as a legal one and if they do, they will recognize that the dictatorship referred to in Art. 48 is not illegal but is law abiding: "The dictatorship of Art. 48 is thus *no law against the constitution*" (emphasis is original) ("Die

Diktatur des Art. 48 ist also *kein Recht gegen die Verfassung*"). On the basis of this and another point, Grau insists that the boundaries of this issue are now clearly delineated. The disagreement is not about the constitutionality of the dictatorship because it is legal. The disagreement is also not about the validity of the dictatorship because it is legally justified. Rather, the disagreement is about how far the Reichpresident's authority extends regarding the instituting of those necessary measures (Grau 1927: 436).

Part II is devoted to discussing the foundations of the claim that Art. 48 cannot be shown to be touchable or reachable. The German term is "Anstasbarkeit," the term for not being touchable is "Unantasbarkeit," and the doctrine of being untouchable is "Unantasbarkeitslehre." Part II is especially difficult to follow and this is partially because Grau appeals to history and partially because he maintains that the problem is logical rather than conceptual. Yet, as he notes, it is a matter of lack of conceptual clarity (Grau 1927: 437–443). Grau returns to the central question about a need for a new law to support Art. 48—would this be a new extraordinary organization to deal with the supposed discrepancy between the constitution as a whole and Art. 48? Grau admits the fact that the paragraphs that make up Art. 48 do not contain many words but they convey an extraordinarily lengthy and complex group of ideas. As he had just done earlier in Part II, he returns again to history to shed light on this complex matter. His examples vary, but Grau's critics might not have been very impressed with his examples. Why would a German citizen be swayed by what happened in France in the previous century? He has a stronger case when he turns to a discussion of the "colorless expression 'measures'" ("farblosen Ausdruckes 'Maßnahmen'"). The expression does not tell the Reichspräsident what he should or should not order. Again, the word "measure" is a "colorless nothing" ("farbloses Nichts"). Grau concludes from all of this that in terms of organization, the general clause of Art. 48 has no significance. Such an organizational norm *can* have a function, but it certainly does not mean that it must have such a function. As such, it is a function but does not command as does a law (Grau 1927: 445–446).

Grau considers how the dictatorship compares to other extraordinary situations. One that seems closest is the "war master" ("Kriegsherr") who can simply implement all relevant measures. Of course, it is the "Kreigsherr" alone who determines what is and what is not relevant. But Grau points out that this is typically a matter of external issues and is not really related to issues between a federal government and its member states. This is another matter of governmental competency, and one of the clearest examples is when a government signs a formal peace treaty. Then it is obvious that it is the federal government that has the competency and not the member states. As another example, Grau points out that the American government has the competency to conclude trade agreements. These may be genuine examples but it is not clear what they really have to do with the necessary measures of Art. 48. It is only when Grau begins to examine the "matter of the Reich's force" ("Sache der Reichsgewalt") that he returns to issues which are clearly pertinent to Art. 48.

Although a dictator is usually depicted as a single individual possessing an enormous amount of power, Grau argues that that interpretation is misleading. It is far more accurate to note that the dictatorship relies upon a huge number of others. In effect, the dictatorship needs bureaucrats in an organization. He refers to this as "a dictatorship organization" ("ein Diktaturbehörde"). Grau spends several pages detailing how these bureaucrats tend to function in the dictatorial organization and what their particular functions are. It is not always clear what relevance these comments have, and Grau's account improves when he returns to the issue of Art. 48.

On the one hand, Grau repeats his earlier assertions that "measures" appear as "colorless" ("farblos") but here he ties it directly to the dictatorial organization (Grau 1927: 450–451). On the other hand, he connects "measures" to Abs. 5—the paragraph that stipulates that further information would be forthcoming through the appropriate Reich law. These lead momentarily to the notion of the alteration of the constitution, but Grau does not elaborate on this. Instead, he focuses on the concept of the "Reichspräsident" as a real person. But again, Grau emphasizes that this actual individual is the "Reichspräsident" but as one who invokes Art. 48, he must make use of his "dictatorial authorities." This is a legitimate point that Grau continuously stresses; however, he then offers a fictional account of a person who orders the demobilization of the troops. His point appears to be that in such a fictive account, the power would be political but in the real Art. 48 the power is legal.

The provisional conclusion that Grau draws is that under Art. 48 the "Reichspräsident" cannot consider a normal approach because it lies outside normal organizations. Instead, the "Reichspräsident" needs an extraordinary organization to implement his "necessary measures." As this shows, the conclusion thus far reached is only provisional and further investigation is warranted. That is the purpose of Part III.

Part III is another lengthy part and like Part II has remarks that are fully relevant to the matter of Art. 48 and still other comments that seem like asides. But the focus here is less negative than the previous part. As the title indicates, it is a setting out of the general clause of Art. 48 ("Zur Auslegung der Generalklausel des Art. 48 R.V.") (Grau 1927: 454).

Thus far, Grau had not specified what he meant by "general clause," but here he indicates that it is comprised by the first sentence in Abs. 2 (see Preuß 2015: 598). Grau adds that next to this "general clause" is the "suspension clause" ("Suspensionsklausel") which states that "he (the dictator)" ("er [der Diktator]") can set aside either entirely or partially Articles 114, 115, 117, 118, 123, 124, and 153 (Grau 1927: 455). Part III is intended to be Grau's investigation into the tension between the "general clause" and the "suspension clause." Grau insists that no constitution "springs out of the blue" but is a derivative of prior constitutions. In addition, any constitution is built upon previous political and juridical theories. As a result, earlier "ideologies" influence a new constitution. That is Grau's justification for considering earlier theses, regardless of whether they were German or from a foreign country

(Grau 1927: 455–457). It is not, however, only legal doctrines that impact a new constitution; historical factors also exert their influence. Here, Grau has in mind Germany's devastating defeat in November 1918, and it was not just Germany's response to it but also its response to President Woodrow Wilson's proposals regarding a new world order. It is in this light that Grau insists that Art. 48 must be understood. This is especially relevant because that article confers extraordinary powers: dictatorship powers. Grau is no doubt correct in his assessment, but his comments on the American and French revolutions as well as the uprising in France in 1830 can be safely left aside. Similarly, his remarks about Germany in 1850 and even in 1871 can be largely omitted (Grau 1927: 458–465).

Grau was undoubtedly correct in claiming that Bismarck's constitution was a direct result of the battles of the previous several years and the struggle for unification. In the same vein, Grau is also correct in his assertion that the Weimarer Reichsverfassung developed in similar fashion. What makes the current debate so different and so important is the tension between the inviolable constitution and the "suspension clause." Grau repeats that he has emphasized the tension between the "general clause" and the "suspension clause"—the former maintains the norm while the latter undermines it. Grau insists that this tension is untenable because the "suspension clause" not only threatens the seven articles but also the entire constitution. This leads Grau to the crucial question regarding which "type" of "exception" this is. He puts this into other words, which he emphasizes: "that *only these seven constitutional articles are under the disposition of the dictator, but the others are untouchable*" ("daß *nur diese sieben Verfassungsartikel zur Disposition des Diktators stehen, die anderen aber unantastbar sind*") (Grau 1927: 467). His answer is that the dictator does not have such unlimited power that he can choose which articles he can suspend and which ones are beyond his reach. Grau suggests that the dictator does not possess such powers. To explain this in more detail, Grau suggests one needs to investigate constitutional norms and their relations to the dictator's grasp (Grau 1927: 468). He maintains that the measures employed and the setting aside of the seven articles is temporally limited and that as soon as the threat has passed, the measures must be stopped immediately. Grau's point is that the "suspension clause" has only a limited applicability and must not be misused (Grau 1927: 468).

Grau next turns to the issue of altering the constitution. Once again, this notion of changing the constitution runs into the issue of the inviolability of the constitution. Critics, like Schmitt, contend that the "suspension clause" has more power than the actual constitution. However, the nature of constitutions in general and the Weimar Constitution in particular hold that the constitution itself takes legal precedence over any specific clause (Grau 1927: 470–471). Grau suggests that there are only two ways in which a "basic right" can be suspended. The first and simplest way is by the announcement that the "basic right" needs to be temporarily suspended. In this, the dictator's assistants can help to clarify what this means and to aid in determining how long the suspension will last. This is the means by which military commanders can suspend certain rights. The second and more complex method is when someone in authority uses some form of "suspension clause" to justify the removal of barriers around "basic rights." The apparent difference between these two is the first means appears to follow legal norms while the second one tends to ignore them. But he suggests that there is only a formal difference between them (Grau 1927: 473–474). What they have in common is that each means is limited in time and limited in scope. They also are limited in what the author of the order of suspension can demand. Grau points out that even in Roman times, the dictator was limited—he could not suspend all rights and the magistrates were not bound by him as they were by the laws. Whether Grau was correct regarding these matters is better left for legal historians to decide. What needs to be explained is Grau's contention that the "suspension clause" runs up against the inviolability of the "general clause" and, as such, must be subordinate to the more basic and more general clause (Grau 1927: 480–481, 484). Scholars like Schmitt misinterpreted this relationship and hence Schmitt and those others were incorrect (Grau 1927: 481–483). His conclusion is that the Reichspräsident does not have dictatorial powers and cannot unilaterally suspend the constitution in total but he can suspend parts, but only for a very limited time (Grau 1927: 485). Grau complains about the difference of opinions about Art. 48, but he hints that it is understandable, given much of its language. He also points to the words regarding more information would be forthcoming—as it never really did (Grau 1927: 487).

Part IV is Grau's conclusion in which he maintains that the law is superior to the power of the dictatorship. He insists once again that the "general clause" regarding the inviolability of the constitution means that the "suspension clause" is, and must be, subordinate to it. In addition, any "dictatorship measures" ("Diktaturmaßnahmen") cannot be laws. This is the case with respect to regular laws and regular rights; it is even more applicable with respect to constitutional laws and "basic rights" (Grau 1927: 490–492). As to the "force" ("Gewalt") that the dictator claims is his, Grau contends that it is not granted by the constitutional organization. In fact, such "force" is usually unwanted and unwarranted. In summary, Grau warns of the tension between the dictatorship and norms and counsels that it may be necessary to place further restrictions on the "dictatorship force" ("Diktaturgewalt") (Grau 1927: 493–494).

Grau's essay is not easy to follow but his conclusion appears sound. While Schmitt and others have argued for unlimited dictatorial powers, Grau sides with those like Anschütz who have maintained that freedom is more important than order and that law is superior to force.

"Reichsexekution"—Kelsen and Flad

The two contributions discussed in this section have a number of things in common. They are both focused on the notion of how and when the Reich is obligated to execute some particular command. They are both wide-ranging so not all of what is contained in both works is relevant, but both deal with Art. 48 and its execution. Finally, both are scholarly works written in legal language and have appropriately lengthy titles. But Kelsen's was an essay while Flad's was a book.

Hans Kelsen's essay has the title "Die Bundesexekution. Ein Beitrag zur Theorie und Praxis des Bundesstaates, unter besonderer Berücksichtigung der deutschen Reichs- und der österreichischen Bundes-Verfassung." A possible translation might be: "The Federal Execution. A Contribution to the Theory and Praxis of the Federal States With a Special Consideration of the German Reich and the Austrian Federal Constitution." Although "Constitution" is singular, it is clear that Kelsen meant both the German and the Austrian constitutions. It is worth keeping in mind that at the time Kelsen wrote this, he was still in Austria and had not yet moved to Germany. It is also worth remembering that Kelsen was not only the author of the Austrian constitution but had recently published his second major work on the philosophy of law.

Both Germany and Austria suffered from the effects of the First World War and both countries saw a revolution in the historical version of a state. Both left behind the old single state idea and became a federal republic. Both had new constitutions that reflected the new form of state: Germany's from August 11, 1919, and Austria's from October 1, 1920. But each state approached the execution of state laws in different ways. It is in this larger sense that Kelsen believed a contrasting account was warranted (Kelsen 1927: 127). Kelsen's essay has six parts but only two of them are relevant here. Several of the others may be of some interest to legal scholars but one in particular is intriguing. Sections III and IV contain a lengthy and sustained examination and reply to a work that Georg Jellinek had published in the 1880s. Jellinek had not yet become the famous Heidelberg constitutional scholar and author of the famous *Allgemeine Staatslehre* (1900). Kelsen's tone is respectful but it is clear that he thinks his own *Allgemeine Staatslehre* (1925) supersedes Jellinek's classic text.

It is Section V that is pertinent here as it focuses on Germany's constitution. Although Kelsen discusses a number of articles from the Weimarer Reichsverfassung, all of them are relevant to the present discussion regarding Art. 48. They will also be of interest later in this chapter and especially in the next one. That is because the issue centers on the tension between the federal government and the "Land."

Kelsen begins Section V with an acknowledgement that thus far there has not been a satisfactory solution to the competition between federal governments and state governments. He suggests that there are three key issues that need to be addressed: (1) the question regarding the legality of an illegal case, (2) the question of the use of force in an illegal case, and (3) what claim is there regarding "parity" between the federal government ("Bund [Reich]") and "member states" ("Gliedstaaten [Länder]") (Kelsen 1927: 167).

Regarding (1), Kelsen indicates that Art. 13 and Art. 15 gives the federal government more weight than any member states. Art. 13 is "Reichsrecht bricht Landrecht"; that is, federal law supersedes any "Land" law. Art. 15 says basically the same—the federal law trumps any state law (Preuß 2015: 595). Kelsen suggests that any discrepancy can be adjudicated by a "state law court" ("Staatsgerichtshof") (Kelsen 1927: 167). His concern is about the illegality of a supposed law and how the federal government can deal with it. But the case that he has in mind is not really about that as it is about when there are two articles that appear to be in conflict. The two articles are Art. 19 and Art. 48. Art. 48 does not need any clarification but Art. 19 does. Art. 19 offers several scenarios in which there are fundamental oppositions: within a member state; between member states; and between the federal government and a member state. It is the "Staatsgerichtshof" that will determine which party is right (Preuß 2015: 596). However, Art. 48 gives the "Reichspräsident" the power to intervene—not the "Staatsgerichtshof." Art. 19 does not stand alone but is part of the entire Weimarer Reichsverfassung. Therefore, either Art. 19 has validity or Art. 48 does. Either Art. 19 limits Abs. 1 of Art. 48 or Abs. 1 of Art. 48 limits Art. 19. He adds that it is little wonder that this problem has generated opposing views by some of the leading constitutional law scholars (Kelsen 1927: 168). There are some scholars (like Triepel) who have argued that the Reichspräsident has the power to execute his decisions while others (like Anschütz) have countered that the Reichspräsident (like all German citizens) is bound to follow the law of the land and especially the law as set out by the highest court (the "Staatsgerichtshof"). Yet it seems that part of the difficulty in determining the real answer is that there are two issues involved. Kelsen insists that Art. 48 Abs. 1 applies not only to the "execution as such," but also to the presupposition of the execution (Kelsen 1927: 168–169). Kelsen asks whether the Reichspräsident is the right person to determine whether a "Land" has not fulfilled its obligations under Art. 48 Abs. 1. This is not an executive decision but a legal one. He points again to Art. 19 where it is the court that must decide such questions. His point appears to be that while the Reichspräsident can execute the decision to intervene, it is the court that should determine whether an intervention is legally warranted. As to the opposing views of Anschütz and Triepel, it is not an easy matter to determine who is has the right argument; instead, a "scholarly" ("wissenschaftlicher") interpretation can be provided for both sides (Kelsen 1927: 169). However, it does seem that Kelsen wants to side with Anschütz and, like him, relies heavily on Art. 19, not to mention 13 and 15. It is, for Kelsen, a question about "binding legal norms" ("bindenden Rechtsnormen") and that is a matter for the courts. Again, Kelsen has no problem with the Reichspräsident carrying out such execution, but he does have a problem with the executive determining a judicial question (Kelsen 1927: 171–173).

Kelsen then moves to discuss this problem within the context of the whole and the "part." The Reich is the whole, or the "entire community" ("Gesamtgemeinschaft"), whereas the "Land" is the part, or the "part community" ("Teilgemeinschaft"). In this sense, the part does not have standing to go against the whole. Nonetheless, Kelsen concludes that while it is up to the

Reichspräsident to perform the "Reich's execution" ("Reichsexekution)," it is the court which determines whether such an incursion into the matters of a "Land" is legally justified (Kelsen 1927: 175).

Whereas we know that Richard Grau was an attorney living in Berlin and was recognized as one of the leading authorities on Art. 48, we know practically nothing about Wolfgang Flad. He is not to be confused with the famous German artist with the same name. What we do know is that Flad thanked Gerhard Anschütz for his encouragement to write *Verfassungsgerichtsbarkeit und Reichsexekution* and he thanked the legal faculty of Heidelberg University for their support in publishing this work (Flad 1929: 3).

As with Kelsen's essay, much of Flad's book has no direct bearing on the debate about Art. 48. Instead, it is about larger legal issues and how they can and cannot be resolved by legal means. It is, however, in the second section of the second chapter that Flad addresses the issue of Art. 48 and, like Kelsen, Flad focuses his attention on the notion of the "Reichsexekution." The previous chapter had addressed Articles 13, 15, and 19 and the following chapter focused on the carrying out of orders. Chapter II is on the relationship between the "Reichsexekution" and the constitutional court. Yet the first section is on the prevailing doctrine of the state and the third section is on the means in which the military executes its orders. These make it rather odd that the middle second section has the title "One Own's Attempt at a Solution" ("Eigener Versuch einer Lösung"). Nevertheless, it is focused on Art. 48.

Just prior to section 2, Flad notes the contradiction between Art. 19 and Art. 48 and how the former limits the Reichspräsident's powers where the latter extends them (Flad 1929: 94–95). The function of section 2 is to reexamine this contradiction, and he begins by assessing the purpose of Art. 19 Abs. II. There it briefly states, "The Reichspräsident carries out the judgment of the state court" ("Der Reichspräsident vollstreckt das Urteil des Staatsgerichtshof") (Flad 1929: 98; Preuß 2015: 596). Flad suggests that it is not the Reichspräsident who determines whether a "Land" is not fulfilling its obligations under Art. 48 Abs. 1, but it is the court that should be determining that (Flad 1929: 99–101). It is noteworthy that Flad takes issue with Richard Grau in that the latter misunderstood the nature of the "Reichsexekution"—the execution is nothing other than the most severe measure of the Reich (Flad 1929: 102, note 1). It is also noteworthy that Flad allows that such determinations are not solely founded upon law but often involve political factors. This is especially true regarding the determination of a "Land" failing to fulfill its obligations (Flad 1929: 106–107). But he suggests that the determination of a threat or real disruption of "public security and order" ("öffentliche Sicherheit und Ordnung") is not a political decision and certainly not a minor one, whereas a real disturbance is far more problematic than the failure to fulfill some obligation and, thus, Abs. 2 is far more important that Abs. 1. In light of this, Flad makes a distinction between "execution" and "intervention" and between "Exekution" and "Diktaturgewalt" (Flad 1929: 108–111). After offering a few historical examples, Flad suggests that any such intervention is always the prerogative of the "Reichskanzler" (Flad 1929: 123). Note, Flad has shifted from the "Reichspräsident" to the "Reichskanzler." This shift is remarkable because he then reverts to referring to the "Reichspräsident" for the remainder of his book. In addition, he confesses that the situation remains unclear and that a solution lays in the hands of the legislators. He concludes with the plea that they set themselves the following goal: "The renewal and grounding of the Reich in freedom and justice" ("Die Erneuerung und Befestigung des Reichs in Freiheit und Gerechtigkeit") (Flad 1929: 154).

Anschütz's Later (1929) Commentary on Art. 48

In 1929, the 11th edition of *Die Verfassung des Deutschen Reichs* was published. This was Gerhard Anschütz's second revising of his commentary and appeared four years after the first revision and eight years after the original edition was published. The 11th edition was almost 700 pages long while the original one was not even 300. Anschütz made changes and additions to many of the articles, but the comments on Art. 48 were massive. To remind the reader of the difference, the 1921 edition had three pages devoted to that article while the 1929 edition had 20 (Anschütz 1921: 106–108, 1929: 239–259). It was not just the quantity that made the 1929 edition different from the 1921 edition; it was also the quality. The first edition did not have a section on literature while the 11th had almost a full page devoted to numerous articles and the few books devoted to Art. 48. These included earlier contributions such as Grau's book and other commentaries. But it included the debate between Carl Schmitt, Erwin Jacobi, and Hans Nawiasky. It also included Kelsen's 1927 "Festschrift" contribution and Grau's 1928 "Festschrift" essay (Anschütz 1929: 240). Anschütz divided his "Literatur" into two sections: Section I covered Absatz 1, which he called "Reichsexekution," and section II was devoted to Absatze 2–5 and he named it "Diktaturgewalt des RPräs und der Landesregierungen." Anschütz's introductory remarks amount to close to three pages; the section on "Reichsexekution" is four pages (with an almost full-page footnote); and the section on "Diktaturgewalt" is almost 14 pages.

Anschütz's introductory section has two paragraphs. Paragraph 1 is rather short and contains some brief comments. He had merely mentioned in the first edition that Art. 48 covers two matters, but in the 11th he emphasizes that Art. 48 governs two different things. Abs. 1 dictates what the Reich can "execute" over a "Land" that does not fulfill its duties while Abs. 2–5 discuss what measures the "Reich" can employ to contain "unusual disturbances" ("ungewöhnlicher Störungen") or combat the "threatening of public security and order" ("Gefährdungen der öffentliche Sicherheit und Ordnung"). The "Diktaturgewalt" confers upon the Reichspräsident the use of "extraordinary dictatorial measures" ("außerordentliche diktatorische Maßnahmen") (Anschütz 1929: 240). Anschütz mentions the history of Art. 48 in the discussions leading up to the formal adoption of that article and he insists that the present examination of both the "Reichsexekution" and the "Diktaturgewalt" are scholarly investigations. He adds that in order to accomplish this, it is important to differentiate the two.

Paragraph 2 is longer and more detailed. Part of it is a brief discussion of socialist-communist revolutionary activities that officials determined were threats to "public security and order" and part of it is the mention of the need for clarity when such occasions arise. And, part of it is an indication that measures can and should be taken whether the activities are covered by Abs. 1, by Abs. 2, or by both 1 and 2. Finally, there is the suggestion that Abs. 3, 4, and 5 are elaborations and clarifications of Abs. 2 (Anschütz 1929: 241–243).

Regarding "I. Die Reichsexekution" Anschütz insisted that Abs. 1 did not cover each and every duty that the "Land" was obligated to fulfill. He listed private law, police regulations, and a number of other areas in which the Reichspräsident would not be required to intervene. Instead, the duties are specifically limited to those which are "*expressly*" ("*ausdrücklichlen*") constitutional or legally written. His point is that the Reich must be capable and ready to execute its duty to intervene, but this also implies that there are genuine grounds to do so. Anschütz points out that to intervene is to make a judgment about matters that are really matters for the "Land" to decide (Anschütz 1929: 243–244).

In addition, the Reichspräsident needs to determine which "*means and ways*" ("*Mittel und Wege*") are appropriate when a "Land" has not fulfilled its obligation. This issue is not only a legal determination, but also an economic one—the Reich's intervention will cost money. If anything, the previous interventions during 1920 and 1923 demonstrated that decisions made by the Reich were, and are, not without legal, political, and economic consequences (Anschütz 1929: 245–246).

In the opening sentence to "II. Die Diktaturgewalt des Reichspräsidenten und der Landesregierungen" Anschütz makes it abundantly clear that he regards the "extraordinary" "dictatorial" force the Reichspräsident can use to be restrictive. As he argues later, it is restricted in terms of place, duration, and degree. This is not just based upon his reading of Art. 48; it is also founded on previous German legal determinations. Specifically, he named the older terms for justifying the extraordinary measures such as "state of war" ("Kriegszustand") and "state of occupation" ("Belagerungszustand") (Anschütz 1929: 246–247). Then, it seemed that the measures instituted were both legal and necessary, in part because they were limited in terms of duration and place. What makes Art. 48 so debatable is that it appears unlimited in terms of time and space but also because it appears to lack any boundaries on its power. What makes this so apparent is that there does not seem to be any judicial review of it. Again, Anschütz emphasizes that this is not just a legal issue but also a financial one. He clarifies that when public security is threatened or harmed, then it is also a matter of the economic impact on the businesses and factories in that area. It is not just the ones who are causing the disturbances who are threatening the economy. Measures intended to restore order that are taken by those authorities will also have their own negative effects

(Anschütz 1929: 247–248). Anschütz mentioned that during 1925, Art. 48 was invoked 135 times. However, he made two further observations. The first was more of a suggestion that the invocation of that article was not intended for real threats. The second was more concrete and that the years the "dictatorship force" ("Diktaturgewalt") was scarcely used between 1926 and 1928. The unspoken hint was that its use was in the past—Anschütz was a great constitutional scholar and a rather good judge of character, but he was too optimistic about the immediate future. As will be discussed in the final chapter, Anschütz was seriously affected by the turn of events in 1933.

Returning to Anschütz's analysis regarding the "content and circumference" ("Inhalt und Umfang") of Art. 48, he focuses on two major points. The first is the notion of "measures" ("Maßnahmen") and the second is "necessary" ("notwendig"). Normally, any measures, whether they are absolutely necessary or not, are subject to judicial review. However, the "measures" instituted under Art. 48 are exempt from legal scrutiny. In this case, they appear to be "completely unlimited" ("völlig unbeschränktes") (Anschütz 1929: 249). Given this, he insisted that it was crucial to ask, "What are 'measures' in the intentions of Abs. 2 and 4?" ("Was sind 'Maßnahemen' im Sinne der Abs. 2 und 4?") (Anschütz 1929: 250). According to Abs. 2, the "measures" that are expressly allowed are the use of "weaponized power" ("bewaffeneten Macht"), and he takes that to mean that the army can be deployed. Anschütz referred to Grau's 1922 book and Schmitt's 1924 paper and he repeats their claims that there is nothing that limits the "dictatorial power" (Anschütz 1929: 250, note 1, 251). Anschütz disputes Schmitt's and Grau's understanding of this power and he maintains that constitutional history reveals that no command has been unlimited—even military orders are subject to limitations. In particular, he takes exception to the "Schmitt-Jacobi Theory" and argues that it has been subject to thorough criticisms. This is largely because the constitution cannot be harmed (Anschütz 1929: 253).

There is a tension between what Art. 48 Abs. 2 seems to allow and what the Weimarer Reichsverfassung indicates as a whole. What the paragraph seems to allow, the constitution does not. There cannot be unlimited power; the constitution guarantees basic rights. Anschütz claims that even when Art. 48 has been invoked, no one claimed that it was unlimited in power and in duration. Instead, it was limited to the location of the disturbance and it was in force only as long as the disturbance lasted (Anschütz 1929: 255–257).

Finally, Anschütz pointed out that the term "einstweilige" means "once" so that the use is limited. He allowed that even state governments have relied on Art. 48 and he referred to the state of Bavaria, which enforced inoculation. But he pointed out that the order applied only to soldiers; more importantly, he insisted that it was strictly unconstitutional. Rather than Art. 48 being unlimited, Anschütz's final determination was that it was constitutionally limited and that it can, and should, be regulated (Anschütz 1929: 258–259).

Anschütz's 1929 edition is noteworthy because of its impressive detail and relative clarity but also because of the references to some of the major participants in the Art. 48 debate. For example, Grau, Kelsen, Nawiasky, and Schmitt were cited two times each (Anschütz 1929: 250, 253/241, 248/250, 259/250, 253). Grau, Kelsen, and Schmitt will continue to be prominent in this debate—Kelsen and Schmitt in the remainder of this chapter and all three scholars in Chapter 6.

Carl Schmitt's "Hüter der Verfassung"

The debate between Carl Schmitt and Hans Kelsen is not just about Art. 48. In fact, Art. 48 plays a rather limited role in this conflict. This debate is also more than about who is supposed to be the "guardian of the constitution" ("Hüter der Verfassung"). It is also about the nature and the function of a government and the role that politics should be allowed to perform in law. While this debate may seem to be about some archaic legal matter, it is more about what a government is intended to do and what law actually means. Two final points: by 1929 both Schmitt and Kelsen were famous and both were highly respected scholars. This debate about governing, law, and politics would increase in tempo and in consequences within three more years. The debate between Schmitt and Kelsen not only has intrinsic value; it also has valuable lessons for today.

Carl Schmitt had a gift for provocative opening lines and the first sentence of "Hüter der Verfassung" is one of them. Actually, the first one gains in importance because of the following one. Schmitt's first sentence reads, "The doctrine of the state from the prewar era hardly talked about a guardian of the constitution" ("Die Staatslehre der Vorkriegszeit sprach kaum von einem Hüter der Verfassung"). The second line is, "In times of inner political security and stability, these types of constitutional-legal problems are uninteresting" ("In Zeiten innerpolitischer Sicherheit und Stabilität werden deratige verfassungsrechtliche Probleme uninteressant") (Schmitt 1929: 161). His point was that during and after the Bismarck years there was such stability that there was no need for any type of discussion regarding protecting or guarding the constitution. It was only after the Weimar Constitution was introduced that difficulties began to occur, and as they increased during the 1920s, the question about the "guardian of the constitution" continued to increase. Schmitt acknowledges that most legal scholars are now concerned with this issue, but he singles out one particular group. He refers to them as "Justiz-Juristen" and he applauds this as a "good descriptive expression" ("gut charakterisierenden Ausdruck") but insists that he did not coin it (Schmitt 1929: 163, note 6).

The term "Justiz-Juristen" is literally "Justice-Jurists," but what it refers to are the jurists who have been associated with the journal *Die Justiz*. This journal is crucial for three reasons. First, it was intended both as a journal for the renewal of German law and as the journal for republican judges. *Die Justiz* had a lengthy subtitle: *Zeitschrift für Erneuerung des Deutschen Rechtswesen. Zugleich Organ des Republikanischen Richterbundes.* Founded in 1925 and continuing until 1933, the eight volumes contain some of the best pro-democracy and republican-minded legal theorists of the late Weimar period (See no name 1925/1926: 2–5). Second, the first issue (1925/1926) had an article that was intended to address some of the shortcomings and discrepancies regarding Art. 48. The main points of this article were to delineate the types of conditions that would count as "state of exception" ("Ausnahmezustand"), and four were listed: (1) danger of war, (2) the declaration of war, (3) imminent danger of internal unrest, and (4) the actual outbreak of internal unrest. This list was intended to provide concrete instances of what counted as a "state of exception" and thus limit what grounds the Reichspräsident could use to justify military intervention. It also served to clarify that the ultimate decider was not the Reichspräsident but the "federal state court" (Staatsgerichtshof") (Verus 1925/1926: 368, 376–378).[1] Third, issue number six (1930/1931) included Hans Kelsen's reply to Schmitt.

To return to "Hüter der Verfassung," Schmitt refers to a polemical work that would appear later in 1929. The article was "Das Reichsgerichts als Hüter der Verfassung," and Schmitt makes clear that he disagrees with those who claim that the decision rests with the federal state court. But here he insists that the court is concerned with the law and he notes that the judge must base his decision on the laws. But that is much different from that which should be the "guardian of the constitution." That is because the judge deals with normal issues but the "guardian of the constitution" confronts an abnormal case (Schmitt 1929: 168–170). Schmitt invokes not only the American constitution and the French one, but in a footnote he mentions the Portuguese constitution (Schmitt 1929: 172, note 38). Schmitt concludes from this "brief overview" that courts are not the ones to protect the constitution and to guarantee its security. He complains that people invoke the term "Rechtsstaat" or the "legal state" but this is a naïve and abstract expression that does not signify much. Instead, he insists that what is needed is someone who can specifically tackle the real danger. It is worth quoting his claim: "The guardian should not [be] against abstract and general [dangers] but rather, should be securing against the wholly specific, actual fearful dangers" ("Der Hüter soll nicht abstrakt und schlechthin, sondern gegen ganz bestimmte, konkrete befürchtete Gefahren sichern") (Schmitt 1929: 173–175). Previously, the constitution needed protection from the executive, but now it needs to be guarded against the "changing parliamentary majority" ("wechselnden Parlamentsmehrheit"). Schmitt bemoans the claim that the essence of democracy is the compromise between majority and minority. Schmitt is at his caustic best when he describes that as "a pretty example" ("ein hübsches Beispiel") and ridicules Hans Kelsen for insisting that it is the essence of the democratic process (Schmitt 1929: 175–176).

Schmitt asks, how is it possible that the "guardian of the constitution" can be found within the sphere of justice and how far can the "guardian of the

1 Unlike most of the articles in *Die Justiz*, this one by Verus lists no first name and there is only the city of Berlin. I have not been able to find anything more about this author.

constitution" be a function of the legal apparatus? His preliminary response is that this is merely the appearance of justice and is only the attempt to clothe the real answer with something else (Schmitt 1929: 176–177). His approach is to compare the danger to the constitution to other, genuine cases in which someone is harmed. He has in mind civil cases and administrative ones as well. These are real cases with real damages and it is the law's duty to determine who should be punished and who should be compensated. But, Schmitt contends that the threats against the constitution do not bear similarities to these ordinary cases. Instead, the threat against the constitution is treason and, as such, lies outside the boundaries of normal justice. That is partially because this is not merely a matter of the state but also of politics. Normal assessments and normal penalties do not, and cannot, apply in these special cases. In light of this, a "Staatsgerichtshof" is not the appropriate venue for adjudicating such cases (Schmitt 1929: 177–178). Schmitt appealed to Anschütz who had limited the law: "The legal state ends here" ("Das Staatsrecht hört auf hier") and he criticized Rudolf Smend, Triepel, and Kelsen for continuing to treat the issue of the "guardian of the constitution" as an abstract legal matter (Schmitt 1929: 180–183).

Schmitt maintains that in order to answer the question about protecting the constitution, there are a number of issues that need to be clarified. He insists that there cannot be a "Rechtstaat" without an independent justice; there cannot be an independent justice without a binding adherence to the law; there cannot be a binding adherence to the law without a genuine separation between the law and what the judges determine. This final point is Schmitt's assertion regarding the political independence of judges. But he also insists that the judge is, and has been, bound to the law in Germany. But he clarifies by distinguishing between a law and a judge's determination by maintaining that the law is general but the judge's decision is particular; that is, it is an application of the general law to a particular case. He further maintains that without this, there is no "due process of law." It is interesting that Schmitt uses the English expression, but he does not explain why he chose it. He also insists that the mark of a "Rechtsstaat" is the independence of the judge and his objectivity—it is his decision but is founded on the objective determination of the facts of the case. This ensures that the legal decision is reached independently from any party position (Schmitt 1929: 186–187). This sounds as if Schmitt is in favor of the "Rechtstaat" but as he continues, he is actually arguing against it. He alludes to the "Rechtsstaat" as nothing more than "abstract formalism" with its simplified logic. "Justice is what a judge does; thus, what a judge does is all justice" ("Justiz ist, was ein Richter tut, also ist alles, was ein Richter tut; Justiz") (Schmitt 1929: 188). This logic is intended to demonstrate the independence of the judge and his allegiance to the law. However, this is, in Schmitt's view, nothing more than a legal fiction, and he specifically identifies this with Kelsen. He ridicules the claim that laws are enforced upon some "foundation" ("Grund") and he scoffs at the idea that the reason is legitimate. Furthermore, he attacks Kelsen's hierarchy of "norms" (Schmitt 1929: 189–191). Schmitt asks how a weaker norm can overcome a stronger one, and he suggests that this is similar to the question regarding how a weaker law can be considered superior to a stronger law. But his larger question has to do with how issues regarding the protection of the constitution can be addressed by abstract and formal norms. After all, this is a question about what is abnormal—the "state of exception" ("Ausnahmezustand") that is at the heart of the dispute over Art. 48. Schmitt does not address this but questions Kelsen's (and others) insistence on the dualism between Is and Ought ("Sein und Sollen"), between norm and actual situation. His larger concern is about the "collision of norms" ("Normenkollision")—what happens when two norms collide with one another? He suggests that there is no way of deciding—and that one cannot simply appeal to some higher norm (Schmitt 1929: 195).

Schmitt returns to the issue of the conflict between a constitutional law and a specific law and he asks how it is possible for a judge to decide this. It is not merely a matter of a higher and a lower law, but is a matter of two totally different types of law. So, it is difficult, if not impossible, for this matter to be decided on just a legal basis. An additional complaint is that Kelsenian formalism is taken to mean that the laws are easy to interpret and so are readily open to the making of decisions. However, concrete laws are often highly complex and full of ambiguities so are at odds with formal legal philosophies (Schmitt 1929: 197). So, a formal legal philosopher thinks that it is merely an act of subsumption, but that notion applies not just to law but to all human judgments. This is tantamount to one who insists, "a horse is not a donkey" ("ein Pferd sei kein Esel"). Schmitt concludes this section with his complaint that the question about the "guardian of the constitution" is not a "legal theoretical" question but is a practical one. Schmitt's use of the term "rechtstheoretische" is another clear reference to Kelsen and the "Vienna School of legal theory" ("Die Wiener Rechtstheoretische Schule") (Klecatsky, Marcić, und Schmabeck 1968).

By 1929, the "Reichsgerichtshof" had been in service for ten years but Schmitt insists that it had never delivered "Verfassungsjustiz," and that is because constitutional debates are more than legal discussions. Instead, they must address the fundamental issue of what a constitution fundamentally is and that means to ask whether it is some type of contract. If it is a contract, then who is party to it?—is it a two-party contract or is it a contract between more than two? If it is a contract among many parties, then are they equal partners? If not, how is the contract valid if one party is regarded as superior and the other one or more are considered subservient? This is because the definition of a contract is between two equals. Schmitt criticizes this because the notion of the constitution as contract replaces the legitimate basis of a "unified people" ("einheitlichen Volkes") for a state with the legal "foundation" of dualism if not pluralism. But, as Kelsen argued, the state is a compromise; Schmitt, however, maintains it is more than that and much worse. Rather, it is a capitulation and an abdication of decisions. In a footnote he directs his readers to his criticism of Harald Laski's pluralistic doctrine of the state that he provided in his article "Der Begriff des Politischen" (Schmitt 1929: 199–202, note 83). The article was published in the *Archiv für Sozialwissenschaft und Sozialpolitik* and it is worthwhile to compare the similarities and contrasts with his famous book of the same title. Schmitt does not pursue this line of thinking but returns to the problem of conflicting laws and the role of the "state law court" ("Staatsgerichtshof").

Schmitt argues that it does not really matter in these types of conflicts between laws whether the constitution is a contract or not. That is because a court cannot determine the outcome in such conflicts— the court is like other courts in conflict, whereas there needs to be an authority that is higher than a court. Instead of being the "Hüter der Verfassung," the "Staatsgerichtshof" is the guardian of the Reich and the Land. That is, it is a guardian of territory and not a guardian of the constitution (Schmitt 1929: 203–206). Furthermore, he suggests that the "Staatsgerichtshof" is the proper forum for injured parties to present their cases, whether they be state, churches, groups, or similar bodies. Schmitt concludes this section with two observations: that the Weimar Constitution was a political decision and that a decision regarding the "Hüter der Verfassung" needs be made by something larger than a fictive justice form (Schmitt 1929: 210–212).

In the fifth section Schmitt addresses the possibility that there could be something higher like a "higher Third" ("höhern Dritten"), but he insists that this would not make it a "Hüter" of the constitution but the "Herr" of it; not a "guardian" but the "master." It is a mistake to regard this as a neutral power that is somehow above the conflict. Instead, Schmitt points out that the head of the state is political and that is the case regardless of whether it is a monarch or a president (Schmitt 1929: 214–215). In an important footnote, Schmitt refers to a sentence from 1829 by the French legal theorist Adolphe Thiers: "The king rules, the ministers govern, the chambers judge."[2] The distinction between ruling and governing occupies several pages of the fifth section and it appears to center on the issue of who rules (that is, has political power) and who governs (that is, has legal authority). It seems also to revolve around the difference between the executive branch and the legislative branch (Schmitt 1929: 215–217). The legislative body is composed of many individuals each of whom has his or her own opinion. It is a deliberative body which means discussions and debates—all of which take time and often result in compromises. However, as all of Schmitt's writings during the 1920s have shown, he was always in favor of the executive branch because he did not need to spend time in discussions with others but would make his decision promptly and unilaterally. This links directly with Schmitt's discussion of majority rule and the supposed need to honor minority interests. As he suggests, these issues are more sociological than they are political (Schmitt 1929: 219–223). In addition, he takes issue with the social emphasis on the "independent and neutral"

2 Schmitt provides the original "Le roi règen, les minitres gouvernent, les chambres jugent" but adds that "jugent" does not mean "justice" ("Justiz") (Schmitt 1929: 215, note 104).

("unabhängigen und neutralen") because that misses what is essentially political. The political is always dynamic and is always changing, that is why the notion of anchoring the state bank and the state railway is misguided. But he also takes issue with the contention that the state must be concerned with the future and with progress. Rather, the state needs to find the proper ground between both extremes and especially regarding the "guardian of the constitution." Furthermore, the notion of "independent" is not clearly defined but has degrees. This fact must be taken into consideration with respect to judges.

Schmitt reminds his readers, "The judicial civil servant is a vocational official" ("Der richterliche Beamte ist Berufsbeamter") (Schmitt 1929: 226). That official has a guaranteed position that involves objectivity and fairness; it differs from the one-sidedness and impassion of the party member. The judge who is dedicated to independence and neutrality is, therefore, unsuited to be the "guardian of the constitution." The person who should be the "Hüter der Verfassung" is the one who is dedicated to fighting for the constitution, a partisan who will passionately guard it. He stresses that the independent jurist is incompatible with the duties of the guardian, and he points to the fact that often the pressure on the constitution is external. He reminds his readers that the Dawes Plan has been imposed on Germany by the victorious powers and it is they who threaten the constitution. No judge is capable of addressing this political pressure and no bureaucrat can defend the constitution (Schmitt 1929: 231–233).

Schmitt's clear conclusion is that the sole individual who should be the "Hüter der Verfassung" is the "Reichspräsident." It is he who has sworn an oath, it is he who has been chosen by the German voters, it is he who embodies democratic principles, and it is he who alone has the authority to defend the Weimarer Reichsverfassung (Schmitt 1929: 234–235). Furthermore, to entrust the legal branch with the highest duty would be tantamount to endorsing an "aristocracy of the robe" ("Aristokratie der Robe") and that would lead to the loss of trust by the German people. But it is the German people who have chosen the "Reichspräsident" so they have implicit and explicit trust that he will protect them by guarding the constitution. Neither the court with its "independence" nor the parliament with its compromise, but it is the executive who decides. Schmitt concludes with the sentence, "By the words and the intention of the Weimar constitution the 'Reichspräsident' is the closest guardian of the Reich constitution" ("Nach Wortlaut und Sinn der Weimarer Verfassung ist zunächste der Reichspräsident der Hüter der Reichsverfassung") (Schmitt 1929: 237). Schmitt would take up this question again in the 1929 article and then the 1931 book with the same title as this essay. Schmitt's *Hüter der Verfassung* will be discussed in the following chapter. For now, it is time to turn to Kelsen's 1931 reply to Schmitt's "Hüter der Verfassung."

Kelsen's 1931 Reply to Schmitt

Hans Kelsen published "Wer soll der Hüter der Verfassung sein?" in 1931 so technically it lies outside the temporal limits of this chapter. However, thematically it is appropriate because it was Kelsen's direct response to Schmitt's article "Der Hüter der Verfassung." Because Kelsen published "Wer soll der Hüter der Verfassung sein?" in *Die Justiz* he was certainly one of the "Justiz-Juristen" that Schmitt had criticized earlier. Although Schmitt and Kelsen had criticized each other's thinking for years, this exchange marked an escalation.

Before turning to that article there is another Kelsen work that sheds considerable light on his conceptions of the constitution and the role that the state court plays in determining constitutional questions. Entitled "Wesen und Entwicklung des Staatsgerichtsbarkeit" ("Essence and Development of the State Court's Jurisdiction"), it was his contribution to the 1929 conference of the German "Staatsrechtslehrer." In the second section Kelsen takes up the concept of the constitution and he ties it directly to the notion of the state. He takes the state to be a construct which allows humans to function together and laws to be the norms which help guide conduct. The constitution is the fundamental norm which guarantees equality before the law and freedom of expression. The constitution is the ultimate guarantee of these rights (Kelsen 1968b: 1819–1821, 1826). As a result, Kelsen wrote that whether a law is legal is something that only a court can determine. And, the only court he has in mind for determining constitutional questions is the constitutional court (Kelsen 1968b: 1838–1841, 1847). The constitution is the guarantor of the rejection of a "document that contradicts the constitution" ("verfasssungswidiger Akte") (Kelsen 1968b: 1863). Although Kelsen tends to keep the legal and the political separate, he insists that it is the constitution that makes any war between the people superfluous and is a "guarantee of political peace" ("Guarantie des politischen Friedens") (Kelsen 1968b: 1868). Given this emphasis on the legal position of the constitution and Kelsen's high regard for the court, it is time to explore Kelsen's answer to the question: who should be the guardian of the constitution?

Kelsen's writings are notoriously difficult, but there are instances where his style is clear and direct. This is the case with the two opening sentences of "Wer soll der Hüter der Verfassung sein?" Both sentences are written in the distinctive Germanic style and are difficult to translate, yet his meaning in both is very clear. The first sentence states, "*Guardian of the Constitution*: In the original sense of the words, that signifies an entity which has the function to protect the constitution against harm" ("*Hüter der Verfassung*: Das bedeutet im ursprünglichen Sinne des Wortes ein Organ, dessen Funktion es ist, die Verfassung gegen Verletzungen zu schützen"). The second sentence can be translated as "One speaks therefore and indeed generally as a rule about a *guarantee* of the constitution" ("Man spricht daher und zwar in der Regel von einer *Garantie* der Verfassung"). Kelsen then indicates that the constitution can be injured in two ways: by active harm or by neglect. The first is when someone or a group seeks to undermine the constitution whereas the second is when someone or a group fails to fulfill a duty that the constitution requires. In both cases, the guardian is chosen to protect the constitution; as a constitutional organ it stands under "*constitutional control*" ("*Verfassungskontrolle*") (Kelsen 1968a: 1873). It is fortunate that this paragraph begins the version in the 1968 collection; it is missing in the original 1931 version.[3] It is unfortunate that the paragraph was not included in the original because it serves as a clear(er) introduction to the essay.

The original version began with a less than clear introduction. Kelsen wrote of the guarantee but he immediately turned to the notion that the parliament or regime would be a possible guardian because it seemed to be a function of the state. But he suggested that in so doing, it would eliminate the proper function of guaranteeing the safety of the constitution.

Kelsen turns to Schmitt's "Hüter der Verfassung" without either naming the author or by indicating the version, but he makes very clear that he thinks Schmitt is mistaken in a number of respects. He regards Schmitt in this work as an ideologist and not a legal scholar; he thinks that Schmitt is mistaken in his defense of a type of monarchy; and he contends that Schmitt minimizes the critical importance of guarding the constitution. Kelsen accuses Schmitt of contradicting himself with the claims that his approach is scholarly when he admits to providing a political theology. His comment is that Schmitt is claiming to provide a legal commentary when he is just promoting his own political values (Kelsen 1931: 577, 1968a: 1874–1875). Just as importantly, Kelsen criticizes Schmitt for ignoring contemporary works and instead is just seeking to ground his theory in nineteenth-century works. It is as if Schmitt intentionally overlooks the movement through that century in order to separate the state from society and politics from economics. In addition, Schmitt provides his notion of a "neutral power," but what he really wants is for the Reichspräsident to be a dictator. All of Schmitt's talk about Art. 48 is nothing more than ideology (Kelsen 1931: 582–583, 1968a: 1876–1879). In addition, Schmitt's ideological tendencies are clothed in a "cluster" ("Menge") of arguments, few of which are systematic. They may lead to an answer to a "legal-political question" ("Rechtspolitische Frage") but they do not provide a useable answer to a "legal-theoretical" ("rechtstheoretisch") one. Schmitt's remarks certainly do not lead to justice (Kelsen 1931: 585, 1968a: 1882). For Schmitt, the question regarding the "guardian of the constitution" is not a legal one; rather, it is a political one—one about power and decisions. But questions about legality are not political; if they were political, there never could be international courts. But Schmitt sees every question as a question of power and every conflict as a conflict over power, and every legal debate as a political fight. Kelsen insists that Schmitt's method is theoretically impossible and that it leads

3 The fact that there was no notification that this paragraph was added sometime after 1931 is not the problem with the 1968 version. The reference listed there is "Die Justiz, 6 Band, 1931, S. 5–56." The actual page numbers are 576–628. The 1968 version also eliminates many passages in which Kelsen had emphasized words, thus lessening Kelsen's impact. In addition, "Wer soll der Hüter der Verfassung sein?" was the introductory essay in the "Doppelheft 11/12" of *Die Justiz*.

to the politicization of law. That is, in Kelsen's view, not "justice" ("Justiz") (Kelsen 1931: 586–587, 595, 1968a: 1883, 1891). Kelsen contrasts Schmitt's monarchial approach and the use of vague slogans regarding "'Freedom', 'Equality', 'Justice'" ("'Freiheit', 'Gleichheit', 'Gerechtigkeit'") with the legal approach which is conceptually clear. Kelsen claims, "That is the ancient, Platonic dilemma: republic or laws, judge-kings or royal legislators" ("Das ist das uralte, platonische Dilemma: Politea oder Nomoi, Richterkönige oder königlicher Gesetzgeber") (Kelsen 1931: 597–598, 1968a: 1893). Kelsen continually emphasizes the word "justice" ("Justiz") in part because that is what was always important to him. But he also emphasized it because it always seemed so unimportant to Schmitt. Kelsen points out that Schmitt's continuous preoccupation is with power and not with justice, with the executive and not with the judiciary. He repeatedly makes the point that his concern is always with justice and Schmitt's continual preoccupation is with power. Kelsen alludes to Schmitt's embracement of the "total state" ("totalen Staates") in opposition to pluralism. Kelsen digresses from his legal thinking to concentrate on Schmitt's political views. While they are not really connected to the question about the guardian of the constitution, they are worth a brief mention. According to Kelsen, Schmitt's "total state" collapses the distinction between state and society; all is subservient to the state. In this, there is almost no difference between the state that Schmitt envisions and the absolute states of the eighteenth century. That also means that Schmitt's comments about political parties are illusionary, because no police state will allow independent political parties to exist (Kelsen 1931: 601–607, 1968a: 1897–1907).

Kelsen complains that the way from the total state to the leader of the state as guardian of the constitution is a path that is not easy to follow. That is because Schmitt's thinking is not so much a legal doctrine as it is an ideology. It is almost a fiction of a unified "people" ("Volk"). In fact, Schmitt's anti-pluralism is an attack on the implicit pluralism embedded in the Weimar Constitution. It also is an affront to the spirit of the constitution—it does not endorse a "homogeneous, indivisible unity of the entire German people" ("homogenen, unteilbaren Einheit des ganzen deutschen Volkes"). Kelsen emphasizes that this type of unity is Schmitt's claim for the Reichspräsident to be the guardian of the constitution. But Kelsen points out that this is not a legal basis but a political one. Kelsen uses Schmitt's own claim that the Reichspräsident should be the "Hüter der Verfassung" because only the Reichspräsident has been chosen by the German people. But as Kelsen also points out, Schmitt's claim is a political one and not a legal decision so it substitutes the question about protecting the constitution with the question about protecting the (unity) of the state. There may be no doubt that the leader of the state is entrusted with the safety of the state, but the state is not the same as the constitution. Politics concerns interests, and the head of the state protects his party's interests. Kelsen points out, "The ideological character of this meaning is clear" ("Der ideologische Charakter dieser Deutung ist offenbar") (Kelsen 1931: 611–614, 1968a: 1907–1910). In contrast, Kelsen contends that the leader of the state could be neutral and that it many ways, that is preferable to Schmitt's belief that the leader represents his party foremost. Despite what Schmitt contends, the head of state is more than a party leader, like judges and bureaucrats, he is also an officer of the state—an official. Yet Schmitt seems to also argue that because the people have voted for the Reichspräsident that that makes him more independent and neutral than any judge. Kelsen counters this claim by pointing out that Schmitt is substituting quantity for quality (Kelsen 1931: 615–616, 1968a: 1911–1912).

Furthermore, Kelsen dwells on the political position of the Reichspräsident and how that political power infects legal decisions. He again reminds us that the Reichspräsident is the leader of the executive branch, not a member of the judiciary. As such, he is not bound by the justices' oath of impartiality. Instead, the Reichspräsident should be regarded as the counterweight to parliament and not to the judiciary. Both the executive and the legislative branches are concerned with promulgating laws and carrying them out; it is the duty of the judicial branch to make sure that the laws are just (Kelsen 1931: 619, 1968a: 1919).

In the final section Kelsen indicates that what Schmitt understood by the phrase "Hüter der Verfassung" was nothing more than his contention that only the Reichspräsident was suitable. What Kelsen takes that to mean is that Schmitt never really regarded this as a legal or judicial question but only a political issue. As a result, Schmitt never really provided any legal arguments against the institution for determining constitutional applicability (Kelsen 1931: 619, 1968a: 1918–1919). Moreover, it is clear that Schmitt is against the pluralistic system and prefers the monarchy. But as Kelsen points out, Schmitt's objection that pluralistic systems are incapable of functioning is also applicable to the monarchical system. Kelsen pointed to the example of Ludwig II of Bavaria. Kelsen did not need to remind his readers that Ludwig the Second was often referred to as "Mad King Ludwig" and he would not need to remind us today that the castles that he is famous for (Schloß Neuschwanstein, Herrenchiemsee, Linderhof) also bankrupted Bavaria. Nor would Kelsen have needed to remind his readers of the mysterious circumstances of Ludwig's death by drowning. If it is a matter of competence then both systems sometimes function and sometimes not. If it is a matter of competency, then it would seem that courts are the proper venue for legal disputes, and in the case of constitutional debates the constitutional court would be the proper place. Instead, Schmitt wants to maintain a particular fiction of the unity of the state, but this is not much more than a "natural legal ideal wish" ("naturrechtliches Wunschideal"). It is also the opposite of what Art. 48 means when Schmitt insists that it is the ultimate function of the Reichspräsident to restore the "unity" ("Einheit") of the state. Rather, Art. 48 is designed to be invoked when the "official security and order is disrupted or threatened." Instead, Schmitt introduced his famous distinction from *Begriff des politischen* between "a foe and a friend" ("ein Feind und ein Freund"). But this is to leave the realm of legal issues and to move to the "mythology" of Ormuzd and Ahriman. Kelsen concludes by maintaining that his critical analysis should not and cannot deal with the question of the expansion of political powers; that question is a political one and is beyond the "scientific treatment" ("wissenschaftliche Behandlung") of the question regarding who should be the guardian of the constitution (Kelsen 1931: 625–628, 1968a: 1920–1922). Kelsen would continue to keep his political advocacy for democracy separate from his insistence on formalism of his legal positivism. In contrast, Schmitt would continue his subsuming of legal issues under political ideals. This clash of positions would manifest itself in the legal aftermath of the "Preußenschlag"—the main focus of the next chapter.

Concluding Comments

This chapter began with a brief overview of some of the major political and historical events of the years 1927, 1928, and 1929. It then provided an account of the most important contributions to the debate about Art. 48. But it also indicated that that debate was part of two larger discussions: what the relation is between law and politics and who should be considered the guardian of the constitution. Some of the articles discussed in this chapter were dry, detailed, legal tracts while others were more provocative, sweeping political papers. Although these three years were relatively stable compared to the first three years of the Weimar government, there was a growing sense that that tranquility was only illusionary or if it was real, it was not likely to last. The debate between Schmitt and Kelsen highlighted the increasing tension between the law and politics and would finally explode in 1932 with the "Preußenschlag." That and the years 1930 and 1931 are the subject of the following chapter.

References

Anschütz, Gerhard (1921) *Die Verfassung des Deutschen Reiches von 11. August 1919.* Berlin: Verlag von Georg Stilte.

Anschütz, Gerhard (1929) *Die Verfassung des Deutschen Reiches von 11. August 1919.* Berlin: Verlag von Georg Stilte. Dritte Bearbeitung. 11. Auflage.

Büttner, Ursula (2008) *Weimar. Die überforderte Republik. 1918–1933.* Stuttgart: J.G. Cotta'sche Buchhandlung Nachfolger.

Flad, Wolfgang (1929) *Verfassungsgerichtsbarkeit und Reichsexekution. Beiträge zur Lehre von den Streitigkeiten zwischen Reich und Länderen und deren Entscheidung.* Heidelberg: Carl Winters Universitätsbuchhandlung.

Gmelin, Hans (1921) "Der Ausnahmezustand." In *Handbuch der Politik. Dritter Band. Die politische Erneuerung.* Berlin und Leipzig: Dr. Walther Rothschild. 156–160.

Grau, Richard (1927) "Diktaturgewalt und Reichsverfassung." In *Gedächtnisschrift für Emil Seckel.* Herausgebern Vom Erich Genzmer, Richard Grau, Walter Grau, Georg Hamburger, Josef Juncker, Ernst Levy and Fritz Schultz. Berlin: Verlag von Julius Springer. 430–494.

Hiller von Gaetringen, Friedrich Freiherr (1993) "Monarchismus in der deutschen Republik." In *Die Weimarer Republik.* Herausgegeben von Michael Stürmer. Frankfurt: Anton Hain Meisenheim: 3. Auflage. 254–271.

Holtmann, Everhard, Koordinator (1994) *Die Weimarer Republik. Der brüchige Friede. Band 2. 1924–1928.* München: Bayerische Landeszentrale für Politische Bildungsarbeit.

Holtmann, Everhard, Koordinator (1995) *Die Weimarer Republik. Das Ende der Demokratie. Band 3. 1929–1933.* München: Bayerische Landeszentrale für Politische Bildungsarbeit.

Kelsen, Hans (1927) "Die Bundesexekution. Ein Beitrag zur Theorie und Praxis des Bundesstaates, unter besonderer Berücksichtigung der deutschen Reichs- und der österreichischen Bundes-Verfassung." In *Festgabe für Fritz Fleiner zum 60. Geburtstag.* Herausgegeben von Zaccaria Giacometti und Dietrich Schindler. Tübingen: Verlag von J.C.B. Mohr (Paul Siebeck). 127–187.

Kelsen, Hans (1968a) "Wer soll der Hüter der Verfassung sein?" In Klecatsky, Marcić und Schambeck. 1968. Band 2. 1873–1922.

Kelsen, Hans (1968b) "Wesen und Entwicklung der Staatsgerichtsbarkeit." In Klecatsky, Marcić und Schambeck. 1968. Band 2. 1813–1871.

Kelsen, K. (1931) *Wer soll der Hüter der Verfassung sein?* Berlin-Grunewald: Dr. Wather Rothschild.

Klecatsky, Hans, Marcić, René und Schmabeck, Herbert, Herasgegebern (1968) *Die Wiener Rechtstheoretische Schule. Ausgewählte Schriften von Hans Kelsen, Adolf Julius Merkl und Alfred Verdross.* Wien, Frankfurt am Main and Zürich: Europa Verlag, Salzburg; München: Universitätsverlag Anton Pustet.

Kolb, Eberhard (2002) *Die Weimarer Republick.* München: R. Oldenbourg Verlag. 6. überarbeite und erweiterte Auflage.

Megerle, Klaus (1994) "Regierungsperiode relative Stabilität Partien, Wahlen und Koalitionen bis 1928." In Holtmann. 1994. 17–64.

Mommsen, Hans (2001) *Aufstieg und Untergang der Republik von Weimar. 1919–1933.* München: Ecom Ullstein List Verlag.

No name (1925/1926). "Was wir wollen." *Die Justiz.* I. Band. Heft 1. 1–6.

Preuß, H. (2015) *Das Verfassungswerk von Weimar.* Herausgegeben, eingeleitet und erläutert von Detlef Lehnert, Christoph Müller und Dian Schefold. Tübingen: Mohr Siebeck. *Gesammelte Schriften.* Dritter Band.

Pyta, Wolfram (2009) *Hindenburg: Herrschaft zwischen Hohenzollern und Hitler.* München: Verlagsgruppe Random House.

Ruck, Michael (1995) "Wirtschaft und Arbeitsgesellschaft im Zeichen der Großen Krise." In Holtmann. 1995. 131–170.

Schmitt, Carl (1929) "Der Hüter der Verfassung." *Archiv des öffentlichesn Rechts.* Neue Folge. 16 Band. 2 Heft. Der ganzen Folge 55. Band. 161–237.

Stammen, Theo (1994) "Weimarer Kultur. Politisierung des Geistes-Republikferne Werteliten." In Holtmann. 1994. 343–387.

Stibbe, Matthew (2022) "Coalition-Building and Political Fragmentation, 1924–1930." In Rossol and Ziemann. 2022. 72–94.

Verus, no first name (1925/1926) "Entwurf eines Ausführungsgesetzes zum Artikel 48 der Reichsverfassung." *Die Justiz.* I. Band. Heft 4. 368–379.

6 1930–1933

The Years of Debate and Debacle

In hindsight it appears possible to trace the path in Germany from the beginning of the first years of the Weimar Republic through the middle years to the final three years. The early years of hyperinflation were followed by a period of relative tranquility, but the increasing political instability and the financial collapse in 1929 contributed to the unrest of the early 1930s. But these early problems and especially the later ones did not mean that Hitler's rise to power was inevitable. But, as Larry Eugene Jones argued in "From Democracy to Dictatorship: The Fall of Weimar and the Nazi Rise to Power, 1930–1933," the imposition of Art. 48 in 1932 helped speed up the dissolution of parliament's power and shifted it into the hands of President Hindenburg and his followers (Jones 2022: 95). That move led to Adolf Hitler being appointed chancellor and then helped pave the way for January 30, 1933.

This chapter differs from the previous four in two different ways. First, its title suggests the time frame from 1930 to 1932 but it will cover some of 1933. One reason for that is the political turmoil that erupted in the early months of that year, and another is that a few of the final essays and books dealing with Art. 48 were published in 1933. Second, this chapter is lengthier than the previous four for several reasons. First, there were more scholars involved in the debate, the history is even more relevant, and most of all, the years encompass the most important event—the so-called Preußenschlag. The chapter has four main parts and one minor one: the first one is the brief, historical overview, and the second explores the debate regarding Art. 48 between 1930 and June of 1932. The third part focuses on the "Preußenschlag" itself and the legal battle that followed. This third part is the lengthiest part of the chapter because it involves much more than any previous discussion. The fourth part contains the final contributions to the Art. 48 debate. The final, and minor, part consists of some concluding comments.

1930–1933: Historic Overview

The years 1925 through 1928 were sometimes referred to as the "golden years," but the period between 1929 and 1933 was and is considered the "crises years" (Bracher 1979: 185). There were crises in the economic sector and in the

DOI: 10.4324/9781003312796-6

social sector, but the main crises were invariably political. This was true in 1930 and 1931 but especially in 1932. Whereas 1932 seemed as if it was going to be the end of the Weimar Republic, the years 1929 and even the beginning of 1930 suggested that there was considerable hope for the continuation of Germany's experiment with democracy.

Much of 1929 was relatively uneventful, and there were some indications that Weimar was a success. On August 11, 1929, Germany celebrated the ten years of the Weimar Constitution. However, the stock market crash in October 1929 and the beginning of the Great Depression in America were being felt as early as November of that year (Ruck 1995: 135). But it was not until the next year that the numbers of unemployed Germans began to swell (Holtmann 1995: 17). Unfortunately, the German government was unable to provide a public safety net that had been promised, and the economic crisis that began in later 1929 meant that more people were unemployed. As Pamela E. Sweet pointed out, long-term unemployment grew to be a challenge for housing—higher prices for those who had been able to purchase a home and higher rent for those who used to be able to cover the rent. Sweet also pointed to a statistic that was even more revealing—that married couples were choosing (or felt forced to choose) not to have children. In 1904 the percentage of workers who were married and had no children was 6.7%, but that climbed to more than 25% during the years 1925 and 1929 (Sweet 2022: 484–485).

There were political disruptions as well. Gustav Stresemann had left his mark on foreign affairs since he had been foreign minister beginning in 1923. He not only served to personify Germany's foreign policy, but also contributed to Germany's sense of stability. As a result, Germany lost more than just a statesman when Stresemann died unexpectedly on October 3, 1929. Stresemann was the "lynchpin" that held the Müller cabinet together.[1]

The year 1929 embodied two trends: the continuing development of the arts and the continuing polarization of politics (Kolb 2002: 98). Kurt Dietrich Bracher discussed the growing political radicalization of this year in detail. The Nationalistische Deutsche Arbeiterpartei (NSDAP) was able to capitalize not only on Stresemann's death and the American stock market collapse, but also on the waning powers of the labor unions (Bracher 1979: 176–179, 184–185).

The year 1930 is often regarded as the year that was the beginning of the collapse of Weimar. It was the year that the longest serving cabinet fell. On March 27, 1930, the social-political government of Hermann Müller fell. This government had been in power for 21 months, but it was also the 13th government in 12 years. Moreover, it had been made up of five parties who could not agree on some of the most important issues of that year, including reparations (Grimm 2018: 262). The year 1930 is singled out because it was in

1 Jones 2022: 97; Stibbe 2022: 76; Bracher 1979: 175. For Stresemann's importance and an overall assessment of his abilities, see Wright 2022: 252–256.

July that parliament was dissolved and some accused the president of abusing his authority (Stibbe 2022: 89). However, Hindenburg's defenders insisted that he had no choice given the problems that Germany faced. While many considered the Communist Party the biggest threat to Weimar's stability, the Nazi Party was steadily growing. The issues that had plagued the party during 1923 through 1926 had largely been set aside, and the party began to grow significantly. At the end of 1929, the NSDAP had 178,000 members but by March of 1930 it had risen to 210,000 (Bracher 1979: 183). September saw the Nazi Party gain a massive increase in votes—it increased from 2.6% to 18.3% (Büttner 2008: 791). It marked the transition from democracy to dictatorship (Holtmann 1995: 17).

While the number of unemployed did rise during 1929, it rose rapidly in the beginning of 1930. By February it was more than 3.37 million. By the end of March, it was clear that parliament was no longer functioning—but that was a result of many factors, including continuing economic crisis as well as the impact of Hindenburg. But it was also influenced by the rise of the NSDAP (Büttner 2008: 389, 399–400; Kolb 2002: 112–113, 119–120). Part of the increase in Nazi Party membership was a result of many Germans' antipathy towards the Young Plan that was determining reparations (Kolb 2002: 123–124), The Young Plan was named after the head of General Electric, Owen Young, and his plan was the second attempt to address the problems that Germany had been facing in meeting its reparations payments. The conference took place during January of 1930 and the German parliament accepted it on March 12. While parliament had officially accepted the Young Plan, many Germans were vehemently opposed to it. Some made their opposition public, while others worked behind the scenes (Jasper 1995: 33–36, 40, 48–49). These hidden movements, alongside agrarian and industrial crises, helped topple the Müller government mid-March (Büttner 2008: 387–395; Mommsen 2001: 350–351). March 30 saw the beginning of Heinrich Brüning's government, which would govern until May 30, 1932. This was one of the longest governments during the Weimar period, but it was filled with crises (Mommsen 2001: 645–649). Brüning was tasked with dealing with the economic crisis caused by the 1929 stock market collapse and the increasing economic problems confronting Germany. Detlef Peukert noted that the economic crisis ended the period of the aftereffects of the post war years and ushered in a new period. He also indicated that the economic catastrophe of the early part of 1930 was so overwhelming that many Germans anticipated the wholesale collapse of capitalism (Peukert 1987: 244–246, 249).

The year 1931 was a continuation of economic and political crises. Unemployment reached almost five million in February and there were bank failures throughout the year (Büttner 2008: 792–794). Peukert noted that many Germans believed that Germany could master these crises, but by the middle of the year those hopes were dashed. Peukert maintained that by that time it was clear that Brüning's government was unsuitable and unable to address the increasing numbers of crises (Peukert 1987: 250; see also Kolb 2002: 233–234). Büttner pointed particularly to the collapse of the third largest bank, the Darmstädter und Nationalbank, in mid-July, which triggered a general banking crisis in all of Germany (Büttner 2008: 794). By early October Brüning's first cabinet was dissolved and was replaced by an even more right-leaning group. The same month saw a 100,000 Sturmabteilung (SA) member march in Braunschweig, and in November the voters in Hessen gave 37% of the vote to the NSDAP, whereas the second largest group, the Social Democrats, only garnered slightly more than 21% Büttner 2008: 795). By the end of the year, the number of unemployed was more than 5.7 million (Büttner 2008: 795).

As indicated in the introduction of this chapter, the focus in the second major part of this account ends prior to June 1932, meaning that only the first five months of 1932 are sketched. The reason for this is two-fold. First, and most importantly, is the "Preußenschlag," and that will require a focus on the actual situation and the ensuring legal and political issues that played out over the rest of the years. Second, the situation in the first several months of 1933 was fundamentally changed from the earlier Weimar years, and so it will be dealt with differently.

The first part of 1932 was filled with crises and conflicts. One crisis was political—how the Weimar government was going to address the increasing conflict between the Left and the Right. Most politicians continued to maintain that the biggest threat was from the Communists, and these critics frequently pointed to the supposed connection between the German Communist Party and the Soviet Union. Others recognized the growing threat from the Nazi Party, and these critics kept alluding to the Nazis' endorsement of harassment and intimidation and outright violence. But the Nazi growth was not just because of people's fear of communism; certain groups were being infiltrated and were being undermined from within. In addition, the NSDAP fed propaganda against the Young Plan (Kolb 2002: 120, 122–123; Mommsen 2001: 407–410). One of the major conflicts revolved around the question of reparations—first with the Dawes Plan (1924–1929) and then with the Young Plan (1929–1931). What counted as a crisis and a conflict were the negative effects of the New York stock exchange collapse and its worldwide consequences. By 1932 the banks had lost money, the industries had shrunk, and people's income was lower than before the crisis (Büttner 2008: 402–403, 829). Thus, the first six months of 1932 were months of economic and political crises—and that is not counting the political crisis of May 1932. That will be addressed later. The change in the approach in this chapter also means including a few publications from 1933. These are included either because they were written in late 1932 but not published until the next year or because they contain comments about the previous year.

The years 1930 to the early months of 1933 were times of political turmoil but would not have the political repercussions and social and economic impacts of much of the remainder of the decade, to say nothing about the

Second World War, the Holocaust, and the radical changes in 1945. The focus here is on Art. 48 and how it played out in the final years of the Weimar Republic.

Art. 48 in the Years 1930 Through June 1932

Although the actual "Preußenschlag" took place during one day, the lead-up to that day and its aftereffects took place over periods of weeks and months. Rather than beginning with Hindenburg's July 20, 1932, decree, we need to start much earlier.

It is not too much to insist that Weimar was primarily based upon the SPD because many of its founding ideals and documents can be traced back to its members in the first half of the 1920s. But with the political conflicts and the economic crises of those first five years, the SPD lost much of its power. The death of Reichspräsident Friedrich Ebert in 1925 was one of the final losses for the SPD. Paul Hindenburg was elected in part because of his reputation as the great war hero but also because he was not formally affiliated with any German party. Hindenburg governed with several different Reichskanzlers between 1925 and 1930, and when he needed to appoint a new Kanzler at the end of March 1930, he chose Heinrich Brüning. Brüning was conservative and Catholic and was well respected (Büttner 2008: 399–401). But the election on September 14, 1930, saw a marked increase for the NSDAP—from 2.6% to 18.3% (Büttner 2008: 419–420). The next two years were both hopeful and difficult for Brüning—he appeared to believe that he was close to his goal when his government collapsed in May 1932 (Büttner 2008: 461–462; Mommsen 2001: 440–442). A major cause of the Brüning government's collapse was the rapid increase in unemployment: from 4 million in the beginning of 1931 to 6.1 million in the beginning of 1932 (Mommsen 2001: 443). By October 1931, Brüning's first government failed but Hindenburg reappointed him. Hans Mommsen chronicled the failure of a major Bremen business and how it had a "snowball effect" (Mommsen 2001: 471–482). The German economy continued to shrink and the number of unemployed continue to rise. Hitler and the NSDAP also continued to attract more and more members and the party's influence rose. January 1932 saw Brüning and Hindenburg engaging in discussions with Hitler (Büttner 2008: 795–796). Brüning supported Hindenburg when he ran again for Reichspräsident on March 13, 1932. Brüning emphasized that Hindenburg was not beholden to any party and should be regarded as an impartial protector of Germany. Hindenburg won with 49.6% of the vote to Hitler's 30.1%. With the second vote on Aril 10, votes for Hitler increased to 36.8% but Hindenburg gained more and was at 53% (Mommsen 2001: 495–496; Schafer 1995a: 340–342). An immediate response to Hitler's increase in support was the April 13, 1932, decree that forbid both the Sturmabteilung (SA) and the Schutzstaffel (SS) (Kolb 2002: 322). By May, the NSDAP had gained majorities in some parts of Germany and the German government continued to lose support. By the end of

May 1932, Brüning's second cabinet collapsed. On the first of June, Franz von Papen was appointed Reichskanzler and Kurt von Schleicher was appointed to the position of minister of defense ("Reichswehrminister") (Büttner 2008: 796). Brüning, Papen, and Schleicher each believed that they had the political power and the intellectual savviness to influence or even control Hitler and his party. These convictions turned out not only to be misguided and wrong; they also had tragic consequences for the last two years of the Weimar Republic (Peukert 1987: 255–256; see Kolb 2002: 232–234). It is, however, a mistake to think that the three shared the same convictions and that what they chose to do and what they chose not to do had similar consequences. In fact, the shift from Brüning to Papen was a major step away from democracy, but the transition from Papen to Schleicher was even more drastic (Schafer 1995b: 355, 358; Schildt 1995: 391, 395). Larry Eugene Jones has recently argued that Papen would never have been chosen except for his friendship with Hindenburg and Schleicher—a friendship which went back to the First World War. Jones also argued that Papen shared with the other two the certainty that their "taming strategy" for Hitler would be successful (Jones 2022: 102–103; see Kolb 2002: 142–143). There is no question that Papen and Hindenburg not only failed to stop Hitler's rise to power; their misconceptions actually helped him. In contrast, it is not so clear how much Brüning contributed to Hitler's rise.[2] But there is wide agreement that Papen's government was unsuccessful in solving Germany's economic problems and that it was ineffectual in slowing Hitler's increasing popularity. Jones provides three grounds that caused considerable difficulties for Papen's new government—all three were based on Hitler's demands. Jones indicated, first, that Hitler insisted on new elections to reflect the increasing popularity of the NSDAP. Second, Hitler demanded that the bans on the SA and the SS be lifted. Third, he insisted that the Prussian government be replaced. Papen arranged to meet all three of Hitler's demands with the assumption that Hitler's party would join his government. Papen scheduled new elections for later in July and lifted the restrictions on the SA and SS. And, he prompted Hindenburg to issue the decree of July 20, 1932, effectively taking over the Prussian government—the "Preußenschlag" (Jones 2022: 103; see Büttner 2008: 464–465). What Jones did not mention was that Hindenburg already had a justification for intervening in the Prussian government.

Hamburg is now an independent "Land" and it prides itself on its history as part of the Hanseatic League. As an indication of this connection, Hamburg's auto license plates have the initials "HH"; that is, "Hanseatiche Hamburg." What is often left out of this history is two-fold. First, Hamburg and much of the surrounding area belonged to Prussia. Second, while Hamburg and Kiel have often been regarded as bastions of the SPD, the area has had its

2 Brüning's role in the rise of Hitler is a matter of continuing controversy. It is beyond the scope of this book to enter into it. For some accounts, see Kolb 2002: 230–232; Büttner 2008: 438–440, 445, 455–459, 461–463; Schafer 1995: 341–342; Jones 2022: 101–102.

share of right-wing-leaning people. These points should be kept in mind when addressing the so-called Altona bloody Sunday ("Altonaer Blutsonntag"). As mentioned earlier, Hitler's second demand of Papen was the lifting of the ban on the SA and the SS. That would allow members of both groups to march in uniform. The ban was lifted on June 14, 1932, and it immediately led to political violence. Büttner indicated that in the month following that lifting of the ban, street violence caused mainly by the SA resulted in the deaths of 99 people. These were street battles between members of the NSDAP and the Kommunistische Partei Deutschlands (KPDs). In Prussia alone, 86 people died in these street battles: 38 from the NSDAP and 28 from the KDP. The NSDAP announced that a huge number of SA members from Altona and the neighboring areas would be marching through the home of the Communists. Some 7,000 SA members marched and were met by the KDP members. According to Büttner, police had accompanied the marchers but were limited in numbers because of vacations and other reasons. As expected, altercations occurred with the end result of 18 men dead—two NSDAP members and 16 innocent civilian bystanders (Büttner 2008: 470–471). The "Altonaer Blutsonntag" gave Papen the excuse he needed not just to meet Hitler's third demand but also to remove one of the last vestiges of pro-democracy and pro-Weimar in Germany.

To remind readers, Art. 48 consists of five paragraphs, but most of the focus has been on the first two. The first paragraph has often been referred to as the "Exekution" paragraph, and that term has not generated much controversy. It was different regarding the second paragraph, which has been called the "Dikaturmaßnahmen." Writing in 1976 Henning Grund indicated that it was a term that generated controversy going back to 1922 when Richard Grau first used it (Grund 1976: 13). Grund also discussed, in more detail than many others, the results which followed Hindenburg's successful reelection on April 10, 1932. Four days later he formally prohibited the military organizations of the NSDAP from public assembly, and this order pertained specifically to the SA and the SS. Hindenburg issued this order "To Secure the State's Authority" ("Zur Sicherung der Staatsautorität"). The basis for this order was the perceived need to avoid a "civil war" between the Right and the Left; that is, between the NSDAP and the KPD. But this was mostly his advisors who were insisting on this measure; Hindenburg himself was more concerned that this would simply further radicalize the Right and would undermine his claim to be above political parties (Grund 1976: 16–17; Pyta 2009: 686–688). Yet Hindenburg was not interested in discussing matters with the KDP; Pyta noted that Hindenburg was ready to discuss governmental matters with the Central Party and the NSDAP, but not with the KDP (Pyta 2009: 692). Hindenburg's prohibition was not successful; the street battles continued and the number of dead and injured increased. Grund insisted that Hindenburg was growing even more convinced that the SA and SS prohibition was not only failing but was a major mistake (Grund 1976: 18–19, 23–25). Hindenburg's concerns appeared justified; the regional elections that were held on April 24 saw the governing parties suffering significant losses, but the NSDAP saw massive gains (Büttner 2008: 447, 457, 796), Büttner described the disintegration of the Brüning cabinet at the end of April and how Hitler and Goebbels were certain that Brüning himself would lose power (Büttner 2008: 459–460). The final chapter of Brüning's second government came on May 30. Franz von Papen became Kanzler on June 1, the same day that Kurt von Schleicher became defense minister. The prohibition against the SA and SS prohibition was rescinded on June 14, 1932 (Büttner 2008: 796–797; Kolb 2002: 143, 322). Within days, the SA began massive displays of force in many parts of Germany but above all, the NSDAP wanted to make Prussia ungovernable (Mommsen 2001: 532–533). Mommsen insisted that the high point of the Nazi-induced unrest occurred on July 17—the "Altonaer Blutsonntag." The antifascist movement had warned about this provocation but the authorities did not heed the warnings (Mommsen 2001: 533–534; Schafer 1995b: 364–365). Grund cautioned against drawing the conclusion that lifting the prohibition caused the increasing unrest, but he did suggest that it was clearly to the benefit of the NSDAP. The NSDAP certainly took advantage of being free to roam the streets and provoke confrontations (Grund 1976: 27–29). The two sides certainly held different views on who was causing the conflicts, but Papen kept maintaining that the KPD was the main instigator. But Grund noted that the Nazis had a far larger membership. Grund noted that the NSDAP had 300,000 SA members and 50,000 SS members as well as one million so-called steel helmet members ("Stahlhelmmitgleider") (Grund 1976: 31). Kolb suggested that the representation of the two sides continued to be debated, but he insisted that Papen's regime was determined to dissolve the Prussian pro-democracy government. These conclusions have been echoed by scholars before and since (Kolb 2002: 236–237; Mommsen 2001: 533–534; Büttner 2008: 470–472; Jones 2022: 103; Grund 1976: 54–58; Boldt 1993: 301–302). Grund provided some details regarding Papen's decision to intervene. Papen had been in Switzerland from mid-June until July 10 when he returned to Germany. Then Papen discussed with Defense Minister Schleicher and Inner Minister Gayl the means of replacing the SPD-led Prussian government. Papen and Gayl traveled to Neudeck to meet with Hindenburg. According to Grund, Hindenburg had long wanted the legal relationship between the Reich and Prussia to be returned to the close connection that it had been under the Kaiser (Grund 1976: 60–64). Peukert emphasized that although Hindenburg wanted Reich and Prussia to be more closely aligned, he was hesitant to act. Peukert also stressed that it was Schleicher, the "Kanzler-maker" ("Kanzlermacher"), who was the driving force behind Hindenburg's final decision.[3]

3 Peukert 1987: 258–259. Schleicher was "Kanzlermacher" because he was able to convince others that Papen should be Kanzler and that he would then become defense minister. But he was ready to take over as Kanzler when Papen fell. This will be discussed later.

The "Preußenschlag"

Hindenburg's order to restore "public security and order" ("öffentlichen Sicherheit und Ordnung") was signed by him on the morning of July 20, 1932. In some ways, it appeared to follow Art. 48 very closely: Hindenburg's order cited Absatz 2 and applied to a large but clearly identified area. It also specified seven "basic rights" that could be suspended under the second paragraph of Art. 48. What it did not specify was how the restoration would be accomplished or for what duration these extraordinary measures would be in place. Finally, and most importantly, the order failed to specify what particular disruptions led to this decision and what basis there was to remove the Prussian government.

The July 20th order was composed of seven sections: a preliminary section followed by six sections. The preliminary section sets out the basis for the implementation of numerous measures based on Art. 48 Abs. 2. These measures apply to the greater Berlin area and the Province of Brandenburg. There are two things to notice about this preliminary section. First, it does not even mention Abs. 1 about Prussia not fulfilling its duties, and second, it does not indicate the reasons for applying only to just these particular areas.

§ 1 delineates the articles that are suspended: 114, 115, 117, 118, 123, 124, and 153, and then points out that these measures limit "personal freedom" ("persönlichen Freiheit") with respect to the freedom to express one's personal opinion, including the freedom of the press and the freedom of association. It limits the freedom of communication including postal service, telegraph, and telephone. Finally, it dispenses with the guarantee that one's living space is free from intrusion and it removes the prohibition against confiscation of personal property.

§ 2 indicates that power is given to the Reichsminister to command the military and that the use of the military and other police forces will reintroduce public security. It also indicates that these groups are authorized to use whatever force they deem necessary.

§ 3 authorizes these groups to use what means they deem appropriate if they meet with resistance against these measures. Those individuals who are arrested for obstructing the restoration of public security will be tried and if found guilty will be fined a determinate amount of money or confined to jail or prison for a set amount of time, or both. These penalties will be determined by the appropriate judicial authorities.

§ 4 discusses the more serious infractions, which include treason, arson, flooding, and disrupting the railways. It spells out in some detail the measures that will be taken against those who lead an uprising or who call others out to resist the proper authorities. It specifically addresses those who use or intend to use weapons.

§ 5 authorizes "extraordinary courts" ("außerordentliche Gerichte") to be formed in order to judge and sentence those who have been accused of attempting to thwart the reintroduction of public security. It bases its claim on a presidential decree from March 29, 1921.

§ 6 states that this declaration is in effect as of July 20, 1932, and is signed by the Reichspräsident von Hindenburg, the Reichskanzler von Papen, and the Reichsminister des Jinnern [Innern] von Gayl.

There is no indication of the duration or what measures the military and the police can use. Despite the fact that the decree is specific, it really does not provide much information about the time, place, and emergency measures that can be legally used.

There was a second, but briefer, document in which Hindenburg and Papen explained the need to interfere with Prussia's internal matters, and it indicates the scope and the limitations of this intrusion. Unlike the aforementioned document, this one appears to be more reasonable and willing to discuss matters with the Prussian officials. In it, Hindenburg named himself to be Reich Commissar ("Reichskommissar") for Prussia and he ordered the members of Prussian ministers to vacate their offices. In addition, he took over most of the duties of the Prussian leadership. Hindenburg indicated that the Reichskanzler was prepared to discuss matters, but he made it clear that Hindenburg and Papen would be in control of Prussia for the duration. He did not indicate how long this decree would be in effect, but it did not really matter because Hindenburg had eliminated the Prussian government and there was almost no possibility that it could ever be reconstituted. It was signed by "Der Reichspräsident von Hindenburg" and "Der Reichskanzler von Papen."

There was a press release that placed the blame on the communist side for the bloody confrontations and for defying the Prussian state's authority. The press release claimed that Prussia was responsible for the break in trust between the Reich and Prussia. It indicated further that the replacement of the regional government with the Reich was the "only way to a quick liberation of the greatest German Land" ("einzige Weg zur raschen Befreidung des größten deutschen Landes").

The correspondence between Kanzler Papen and Prussian Minister President Braun did not indicate any flexibility or willingness to compromise. Papen's letter was brief and direct: Braun and his ministers were being summarily dismissed. Braun's reply was lengthier but no less direct: he objected to Hindenburg's decree on several grounds. First, the declaration was illegal because it was a misreading of the Weimar Constitution and particularly Art. 48. Second, the Reichspräsident and his ministers had no authority to remove the Prussian government. Third, Braun demanded that he be allowed to continue the Prussian measures to restore "public security and order" in his own "Land." Fourth, he appealed immediately to the high court. Papen dismissed Braun's concerns and justified his intrusion on the basis of Hindenburg's decree of July 20. He repeated a few of the passages from that document and concluded with the claim that he had already made official the grounds for such emergency measures (Brecht 1933: 481–486).

The Prussian leadership lodged its initial objection to the Reich's intrusion and was joined two groups of the Prussian government. The Freistaat Preußen was also represented by the Sozialdemokratischen Partie Deutschland (SPD) as well as the Zentrumsfraktion (Zentrum) against the Deutsche Reichs. The decision was handed down on July 25, 1925, only four days after the Reichs' document. The decision was from the "Staatsgerichtshof" located in Leipzig, was approximately four and a half pages in length, and was composed of two sections, designated as A and B. The decision was signed by the seven judges of the "Staatsgerichtshof."

Section A set out the measures that the Reich had taken, mainly forcing Braun and his ministers into "retirement." Braun appealed to Abs. 1 and Abs. 2; regarding the first one, Braun insisted that Prussia was fulfilling its duties and that Abs. 1 was not a sufficient ground to interfere with Prussia's government. Recall that Hindenburg did not appeal to Abs. 1, but Braun was probably wise to address that issue. Regarding Abs. 2, Braun insisted that it was unnecessary for the Reich to interfere with Prussia because the "Land" was in the process of restoring "public security and order" ("öffentlichen Sicherheit und Ordnung") and that this intrusion was not just unwarranted but was based upon "arbitrariness" ("Willkür"). The Prussians made a four-point argument against the Reich: (1) the Reich had no standing to replace the Prussian ministers, (2) the Reich did not have the authority to interfere in Prussia's internal affairs, (3) the Reich needed the permission of the Prussian government before attempting to take over Prussian offices, and (4) forced retirement is not justified, even if it is only temporary (Brecht 1933: 487–488).

In Section B the "Staatsgerichtshof" noted the opposition between Reich and "Land" and maintained that that court was the proper legal venue to adjudicate between one "Land" and another "Land," but especially between Reich and Prussia. The court's decision caused an immediate outcry and Prussia was determined to get that decision overturned. Prussia filed a response rejecting that decision and demanding that a full court take up its case. The court agreed to do so and Prussia's case against the Reich was scheduled for October of the same year.

The October 1932 Court Case ("Preußen Contra Reich")

The actual court proceedings began on Monday, October 10, 1932, at 10:30 a.m. It would continue for the next four days of that week, with each session beginning at 9:30 a.m. The main proceedings concluded late on Friday the 14th of October but met again on Monday the 17th. The 25-page decision was delivered on October 25, 1932. The book that contains the proceedings appeared in 1933. It contains the transcript of the trial as well as a number of supporting documents. It provides a clear view of the debate between those siding with the Reich and the implementation of Art. 48 and those whose values aligned with the Prussian democrats who decried such extraordinary measures. The volume is slightly more than 500 pages of rather small print.

It is neither easy to read nor follows all of the lines of thinking. That volume itself could be the subject of another complete book. What is intended here is to give a very brief overview of the relevant parts pertaining to Art. 48.

The full title is *Preussen contra Reich vor dem Staatsgerichtshof. Stenogrammbericht der Verhandlungen von dem Staatsgerichtshof in Leipzig vom 10. bis 14. und vom 17. Oktober. 1932. Mit einem Vorwort von Ministerialdirektor Dr. Brecht.* "Dr. Brecht" referred to Arnold Brecht who was part of the Prussian government. He agreed to write a foreword because he was convinced that the account should be accessible to a larger audience and because he was impressed with the accuracy of the transcription. Nothing was omitted or altered. The only changes to what was said in the Leipzig courtroom were the few instances in which a speaker was not understandable or some phrase was not correctly heard. Although Brecht sided with the Prussians, he thought that both sides put forth some compelling arguments. He did ask that the publisher change the title, *Preussen contra Reich*, because he thought it was not accurate. Brecht insisted that Prussia was not against the Reich, but rather, was fighting for the Reichsverfassung and for the Reich. Brecht regarded "Problem Reich-Preußen" to be more accurate. The publisher noted in his "Vorwort" that it was too late to have changed the title (Brecht 1933: VII, XVI).

After opening the first day's proceedings, the Reichsgerichtspräsident Bumke listed the points of contention and then noted who was representing each side. For Prussia, these included Anschütz, Giese, Nawiasky, and Hermann Heller. For the Reich, these included Schmitt, Jacobi, and Bilfinger. After noting the bad acoustics and appealing for speaking clearly, Bumke asked that both sides be respectful during the course of the trial. Brecht asked to address the issue and explained that Prussia was not objecting to Hindenburg's decision—he expressly stated that they did not question Hindenburg's will and motive. But Brecht did insist that Prussia was questioning the *legal* basis for these measures and not the *political* grounds (Brecht 1933: 1–2, 8).

The first day's proceedings began at 10:30 in the morning and lasted until 8:00 in the evening with a lengthy break midday. Arnold Brecht was the first speaker and he talked for hours until that midday break. Much of Brecht's talk focused on the political developments since the fall of 1930, and he pointed to the problems that the NSDAP had been causing for Prussia and for much of Germany. His speech contained numerous passages from the press and from the radio. He discussed the numerous times that public security had been threatened and the Reich did little or nothing to intervene. He pointed particularly to the "Bloody Altona Sunday" and he posed the question regarding the importance of law versus politics. But Brecht complained about the July 20 decision to take over Prussia—he pointed out that Prussia had some 40 million citizens and was a "Land" the size of France. Yet, the Prussian Ministerpräsident was not treated with respect—Papen sent his letter to Braun's apartment where he was vacationing and not to his office (Brecht 1933: 10–19). Papen was just as discourteous to Severing and the other ministers. The first time that anyone bothered to offer any justification for the emergency decree came in the afternoon in a radio address. Papen laid most of the blame on the Communist Party, but Brecht questioned the legality of such a claim. Was this not a political claim? Brecht argued that the Communist Party's influence could not be considered to be threatening; if anything, its influence was diminishing. Brecht pointed out that in 1930 there were 3.1 million votes for the KPD but by April 1932, it had dropped to 2.8. The recent increase in the power of the Communists was not through their efforts; rather, it was the Reich's decision to remove the prohibition against the SA and the SS. Brecht concluded with the insistence that Prussia had been mistreated and in particular by removing its officials. Brecht was willing to go into detail but wondered about the need for a break—a suggestion that Bumke highly recommended (Brecht 1933: 23, 27–28).

After the break Brecht briefly returned to that topic but was followed by the Reich's Ministerdirektor Gottheiner who contradicted Brecht. Gottheiner defended the Reich, insisted that Prussia had been warned repeatedly about the street fighting, and minimized Brecht's claims of disrespect by suggesting that these were little formalities. Further, Gottheiner indicated that there was a formal letter to Braun that stated the justification. At this point, there was a major commotion and Hermann Heller asked to speak.

Heller objected to the marked contrasts in which the SPD and the Communists were treated in comparison to the National Socialists. Whereas the publications of the Left were vocally and often viciously condemned, the works and leaflets of the National Socialists were left alone or even defended. Heller pointed to a letter that indicated that the Reichspräsident maintained that the Papen government was not a transitional one but represented a new direction, one that would be heavily influenced by the "strong cooperation of the national socialist powers" ("starker mitwirkung nationalsozialitischer Kräfte."). Heller insisted that this letter was authentic and revealed the true intentions of Hindenburg, Papen, and Hitler (Brecht 1933: 35–38).

When Brecht returned to speaking he acknowledged the difficulty for the Reich to control 17 different "Länder," but he objected to the way in which the Reich had portrayed Prussia. The Prussian state minister never intended to place the Communists and the National Socialists on the same level; that was a "favorite expression" ("Lieblingsausdruck") of the Reich's campaign against Prussia (Brecht 1933: 45). Brecht's assumption seemed to be supported by the court president's siding with Gottheiner against Brecht regarding publications by the Left and in particular by Severing. Heller again interrupted. This seemed to be over rather minor points, but one of the other judges made an interesting observation. Triepel pointed out that all this discussion about the threat from the Left was undermined by some statistics. The vast number of weapon permits were not granted to the KPD but to the National Socialists (Brecht 1933: 52, 55–56)!

At this point a Professor Peters referred to Carl Schmitt who had written about the two powers, the Reich and Prussia, and he suggested that Schmitt had indicated that the Reich was well within its rights to try to influence Prussia. Peters referred to a number of Schmitt's works: in *Legalität und*

Legitimität Schmitt had argued that laws applied during normal times but not during abnormal times. That is why Schmitt believed that the Reich was correct to invoke Art. 48. But it is also interesting that in "Hüter der Verfassung" Schmitt did not think that the Staatsgerichtshof had jurisdiction over constitutional issues. Finally, Peters noted that Schmitt seemed to suggest that this dispute was between not only Reich and Prussia but also between parties and factions. No one appeared to have addressed any of Peters's three Schmittian points; instead, the discussion returned to the debate about Left and Right propaganda. As the hour grew late, the discussion grew more heated, so it was finally time to adjourn (Brecht 1933: 56–57, 67–68).

The second day's proceeding began at 9:30 in the morning and concluded at 7:00 at night. It began with a heated discussion about whether the National Socialists could be considered witnesses for the support of the Reich cabinet with Brecht arguing against it and Bumke suggesting that he would allow it. Heller joined with Brecht, but Bumke indicated that Brecht's and Heller's views did not totally agree. This prompted Bumke to ask Heller to address the situation in Prussia on July 20—did Heller believe that the "public peace, order and security" ("öffentliche Ruhe, Ordnung und Sicherheit") was *not* disturbed? Heller's answer was revealing: "the public peace and security has been constantly disturbed in all of Germany since 1914" ("die öffentliche Ruhe und Sicherheit in ganz Deutschland seit dem Jahre 1914 dauernd gestört ist"). Heller's complaint was that it is wrong for the Reich to intervene solely in Prussia when there have been far worse disturbances of the public peace in other parts of Germany (Brecht 1933: 74–77). Just as notable was the request from a Dr. Badt to introduce two pieces of information. One, he said, was not essential but was still telling. As he left the proceedings yesterday evening he noticed a National Socialist placard attached to a post and each part began with "Herr Reichspräsident" and the main point was that they had been ready to declare that they tolerated Papen's government. Badt noted that that explained that the National Socialists were not bystanders in this matter, but openly sided with the Reich. Badt's second and more essential point was that the Reich had not just decided in July to intervene in Prussia; it had been planning on doing that for a long time (Brecht 1933: 79–80). Much of the second day's proceedings dealt with minor and bureaucratic points. But Heller alluded to a crucial difference: Prussia was focused on legal issues whereas the Reich was preoccupied with political matters. Brecht added that a Prussian was both a public official and a private individual and that the Reich was confusing the two (Brecht 1933: 105–107).

After some further discussion about minor points, the court adjourned until 4 p.m. Then the first main issue was to compare the development of Art. 48 with Western countries. Here, Gerhard Anschütz added his voice for the first time. He reminded the court that Baden and Bavaria were involved in these proceedings on the Prussian side. Dr. Jan addressed the court from Bavaria and expressed the wish that the proceedings focus more on the future than on the past. Having said that, he spent most of his lengthy speech on the legal history in Bavaria. It may be worth noting that many of the speakers indicated that they wished to make a "brief comment" ("kurze Bemerkung") and the proceeded to talk for ten-plus minutes (Brecht 1933: 112, 117–118). Nawiasky then was permitted to speak, and he pointed out that Carl Schmitt and Bilfinger had made their preferences for the Reich well known. Nawiasky pointed specifically to Schmitt's *Der Hüter der Verfassung* in which he insisted that the Reichspräsident was the guardian of the constitution (Brecht 1933: 118–120).

Gerhard Anschütz again addressed the court and said that he was doing so along with some of the other professors in response to Bumke's request that he clarify the meaning of Art. 48 Abs. 1. Anschütz began by indicating that he was not in the position to offer a wide-ranging lecture over the matter but would be limiting his comments to the issue of "Reichsexekution." He clarified further that he was not going to discuss the limitations or boundaries but would discuss the presuppositions. He reminded the court that Art. 48 Abs. 1 specifically addresses the situation when a "Land" has failed to fulfill its duties. In addition, this failure must have caused some damage or inflicted some injury. Anschütz noted that Abs. 1 comes into play only if both parts apply: that the "Land" has failed to fulfill its duties and that this failure has resulted in some form of damage. But Anschütz insisted that the type of damage makes a difference and that the claim that Carl Schmitt was making that Prussia's lack of fulfilling its duties somehow adversely affected the homogeneity of Germany was not applicable. What was applicable was that, in his opinion, the measures that the Reich took in response to whatever duties Prussia had failed to fulfill were clearly not legally justified (Brecht 1933: 124–129). It is at this point that Carl Schmitt was permitted to speak. Schmitt made two points: one in response to the emphasis on the politics behind Art. 48 and one in response to the explanation of the "Reichsexekution." Schmitt agreed that many of the decisions to employ force are based upon political factors but that does not undermine their legality. He objected to "Exekution" on the basis that Art. 48 Abs. 1 does not speak of that but talks only of the "Land" not fulfilling its duties. Schmitt further contended that Anschütz erred in not recognizing the danger to Germany's unity and that he was mistaken in his insistence on separating Abs. 1 from Abs. 2. Germany's unity had been threatened repeatedly since 1919, and these threats had only grown worse. Both paragraphs must be taken together because both deal with restoring "public security and order" (Brecht 1933: 130–133).

Hermann Heller was to address the issue of injury but before doing so, he responded to some of Carl Schmitt's points. Heller stated that Schmitt's points about the Holy Roman Empire and what occurred in the first decades of the nineteenth century were not relevant. Furthermore, he suggested that Schmitt's insistence on "situation relevance" was misplaced. Heller also objected that Abs. 1 does speak to "Reichsexekution" and that "execution" and "intervention" are two totally separate things. Finally, Heller questioned Schmitt's implication that the "Reich's" intervention into the internal affairs of

Prussia was necessary in order to preserve the "Reich." Dr. Peters then spoke, and among the points he made was the need to keep Abs. 1 and Abs. 2 conceptually separate but that with respect to public security they could be linked (Brecht 1933: 136–141).

The third day began at the usual 9:30 but concluded at 7:30. After a brief discussion regarding a letter that Braun sent to Bumke about the proceedings and their ambiguity, Bilfinger attempted to clarify Art. 48 by pointing to the claim that the Reich was and is in danger. Bilfinger countered the Prussian position that whatever unrest was occurring in Prussia was not affecting the Reich. Bilfinger insisted that this was not merely unrest but that it was a massive and continual bloody unrest. As such, what was happening in Berlin was a direct threat to the public security of the entire Reich. He emphasized the importance of the constitution: "The Constitution of Weimar must still more be emphasized" ("Die Verfassung von Weimar muß das doch viel mehr betonen") (Brecht 1933: 147–150). Yet at the conclusion of his lengthy speech Bilfinger appeared to suggest that a decision from the court was not entirely necessary. Bilfinger not just took issue with Anschütz and Triepel, he also seemed to select parts of his argument in favor of the Reichspräsident from Hans Kelsen (Brecht 1933: 157). Anschütz objected to Bilfinger's selective use of passages and in particular the misuse of Anschütz's *Kommentar.* In particular Anschütz contended that Bilfinger claimed that Anschütz's commentary on Art. 48 could be construed to support the Reichspräsident's intervention in almost any matter—a contention that Anschütz vehemently denied (Brecht 1933: 161–162).

Hermann Heller wished to provide a theoretical clarification regarding the relationship between Abs. 1 and Abs. 2. He claimed that Abs. 1 was a subjective opinion about disruption and only if that was really met could Abs. 2 be triggered. In Heller's view, that had not occurred. Peters agreed mostly with Heller but added that they are speaking not just about facts, but also about law. He criticized Bilfinger for suggesting that Art. 48 was somehow a faulty construction and then intended to use it against Prussia. Peters pointed out that several of the paragraphs in the Weimar Constitution were also open to interpretation, but that did not render them defective (Brecht 1933: 169–171). Peters was not the only speaker to roundly criticize Bilfinger. Jan, Nawiasky, and Giese also criticized Bilfinger's understanding of obedience (Brecht 1933: 170–175).

Carl Schmitt then interrupted to argue against Giese's interpretation of obedience. Schmitt attempted to use a minor work from Walter Jellinek to bolster his claim that Prussia had failed to fulfill its duties by not obeying the law that mandated peace and security. Schmitt pointed expressly to the danger that the Prussian unrest was causing all of Germany. Like Bilfinger, Schmitt invoked the Weimar Constitution to support the Reichspräsident's legal right and moral duty to stop the Prussian danger (Brecht 1933: 175–181). Heller responded to Schmitt by asking how is it that Schmitt can maintain that the Reich can interfere only in instances of "extraordinary danger" ("außerördentlicher

Gefahr") and then insist that the Reich has the legal right to interfere in the everyday activities in Prussia (Brecht 1933: 186–187).

Much of the remainder of the day's proceedings revolved around historical issues. These discussions revealed a level of ignorance of historical events; they also revealed a lack of understanding the speakers' various points. They also revealed a whole series of repetitions and a series of digressions. As an indication of the confusion, they not only disagreed about what duties officials had and have, they were also debating whether it was time to end the day's proceedings (Brecht 1933: 212–214, 219–221).

The fourth day's proceedings began again at 9:30. The day began with Bumke indicating that Abs. 1 had been dealt with and he expected the discussion about Abs. 2 to be rather brief. He was wrong about both points. This was partially because Bilfinger spoke at length but not about Art. 48. It is with some understatement that when Bilfinger finally finished, Bumke admitted that it was a speech that was difficult to follow (Brecht 1933: 224–229). Bumke asked that the following speakers try to stay with the proper topic and keep their remarks to Art. 48 Abs. 2. When Bumke himself ended his speech, Nawiasky responded. He appreciated Bumke's concern about speeding up the court case but insisted that this was not a regular court case. Nawiasky maintained that this was not only the most important constitutional case in Germany, but was the most important constitutional case in the world. He pointed out that this case involved power versus law (Brecht 1933: 232–233). Later Nawiasky addressed Jacobi's early contention that "Exekution" does not apply in this case. Nawiasky indicated that there are three cases in which "nicht Exekution" would apply. First, when it is not necessary to insist on particular protection. Second, if one considers "Reich compulsion" ("Reichszwang") to be the same as "administrative compulsion" ("Verwaltungszwang"). Third, when the state does not demand payment. But Nawiasky argued that none of these three applied, and even though "Exekution" may not be expressly spelled out in the first two paragraphs of Art. 48, it is certainly more than implied. Nawiasky suggested that if a "Land" refused to contribute its share of the money to the Reich, does anyone think that the Reich would be satisfied with that refusal? Nawiasky pointed out that the Reich would certainly demand its share and would "execute" some way to get it—even if the Reich did not label it "Exekution." Nawiasky may not have been known for his humor but several of his remarks and his illustrations prompted laughter (Brecht 1933: 240, 241, 244).

Erwin Jacobi responded to Nawiasky with the complaint that Nawiasky's "friendly words" in his "interesting speech" did not really obscure the fact that it was a highly personal attack. More substantially, he accused Nawiasky of misconstruing Jacobi's notion of "Exekution." It was not Nawiasky who then interrupted Jacobi but Heller who did it twice. Heller had interrupted the first time to ask about the Reich because Jacobi was placing all the blame on Prussia. The second time was in reaction to Jacobi's allusion to a vote of no confidence, to which Heller asked about its relevance.

Heller was allowed to speak and he focused on the Reich Constitution and how Papen had often expressed the wish to change it. Heller asked then what would happen to Art. 48? Heller's larger issue was with Bumke. Bumke continued to appear to side with the Reich and so Heller wanted clarification; especially since Bumke was apparently intent on evading Heller's question. Heller insisted that he needed to know Bumke's actual position so that Heller would know how to defend his own claims. Heller brought up the American Civil War and that President Lincoln made use of his presidential powers so long as the war continued. Heller also pointed to the interference with rail strikes in the United States during the 1890s. Heller's point was that even during the most violent conflict and most disruptive strikes, the executive branch interfered only when absolutely necessary and only for a determinate time. Heller was contrasting that with the extraordinary measures that the Reich had been taking since July (Brecht 1933: 246–252). There was a very lengthy discussion about officials and the limitations of their duties, which was then followed by a lengthy break (Brecht 1933: 272).

When the court reconvened Bumke again appeared to side with von Papen and von Schleicher. Bumke appeared to minimize the role that Hitler and the National Socialists had been playing in provoking the unrest and was suggesting that the blame lay with the SPD and with the Zentrum Party. Brecht responded with the objection that it was unfair to accuse Prussian democrats of causing disruptions when the Reich itself was also responsible. Bumke claimed that he had made it clear that he finds that both sides were equally responsible. After some discussion Bumke returned to the theme and allowed that these questions regarding law and power were no doubt difficult to answer (Brecht 1933: 272–275, 279). Several speakers then insisted that each "Land" was governed by a government that the voters had chosen and the voters' choice and voters' trust went hand in hand. One pointed to Hugo Preuß as "father of the Reich Constitution" ("Vater der Reichsverfassung") and Gerhard Anschütz in "his Commentary" ("seinem Kommentar") as insisting on the need for choice in order to secure trust; only when voters know that their votes matter do they have trust in the government. But by interfering with the Prussian government, the Reich was rejecting the voters' choice and undermining voters' trust (Brecht 1933: 282–283). Although Bumke had suggested much earlier that the court had finished its discussions regarding Art. 48 Abs. 1, only now had he concluded that they have completed that discussion (Brecht 1933: 286). It is telling that Bumke did not even attempt to offer a summary of the preceding days' extensive discussion regarding Abs. 1.

When the court reconvened the afternoon of Thursday, Bumke immediately explained that there were two issues which needed to be addressed. The first one concerned the inequality of intrusion; that is, how different had it been when the Reich intervened in other regions in comparison to the measures it had used in Prussia. The second one concerned the question of guilt of the Reich when it had lifted the prohibition of wearing SS and SA uniforms in public. Brecht spoke to the first point and said that if the Reich had indicated that it would be forced to involve itself in Prussian matters if Prussia did not restore order, then that would have been a signal for Prussia to act. But, the Reich did not indicate that but simply ordered the dissolution of the Prussian government. The Reich had previously faced similar situations and had always issued some kind of ultimatum. Brecht's point was clearly aimed at the inequality of intrusion that was to the detriment of the Prussian government. Regarding the question of guilt, Brecht indicated that much, if not most, of the guilt lay with the Reich because it had to have been aware that the removal of that prohibition would certainly lead to violent clashes (Brecht 1933: 286–288).

Bumke turned to Carl Schmitt to reply on behalf of the Reich. As Schmitt had a tendency to do, his reply was composed of two parts: a conceptual one and a practical one. He had problems with the formulation of Bumke's first question because it could be interpreted differently; that is, the misguided attempt to treat unequal things equally. He objected to this equality principle. He complained about the second question because it already presupposed the answer with the phrase "Reichsmißbrauchs." It is not right to insist on guilt before the matter has been discussed. Heller provided a rejoinder: as much as Schmitt was penetrating in his analysis he accused us of contesting issues that we have not contested and he insisted that we hold positions that we have never maintained. As an example, Heller pointed out that he and the others have never objected to the normal police intervention to restore order and peace. But Heller continued that the Reich's intervention was totally unlike other interventions. Heller suggested that what Schmitt was defending was basically that the larger the state was, the fewer rights it had; and the smaller the state was, the larger the rights that it had. "Oldenburg may allow itself everything. Prussia absolutely nothing!" (Oldenburg darf sich alles erlauben. Preußen gar nichts!") (Brecht 1933: 288–293). Brecht agreed with Heller and clarified that it was not just the small state of Oldenburg but many other small states. Brecht added that the complaint about Hindenburg's intervention on the side of the National Socialists did not originate with Heller but came from the Reichs-Bank. Brecht reminded the court that it was Hindenburg as Reichspräsident who had lifted the prohibition which was followed by the unrest in Prussia. To this, Bumke demanded that the Reichspräsident be left out of the discussion. Bumke's demand was another indication of the court's allegiance with the Reich (Brecht 1933: 294–295). The debate turned to more trivial matters, which finally prompted Bumke to ask that the speakers cease from discussing such matters because "It leads us not a step further" ("Es führt uns nicht einen Schritt weiter") (Brecht 1933: 300).

Gerhard Anschütz bemoaned the mounting introduction of politics into the legal proceedings and the increase in personal attacks. He sought to reduce the elevated temperature of debate and to return the court to its rightful task of determining a legal decision. He insisted that the phrase "public security and order" ("öffentlichen Sicherheit und Ordnung") was not too narrow but was too broad. Anschütz also argued that the phrases dealing with purpose, appropriate, and justifiable were similarly too broad and too subject to too many different interpretations (Brecht 1933: 301–307). The day ended at 7:30 p.m.

The fifth day's proceedings began at the usual 9:30 but this final session ended at quarter to eight. It marked the end of a long week of intense debate over the meaning of Art. 48 and the right, or lack of right, for the Reich to use that article to justify its emergency decree. Bumke opened the day by indicating that he believed that Carl Schmitt wanted to speak first. Schmitt acknowledged that request and indicated that he would not misuse the first hour of the day's session. Schmitt immediately responded to Anschütz's remarks from the end of the previous day's session. Anschütz had argued that the Reich had overstepped its boundaries by interfering in Prussia's internal affairs. The Reich did this by suspending the seven "basic rights" and by intervening with military force. Schmitt spoke for most of the hour, but his points can be condensed to the point that the Reich did not overstep its boundaries because it was necessary for the security of the Reich to intervene (Brecht 1933: 311–322). Brecht was permitted to respond for the Prussian side and he pointed to works from Schmitt, Jacobi, and Richard Grau who had all endorsed dictatorships (Brecht 1933: 322–327). Nawiasky followed with the observation that Art. 48 Abs. 2 does not endorse a dictatorship nor does it permit compelling force; it speaks only of "measures" ("Maßnahmen"). Nawiasky also insisted that the Reich is granted the legal right to interfere only when there are certain presuppositions in that "Land" but he insisted that those presuppositions had *not* been met. Therefore, the Reich did not have that right. Even if the Reich had the right to intervene, it would still not have the right to what was basically a permanent intervention (Brecht 1933: 328–335, 338). Peters added his voice to that of Nawiasky and maintained that the dismissal of six Prussian ministers had nothing whatsoever to do with restoring "public security and order" ("öffentlichen Sicherheit und Ordnung") but was instead motivated by non-legal factors (Brecht 1933: 343). Jacobi did not respond directly to the speeches by Nawiasky and Peters, but he complained that they were referring to "almost mythical becoming Schmitt-Jacobi Theory" ("beinahe mythisch geworden Schmitt-Jacobische Theorie"). Rather than addressing Abs. 2, Jacobi continually referred to Abs. 4 (Brecht 1933: 344–345). Heller spoke briefly and then was followed by Giese who did not specifically refer to the "Schmitt-Jacobi Theory" but did allude to their endorsement of a dictatorship (Brecht 1933: 347). Jacobi and then Schmitt responded to the accusations that both were dealing with political issues and not legal matters. Schmitt in particular insisted that he was there speaking as a "jurist for jurists" ("Jurist für Juristen") and that he objected to the "caricature of the so-called Schmitt-Jacobi Theory" ("Karikatur der sogenannten Schmitt-Jacobischen Theorie"). He also complained that the discussion had degenerated to the "completely empty terminological conflicts" ("völlig leere terminologische Streitigkeiten"). Schmitt concluded by insisting that he was speaking from the national standpoint (Brecht 1933: 350–353, 355). Schmitt was speaking for himself because others continued to bring up matters from the United States and Switzerland until it was finally time for the midday break.

When the court reconvened Brecht wanted to discuss the legitimacy of removing the officials from their offices. He suggested that Carl Schmitt had argued in 1924 that such a move was illegitimate if not illegal. It seems odd that Schmitt, who was always ready to reply to any remark, chose not to comment (Brecht 1933: 358–360). Nawiasky did want to respond to a comment that Jacobi had made—Nawiasky countered that Art. 48 did not specify any military intervention; it only indicated the use of the police (Brecht 1933: 362–363).

The remainder of the session was devoted to reconsidering the limits of Art. 48 and the role that the Staatsgerichtshof should be playing in determining whether the Reich was entitled to interfere in Prussian affairs. It was also focused on whether the Reich overstepped its authority when it suspended the seven "basic rights" and removed the six Prussian ministers. Some of this discussion remained mostly congenial but again there were flare-ups of personal attacks and less than professional behavior. Friday's proceedings ended at quarter after 7 with Bumke reminding the participants that the court would reconvene on Monday, October 17, at 10:30 a.m. (Brecht 1933: 391).

The sixth and final day of the court case did begin at 10:30. Brecht condensed the previous week's position into one sentence: "that Art. 48 Abs. 1 was *not* applicable, however in regards to Abs. 2 it was indeed applicable, but not as it was used in comparison to how it should be and could be applied" ("daß Art. 48. Abs. 1 *nicht* anwendbar war, daß gegen Abs. 2 zwar anwendbar war, aber nicht so angewendet werden durfte und konnte, wie er angewendet worden ist"). Much of what Brecht goes on to say was a repeat of what he and his fellow Prussians had argued. But he repeated with more emphasis his claim that the Reichskanzler had clearly overstepped the boundary in removing the six Prussian ministers. Furthermore, he objected to the claim that much of the blame for the unrest lay on Prussia when it was the National Socialists under the leadership of "Papen-Hitler" which had caused the unrest (Brecht 1933: 393–402). Others added that the political leaders of the Reich had encouraged attacks on workers and Communists. One of them reminded the court that these politically organized and secretly sanctioned attacks led to more violence, including the 17 dead Communists at the "Bloody Altona Sunday." Instead of taking another look at how the Reich might have dealt with the Prussian disturbances, it does not even contemplate that perhaps it overstepped its authority (Brecht 1933: 404–406). Heller added to this by pointing out that what Prussia has been accusing the Reich of is not so much a legal matter. Rather, the Prussian authorities have pointed to the political motive behind their measures. Heller specifically drew attention to the Reichs' focus on the SPD and insisted that it was mounting a threat against security. That was not just false but appeared to deliberately overlook the genuine threats from the National Socialists. Peters again mentioned that the removal of the six Prussian ministers had nothing to do with the disturbance of the peace but was a purely political move (Brecht 1933: 406–410).

After the conclusion of those remarks, Bumke moved to discuss the actual claims of the Prussian representatives. Bumke asked that the representatives agree that their claims that the Reich had overstepped its bounds was a correct assessment. Heller and Peters answered that it was basically correct. But von Jan spoke for Bavaria and suggested that the word "Streit" may not be the right word. He explained that there can be a "Streit" between two individuals and there can be a "Streit" between two "Länder." But there cannot be a "Streit" between the Reich and Prussia because they are not two similar states (Brecht 1933: 416, 422–423, 428–433). Shortly thereafter the court adjourned and reconvened at quarter after four that afternoon.

Erwin Jacobi then spoke for the Reich and objected to how the Prussian representatives were arguing for their side. Jacobi was suggesting that Bavaria and Baden were not in a position to side with Prussia because they were not involved in the Reichs' measures taken in Prussia (Brecht 1933: 434–447). Nawiasky countered that the other "Länder" had the right to side with Prussia because the Reich was acting as a dominating force and expected the "Land" to be submissive. The Reich was not using legal measures but was imposing its will by force. Nawiasky repeated what he had mentioned much earlier and that what Jacobi was wrong to deny that another "Land" had standing to join Prussia. He maintained that the other "Länder" such as Bavaria did have legal standing because they were equals in the "federal" government. Heller added that Jacobi was wrong to suggest that it was a "fiction" to allow other "Länder" to join. If Jacobi is intent on pointing to voter mistrust, then the Reich is just as guilty as any "Land." Heller also pointed out that in von Papen's declaration from July 20, 1932, there is mention only of "Reichskanzler" and not of any "Reichskommisar." Heller pointed further to the politics of that declaration (Brecht 1933: 448–452, 458).

Jacobi and then Bilfinger claimed that they were being misunderstood. In particular Bilfinger insisted that he had attempted to clarify what "Exekution" meant. Carl Schmitt did not elaborate on Bilfinger's point but instead pointed out that there was only one case of the three in which the Reich and the "Land" could be brought before the Staatsgerichtshof and that was the one between Reich and "Land." Those between two "Länder" should be tried before the Haag (Brecht 1933: 466–467). Slightly later there was another debate between Brecht and Jacobi. Brecht complained that according to Jacobi, Prussia itself should not be allowed to contest the Reich. Brecht's response was that since the Reich has intervened in Prussia's affairs, it certainly has the right to contest the Reichs' actions in court. Brecht then asked when a decision might be expected. Before Bumke answered, Jan objected that the lawyers for the Reich have been claiming that the Prussian case was too abstract. Jan pointed out that their case was in fact concrete but that the words from Art. 48 Abs. 1 "The Reich is permitted"

("Das Reich darf") was really abstract. Bumke simply acknowledged that a decision was a pressing matter and that the court would inform the lawyers for both sides when a decision had been reached. He thanked everyone and declared the proceedings over at eight in the evening (Brecht 1933: 473, 476–477).

The decision was handed down on October 25, 1932, and was lengthy and complex. It was lengthy at almost 30 pages and it was complex because it was composed of numerous groups, subgroups, and sub-subgroups. The title and its subtitle indicated its limits and its preferences. The title is "Decision in the Main Issue" ("Entscheidung in der Hauptsache") which indicated that it was limited to one main issue. The fact that the Court issued its rulings "In the Name of the Reich" ('"Im Namen des Reichs!") more than suggested that it was more than inclined to side with the Reich over any specific "Land." After all, it was the *Reichs*gerichts (Brecht 1933: 492–493). The Court pointed out that after Prussia lost its case on July 25, it brought it again. If the court's decision was expected to be fair, its claim that Prussia failed to fulfill its duty by not dealing with the "bloody Communist unrest" ("blutigen kommunistischen Unruhen") dispelled that expectation (Brecht 1933: 496). The Staatsgerichtshof determined that the Communists were committed to fomenting a civil war and that Prussia had failed in its duties to stop that unrest. The court also insisted that the Prussian government was politically motivated in not following the Reich's insistence that it quell the violence (Brecht 1933: 495–496). But the Staatsgerichtshof also concluded that the Reich did overstep its authority when it intervened in Prussia. It did so first by using forces other than the police and, second, by intervening only in Prussia when its peace was no more threatened than in other "Länder." The court emphasized that this second point violated the "federal state equality principle" ("bundesstaatliche Gleichheitsprinzip") (Brecht 1933: 498). It may have been this principle that the court was thinking about when it devoted several pages of its decision to Baden and to Bavaria (Brecht 1933: 501–507). If much of the decision appears opaque, it is because it was. Much of the testimony from both sides was often hard to follow; but that was mostly understandable compared to the court's decision. One instance is where the court decided that the Prussian ministers were not entitled to bring suit because they were acting as individuals and that only ministers could have standing. But that ignores the fact that they could not act in their official capacities because the Reich had relieved them of their offices (Brecht 1933: 510). Regarding Art. 48 Abs. 1, the court found that the Reich did not have the right to interfere in Prussian affairs. Regarding Abs. 2, the court found that the Reich did have the right to interfere in the pursuit of restoring "public security and order" ("öffentlichen Sicherheit und Ordnung"). The court grounded its decision on the basis that the opposing political groups were engaged in bitter street fighting that was leaving some dead and many injured. Since Prussia either could not or would not take measures to restore peace, the Reich was legally entitled under Abs.

2 to use all measures including weaponized force to restore that peace. The Reich did not overstep its authority. The court did acknowledge that the tension between Reich and "Land" was extremely problematic, and it appeared to admit that perhaps the Reich could have acted in a less forceful manner (Brecht 1933: 513–517). The fact that the court's decision was split and its reasoning was less than compelling resulted in criticism from both sides.

The Immediate Aftermath

This section of this chapter has two components. One is an examination of Kelsen's assessment of the outcome of the October trial with a brief response to Kelsen. The other is devoted to a series of comments by Ernst Fraenkel.

Hans Kelsen did not participate in the Staatsgerichtshof's proceedings of October 1932. He did publish his reaction to the court's decision in the second issue of *Die Justiz*. Kelsen pointed out that the emergency decree specified Art. 48 Abs. 2 as was needed to restore the "public security and order" in the area of Prussia. But he added that it implicitly appealed to Abs. 1 as well—the "Reichsexekution." Both paragraphs allow for the use of weaponized force to reintroduce security, but the emergency decree did not indicate which duties Prussia supposedly failed to fulfill. Kelsen made it perfectly clear that he objected to the implementation of Art. 48 and the court's determination. Kelsen indicated that it signified nothing more and nothing less than undermining "both *organizing fundamental principles* of the Weimar Constitution" ("beiden *organistorischen Grundprinzipien* der Weimarer Verfassung"); namely, the "principle of a *Federal State*" ("Prinzip des Bundesstaates") and the "principle of *democracy*" ("Prinzip der *Demokratie*"). Kelsen insisted that both are interconnected and that the decision violated both principles because it reduced the importance of the individual state and that it valued central (executive) power over democracy. As he put it, "Centralization of functions is simultaneously the process of undoing democratization" ("Zentralization der Funktionen ist zugleich Entdemokratisierung") (Kelsen 1932: 65–68). Kelsen maintained that there were two related questions: first, was the Staatsgerichthof's decision the correct one and, second which is even more fundamental, what is the legal function of a Staatsgerichtshof?

Kelsen addressed the first by pointing out (as others had) that the emergency decree of July 20 did not indicate which duties Prussia had failed to fulfill. Furthermore, Kelsen pointed out that the Staatsgerichtshof failed to clarify many issues; in fact, it had failed to even mention them. One of them was the issue of whether a "question of activity" ("Tatfrage") can be a "question of law" ("Rechtsfrage"). He points this out because it displays the tension between Art. 48 Abs. 1 which focuses on something that a "Land" has done, or in this case, not done—which is a "question of fact." In contrast, Abs. 2 is a "question of law" having to do with the legal authority to intervene. Kelsen maintained that it is crucial to point out that these are different matters—the first a matter of fact and the second a matter of law (Kelsen 1932: 70–71).

Kelsen then turned to the issue of power and questioned the claim that the Reich was legally entitled to take over all of the functions of the Prussian government. He based his question on the fact that there was a conflict between two constitutions: the Reichsverfassung and the Prussian Verfassung (Kelsen 1932: 78–80). Kelsen again pointed to the two different governments and criticized the claim that Prussia had harmed the Reich. After all, the disturbances were within Prussia and not in other parts of the Reich (Kelsen 1932: 81–84). Kelsen then criticized the court's decision for being almost contradictory: it claims that the Reich was within its legal rights but also that it acted beyond them. In effect, the court determined that the Reich both acted in accordance with the Constitution and in violation of it. What makes the decision even worse was that the court refrained from identifying exactly in what ways the Reich acted legally and in what ways it did not (Kelsen 1932: 84–87). Kelsen placed much of the blame on the Weimar Constitution itself for not clarifying the rights of the "Lands" vis-à-vis the rights of the Reich. Furthermore, Kelsen criticized the Staatsgerichtshof for not functioning as a court as much as a place for mediation. In Kelsen's legal opinion, the Staatsgerichtshof chose to find what it thought was a "compromise," but this attempt at finding the "golden middle way" ("goldenen Mittelweg") was not going to save the Weimar Constitution (Kelsen 1932: 90–91).

In the same issue of *Die Justiz* in which Kelsen published his critique of the Leipzig court's decision, a criticism of Kelsen appeared under the name "Civis." Civis noted that it is difficult to criticize the court since the court had not really spelled out its reasoning. But that did not prevent Civis from attacking Kelsen. Much of Civis's attack was personal: Civis objected to Kelsen's tone, his reasoning, and his conclusion. Civis concluded with the observation that one could fruitfully criticize the Staatsgerichtshof's decision, but Kelsen did not do so. But, Civis also did not offer a fruitful criticism of the decision, mainly because he appeared to agree with it in total (Civis 1932: 92–97, 99, 104–106). Civis's Kelsen critique seemed designed to cast doubt on Kelsen's writings more than it was intended to shore up the court's decision. Hans Kelsen would then leave Germany for Switzerland while Carl Schmitt would move to Berlin. Schmitt would later part ways with the Nazis while Kelsen would later find some comfort in the United States. Something similar can be said about Ernst Fraenkel's later life in America.

Ernst Fraenkel's comments are highly instructive because he was a well-respected legal scholar and provided an objective account of the "Preußenschlag." The first installment appeared in the first "Heft" of volume 8 of *Die Justiz*. Fraenkel began by commenting that he was writing this during the first day of the Staatsgerichtshof and noted that it was the "legal conflict [between] Free State Prussia against the German Reich" ("Rechtsstreit Freistaat gegen Deutsches Reich"). He allowed that no matter which way the Leipzig court decided, it would be massively criticized. He noted that the understanding between the people and what justice is was becoming increasingly more difficult. He also noted that the demand that all are equal before the law was becoming more suspect. Fraenkel admitted that justice seems abstract in times of massive unemployment and political unrest. He placed much of the blame on the Reich but he also allowed that parliament had been considered as being unproductive. Fraenkel introduced a new phrase: "authoritarian democracy" ("autoritären Demokratie"), and he suggested that whatever wakens the German "Volk" to the realities will have done it a great, if involuntary, service (Fraenkel 1932a: 53–58).

Fraenkel's second "Chronik" appeared in the double-edition 2/3. This one is not as objective in that he wrote about the two instances of law versus the "established power" ("etabilierte Macht"). He emphasized how in the "case Reich–Prussia" ("Sachen Reich–Preußen") that it appeared that the Staatsgerichtshof had sided with the Reich and he warned of the consequences of that decision. Above all, he warned about the infringement on freedom of opinion and expression. In concluding, Fraenkel noted that the readers of *Die Justiz* should be aware that the Weimar Constitution is in its moment of deepest crisis. This was finished on November 27, 1932 (Fraenkel 1932b: 133–139).

The third "Chronik" appeared in Heft 4 and it mostly ignored the Prussian–Reich conflict. What Fraenkel did mention was that his chronicle was both forward-looking and backwards-looking and that he was both depressed and elated about how some legal battles were shaping up (Fraenkel 1932c: 189–192).

Fraenkel's fourth and final "Chronik" appeared in the penultimate edition of *Die Justiz.* His beginning and his ending said the most: he started with "Womit beginnen?" ("Where to start?") and he noted that it was eight months since von Papen had signified a major shift in German politics and governing—from the party state to an authoritarian regime—yet Papen himself was forced to resign. It was the Prussian government that had underscored the discrepancy in Art. 109. It stated, "All Germans are equal before the law" ("Alle Deutschen sind vor dem Gesetze Gleich"), yet what the law stated and what the administration does is not the same. But Fraenkel insisted that there were millions of German voices which will cry out against the new arbitrary rule and that the battle between "a regime of Arbitrariness" ("ein Regim der Willkür") and justice with equality for all. Fraenkel concluded with the phrase praising "law and freedom" ("Recht und Freiheit"). Fraenkel dated his final "Chronik" February 25, 1933 (Fraenkel 1932d: 281, 284).

Having concluded the discussion of the "Preußenschlag" and its aftermath, it is time to return to the discussions regarding Art. 48 that were published in the second half of 1932.

Art. 48 in the Second Half of 1932

Richard Grau has played a major role in this story of Article 48. His major book and his several essays have been explored in previous chapters. There are two critical essays contained in the *Handbuch des Deutschen Rechts* that

Anschütz and Thoma had published in 1930 and in 1932.[4] Grau's two lengthy essays are found in the second volume; that is, the one published in 1932. The fifth main part of that volume is entitled "The Functions of the State Power" ("Die Funktionen der Staatsgewalt") and it was composed of 29 essays. The authors included Richard Thoma, Walter Jellinek, Erwin Jacobi, Leo Wittmayer, and Grau. That Grau contributed two essays was not unusual; Thoma wrote two (§ 71 and § 76), Jellinck wrote two (§ 72 and § 73), Walther Schoenborn wrote two (§ 82 and § 83), Eduard Kern wrote two (§ 95 and § 96), Jacobi wrote two (§ 77 and § 78), and Johannes Heckel wrote three (§ 87, § 88, and § 89). All 29 focused on law, the courts, administration, and amnesty, but several were focused on power and force. Both of Grau's essays concerned the use of force by dictatorial powers; however, the first one was on the Reichspräsident while the second one was on the "Länder." The first one was not at all surprising given what had transpired throughout the Weimar Era, but the second one seemed odd at the time and even more so today. Even Grau must have been aware of how strange this must have appeared because he devoted only five pages to the second essay while the first one took up 26 pages.

Grau's first essay (§ 80) has three main sections. Section I is a brief, four-page introduction, section II is the longest at ten pages and covers the central points of Art. 48, while section III concerns the organization and the position of the dictatorship.

Section I places the concept of dictatorship within its proper context. Grau insisted that Art. 48 paragraph 2 concerning dictatorial powers is not some transconstitutional attempt at national unity but rather is firmly embedded within the Weimar Constitution. Grau emphasized that that article was expressly intended to guarantee the security and protection of public life and with it the security of the constitution itself. It is a remark like this that prompted the debate about who or what should be considered the guardian of the constitution—a debate that will be discussed later in this chapter.

Grau suggests that a dictatorship is neither as restrictive nor as expansive as it has often been characterized. Rather, it is considered in Art. 48 as a limited and temporary introduction of special a measure to ensure against the

4 Hans Nawiasky published two reviews of the *Handbuch des Deutschen Staatsrechts* in the *Archiv des öffentliche Rechts*. The first one covered the early sections, and Nawiasky noted that the large number of authors meant that there would be major differences of opinion. He suggested that it might be considered a drawback for a non-scholar but is to be welcomed for an advanced scholar. In his second review, Nawiasky praised a number of authors for the clear and comprehensive accounts. He singled out Anschütz and several others. He suggested that the differences of opinion that he mentioned in his earlier review continued with the later sections. Again, he stressed that it would be a problem only for a novice. A second possible danger might be a repetition, yet Anschütz and Thoma were able to reduce that to a minimum. Nawiasky repeated his praise for the work as a whole and underscored the need that the *Handbuch* certainly satisfied (Nawiasky 1930: 235, 1931: 299, 302).

"bank-rot" of the Weimar Republic. This is what he refers to as the "Reichs' execution" ("Reichsexekution"), but he means the carrying out of specific measures and not the execution of any regime. He emphasized what he had said in earlier publications, that when rules are broken and peace is threatened, then dictatorial powers are not just justified but are necessary. Grau also insists that these measures are not legally questionable but are firmly within the reading of the Weimar Constitution. He justifies this by contrasting the flexibility of what Art. 48 states and the rigidity of the Bavarian army's introduction of military law during the final years of the world war. A further contrast was that the Bavarian military had taken upon itself the authority whereas in Weimar the authority was built into the constitution and by extension by parliament. Another contrast was that the Bavarian instructions were extensive in contrast to the limited application of Art. 48 (Grau 1932a: 274–275).

The fact that there can be such unrest in an area is a partial indication of the weakness of that area's governing body, and that weakness underscores the justification for the intrusion of the federal government's suspension of certain "basic rights" ("Grundrechte"). But Grau also pointed out that such measures would not be introduced in a wide variety of cases: in disputes over banking practices, in arguments regarding government spending practices, or debates about tariffs. These are typical issues that would not warrant the introduction of dictatorial powers.

The issue of the competency of the dictatorship is founded upon Art. 48 itself. This particular paragraph is very dense and difficult to follow. What Grau seems to be suggesting is that there is a fundamental difference between assessing the competency of a "normal" government and appraising the competency of an emergency dictatorship. It is the distinction between regularity and exception. This applies not only to the federal government but to each of its member states as well. In Grau's assessment, security and order are the highest and most important things that every state is obligated to ensure (Grau 1932a: 276–277).

Grau's explanations regarding the presuppositions of the introduction of dictatorial powers is far clearer: it is justified whenever there is the disruption or the threat of disruption of "public security and order" ("öffentlichen Sicherheit und Ordnung"). This is not some abstract presupposition but is actually about material conditions. Grau admits that determining when there is a disruption is not always easy to do and there are various factors that can influence that decision. He admits that it is far more difficult to ascertain whether there really is a threat to public security and that such a determination can be regarded as subjective. However, he does insist that such cases of actual disturbance and such instances of genuine threats can be determined. It is the obligation of the dictatorial powers to make clear what basis it has for determining whether there is actual disruption or a genuine threat. In other words, the user of dictatorial power must justify its actions. In so doing, it shows itself to be a preventive dictatorship and not a repressive one (Grau 1932a: 277–278). He clarifies this by indicating that such instances are not your typical instances in which the police can take charge and remedy the situation. Instead, the danger must be recognized as being real and to be so extraordinary that it calls for extraordinary measures to combat it. Grau repeats that in these situations, the dictator not only has the justification for intrusion; but also is actually obligated to do so (Grau 1932a: 278). Grau has finished with his overall introductory remarks and turns to his examination of specific aspects of Art. 48.

Section II begins with Grau's announcement that there are two aspects of the use of force as set out in Art. 48 that require special consideration: the right to use weapons as force and the suspension of some of the "basic rights." However, instead of discussing those two aspects, he turns to discussing the general clause and what "necessary measures" ("nötigen Maßnahmen") means. He also mentions how the dictatorship can limit freedom of movement and impose other measures that are designed to be implemented for a restricted time frame. The question of the legality of these political actions can be decided in their favor by the judiciary; after all, the judges are independent and not political.[5] Grau is on more solid ground when he indicates that the application of the "necessary measures" "fit" their actual purpose; that is, to restore "public security and order" ("öffentlichen Sicherheit und Ordnung"). These measures can, and should, be ratified by parliament to give it additional legitimacy and legality.

There is no question that Grau places the central government over any regional powers. In fact, he questions the basis for even claiming that the dictatorial powers would be acting in the "name of the Land" ("im Namen des Landes"). To help forestall complaints from the "Länder" regarding the dictatorial measures, Grau repeats that such measures are for a limited time and are not to be considered as continuing and certainly not as permanent. If these measures need to be extended, then the parliament or possibly the judiciary needs to grant the approval.

In a paragraph printed in small font, Grau briefly discusses the appropriateness of the dictatorial measures. On the one hand, it is evident that the determination that the dictator needs to intrude is a personal one as is the decision as to what counts as "necessary measures." On the other hand, the dictator is cognizant of his power—it should not be either too extensive or perceived as being too weak (Grau 1932a: 280–281).

This seemingly minor paragraph leads into Grau's crucial discussion of the binding of the dictatorship to the Reichsverfassung. He is blunt in insisting that just because the force that the dictatorship uses is based upon the constitution does not imply that that dictator is bound by the content of the

5 Grau's claim that judges are not political and are independent is a claim that can be, and often is, hotly contested. Even in the United States, there has been considerable debate about the independence of the states' judiciary, not to mention the claim that the Department of Justice can, and often is, a "weapon" of the ruling party.

constitution.[6] His point apparently is that the constitution is an "abnormal" type of organizational "institution" or "entity" that grants the authority to the dictator to use force in extraordinary circumstances. Those extraordinary circumstances mean that the dictator is not bound by the "normal" organizational institution. Grau justifies this by considering the language from the Prussian Constitution of 1850 as well as from the Reichsverfassung from 1871. In addition, Grau emphasized that most aspects of governing are continuing to function: meaning the Reichspräsident, the Reich regime, the Reich government, and the "Land" government. These "ordinary" parts of government cannot be allowed to intrude on the necessary powers that the extraordinary circumstances demand (Grau 1932a: 282).

This is directly connected to Grau's explanation covering the suspension of some "basic rights." That he discusses this is not unusual, given what Grau had written in earlier works; what is unusual is that he does not discuss individual rights. Instead, his discussion is peculiarly abstract except when he was mentioning the suspension of certain tax laws and when he was referring to the use of the German postal service. His point is that the suspension of some "basic rights" should not be regarded as being particularly dangerous and should be considered only as temporary necessary measures. At first glance, it seems that Grau was concerned with how the citizens would react to the suspension of some "basic rights," but a second glance reveals that he had no such concerns. Although such a suspension would impact the citizens' lives, that impact is less important than the necessary suspension of any "basic rights." Grau is not totally dismissive of "basic rights" but again what is far more important is the reestablishment of "public security and order." Although he does not make the point here, the assumption is without "public security and order" there are no "basic rights" (Grau 1932a: 283–284). Grau then spends several pages discussing the minutiae of legal decisions that had some relevance to his defense of dictatorship. What is far more relevant and much more interesting is when he moves to examine the relationship between dictatorship and justice. It is noteworthy because justice is applicable during normal circumstances and the Weimar Constitution specifically prohibited dictatorship (see Articles 103, 105, and 106). Moreover, it needs to be stressed that the dictator determines his course of action merely by himself; whereas the judge is fully independent and submits only to the law (Art. 102). Grau realized that his position was not tenable, but he suggested that Art. 105 did not really mean what it said. He tried to finesse this difficulty by arguing the Art. 105 applied to the person and not to the institution and that the institution of justice can be subsumed under the dictatorship (Grau 1932a: 287–288).

Believing that he had dispensed with legal obstacles to a dictatorship, Grau then moves to discussing the "organization of the dictatorship." Here, Grau

6 "*Die Bindung der Diktatur an den Inhalt der Reichsverfassung*. Daraus allein, daß die Diktatur eine aus der Verfassung hergeleitete Gewalt ist, folgt noch nicht, daß der Diktator *an den Inhalt der Reichsverfassung* gebunden ist" (Grau 1932a: 281).

insists that the organization and the administration are solely the option of the dictator—in this case, the Reichspräsident. He has the right to appoint people from his own government in order to assist him. He also has the right to appoint people from a "Land" government if he thinks that that individual will be able to assist him. In other words, it is simply a matter of who can be of use to him. That is why Grau emphasized a "helper" who shares the same goals. It is also why Grau had no particular interest in distinguishing between an immediate organization and a mediate one. For Grau, it is only an issue of purpose and expediency (Grau 1932a: 289–291). His defense is striking especially when he concluded with the question of whether the dictatorship is subject to review or to control. He basically insisted that neither the parliament nor a court has any legitimacy is judging whether the dictator has overextended his authority. It also helps explain why, with one minor exception, Grau chose to ignore the thorny issue of what counts as "weaponized power" ("bewaffeneten Macht"). He leaves that decision of what counts or what is legitimate to the dictator—again neither issue is a matter for any court (Grau 1932a: 291). The closest that Grau comes to allowing that a court has any jurisdiction over a dictatorship under Art. 48 is under the purview of the "State Court" (Staatsgerichtshof"). This court is legitimate to decide because it is supposedly free from political influence and is not liable to pressure as in other courts (Grau 1932a: 294–295). If Grau had appeared to be impartial about the dictatorial powers supposedly authorized by Art. 48 in his 1922 book, by 1932 he had mostly abandoned that impartial scholarship for a full-scale justification of dictatorial force. The fact that this power can only reside in the central government and specifically in the hands of the Reichspräsident is made clear in his second contribution to the Anschütz and Thoma *Handbuch.*

Grau began his second essay in the *Handbuch des deutschen Rechts* (§ 81) in the same way that he began his first (§ 80) by discussing the role of a dictatorship within the limits of the constitution ("Stellung der Diktatur der Landesregierungen im Verfassungsleben"). But Grau contrasted the dictatorial powers of the Reichspräsident with that of the regional governments—the Reichspräsident's dictatorial powers were not only grounded in the Bavarian orders during the First World War but were embedded in the unitary nature of the presidency itself. Grau looked to Art. 48, but not to the first or second paragraphs but to the fourth one. There it states that a government of a "Land" has the right to introduce extraordinary measures when a certain part of the region is threatened. However, Art. 48 paragraph four is rather limited: it is limited it terms of place, time, and extent. It is limited to just that part of the "Land" that is threatened, it is limited to the time that the threat is active, and most importantly, these extraordinary measures can be curtailed at any time by the Reichspräsident or by the parliament (Grau 1932a: 295; Anschütz 1929: 239). Grau contended that the introduction of paragraph four was made primarily, if not solely, to appease the members of the constitutional committee from smaller "Länder" and that it was a means to secure their approval to Art. 48 that they would have opposed. He suggested that it would appeal to their sense of federalism and would limit their fears about a strong central authority. To bolster his contention, Grau pointed to the political function of that paragraph and he cautioned his readers not to lose sight of its political significance (Grau 1932b: 296).

Grau then turned to examine the presuppositions in allowing the "Land" to introduce dictatorial measures. He pointed in particular to the phrase "danger in postponements" ("Gefahr im Verzüge"). He objected that this meant that an extraordinary measure could be introduced to counter an ordinary institution and he emphasized how dangerous this could be. But he added that even the authors of paragraph four recognized this danger and so they limited it in several ways. The main one is where the Reichspräsident can intervene; thus, Grau insisted that the "Lands'" dictatorial powers were extremely limited in contrast to those of the Reichspräsident. This is also shown by how limited the "Land" is in legally using weapons to restore order. It is also shown by the notion of "for its area" and "temporarily." In contrast, the Reichspräsident is not hampered by these limitations. Instead, the Reichspräsident is authorized to eliminate or to alter whatever extraordinary measures that any "Land" has implemented. In other words, the dictatorial powers of the Reichspräsident trump any dictatorial measures instituted by any "Land."[7] This would be Richard Grau's final writing on Art. 48, and it is fairly evident that even in his 1922 book, he favored the use of Art. 48 and that inclination only intensified over time. Grau shared that with Carl Schmitt and others; however, Anschütz and Thoma were joined by Walter Jellinek in their objections to the imposition of the dictatorial Art. 48.

Anschütz (and Jellinek)

In 1932 Gerhard Anschütz and Walter Jellinek published two separate accounts of a financial document. Their accounts and their positions need some clarification. Both Anschütz and Jellinek were professors of "public law" ("öffentlichen Rechts") at the University at Heidelberg. Anschütz had been there for many years, and Jellinek came in 1929. He had been at Kiel from 1919 until moving to Heidelberg. Walter Jellinek was not your typical professor of jurisprudence. He was born in Vienna in 1885 to Georg and Camilla Jellinek. Despite having an exemplary publishing record, Georg left Austria because his Jewish background closed most doors to Austrian professorships. Georg taught at Heidelberg until his premature death in 1910—he had been a close friend of Max Weber and along with his wife was part of the Weber circle. Georg Jellinek's *Allgemeine Staatslehre* was the standard work until Kelsen's work was published in 1925. Walter had edited the third edition of his father's magnum opus in 1914. Like his father, he was discriminated

7 Grau 1932b: 297–300. It is noteworthy that Grau cautions any "Land" about using dictatorial measures because its citizens will be liable for any and all costs that such measures would incur.

against because of his Jewish background and was forced to retire from teaching in the mid-thirties. After the war, he was reinstated at Heidelberg and helped Germany rediscover its democratic principles and values. As to the two accounts and their connection to Art. 48: the title of the collected two was *Reichskredite und Diktatur* and Anschütz and Jellinek point to the claim that the Reichspräsident has the legal right under Art. 48 Abs. 2 and 5 to unilaterally reduce the state's debts. Anschütz was convinced that the Reichspräsident had no power under Art. 48 to use dictatorial measures to help the German "credit situation" and he agreed with Dr. Kühnemann. Anschütz praised Kühnemann not only because of his legal appraisal of the matter but also because of his "strict legal state conviction" ("strenge rechtsstaatliche Gesinnung") (Anschütz und Jellinek 1932: 7). Anschütz referred to his commentary on the Weimarer Reichsverfassung and particularly to his third edition account of Art. 48. Anschütz insisted that the article does not give the Reichspräsident dictatorial powers except to restore public security and order. Obviously, making Germany's financial matters more attractive does not come under that label (Anschütz und Jellinek 1932: 8–14). Anschütz spent the remainder of his essay to explain that laws are laws and that they regulate power. Even an Art. 48 does not give the Reichspräsident "limitless, uncontrolled, and uncontrollable power" ("schrankenlosen, unkontrollierten und unkontrollierbaren Macht"). The Reichspräsident has his power and parliament has its power—and parliament has not only the right to limit the Reichspräsident's inclination to dictatorial powers; they are the responsible authority to do so (Anschütz und Jellinek 1932: 17–22).

Walter Jellinek's contribution differed in several ways from that of Anschütz. First, it had a shorter and more understandable title: "Monetary Acquisition Through Credit on the Basis of a Dictatorial Measure of the Reichspräsident" ("Geldbeschaffung durch Kredit auf Grund einer Diktaturmaßnahme des Reichspräsidenten"). Second, Jellinek provided a detailed table of contents for his 17-page essay. Third, his essay has four parts: an introduction, a section in which he agrees with Kühnemann and a section in which he disagrees, and a fourth concluding section. But like Anschütz, Jellinek relied on his earlier work, in this case the third edition of *Verfassung und Verwaltung des Reichs und der Länder* (*Constitution and Administration of the Reich and the Lands*). There Jellinek maintained that the changes in credit or in monetary acquisition could be done "only on the basis of a Reich law" ("nur auf Grund eines Reichsgesetzes") (Anschütz und Jellinek 1932: 25). This is a direct quotation from Art. 87 of the Weimarer Reichsverfassung, and Jellinek agreed with Anschütz that the Reichspräsident's claim to dictatorial power is contradicted here by Art. 87. Jellinek then offered five points in which he agreed with Kühnemann. The first four were connected to constitutional law; in the fifth one Jellinek argued that the Reichspräsident did not have jurisdiction over credit with respect to Art. 48. Jellinek returned to the passage from Art. 87 that he had earlier quoted and here emphasized "nur" ("only"). He insisted that this "little word" ("Wortchen") was definitively applicable to laws. The Reichspräsident can enforce the laws, but only parliament can make them (Anschütz und Jellinek 1932: 30–32). Jellinek concluded with the insistence that Art. 48 Abs. 2 applied only to situations in which "public security and order" is threatened or disrupted and that Art. 87 ensures that such measures do not, and cannot, apply to monetary issues. Jellinek recognized the danger of the lack of German credit-worthiness but he insisted that this issue must be dealt with in a reasonable and responsible legal way (Anschütz und Jellinek 1932: 39–40).

The following year saw the publication of the final edition of Gerhard Anschütz's constitutional commentary. It is intriguing to contrast his positive and hopeful comments from January 1, 1921, for the first edition to the negative and resigned remarks of the foreword to the 14th edition. Written in February 1933, Anschütz noted how the publication of the two volumes of his and Thoma's *Handbuch des deutschen Staatsrechts* were delayed and that the third edition of his *Kommentar* from 1929 was still published without the new version for the editions 11 through 13. His new edition was appearing during the time of heavy political struggles and disruptions because the Weimar Constitution was being threatened. He admitted that he did not know whether the Verfassung would come through intact or in pieces and acknowledged that writing a new edition took "no small amount of trust and confidence" ("kein kleines Maß von Vertrauen und Zuversicht"). Anschütz also admitted that the Weimar Verfassung had its defects, but he insisted that it was elastic and changed when circumstances warranted such changes. He closed with the hope that this dependence in the belief in the constitution "must and will teach a—perhaps near—future" ("muß und wird eine—vielleicht nahe—Zukunft lehren") (Anschütz 1933: V–VI).

A brief contrast between the numbers from the first edition of 1921 and the 14th from 1933 help demonstrate the importance and the impact of Art. 48. In the first edition, Anschütz devoted a total of just under three pages to Art. 48. The first edition did not contain a bibliography whereas the 14th did. It was almost a full page of petit print and was divided into two sections: one on Abs. 1 ("Reichsexekution") and one on Abs. 2–5 ("Diktaturgewalt"). This difference reflected the change from 1921 where he did not formally distinguish among Art. 48's five paragraphs (Anschütz 1921: 106–108, 1933: 268–269). In 1933 his examination of Art. 48 had increased to 33 pages, thus ten times the number of pages from the first edition. In the 1933 edition, he maintained that the five paragraphs were concerned with two different matters. Abs. 1 focused on the "Reichsexekution" against "Land" which did not fulfill its duties. Abs. 2 through 5 focused on the measures that can be taken in the fight against "unusual disruption or endangerments" ("ungewöhnlicher Störungen oder Gefährdungen") of the public security and order. These measures are to be regarded as extraordinary because they are "dictatorial measures of the Reichspräsident" ("diktatorische Maßnahmen des RPräs"). After providing the entirety of Art. 48 and the "Literatur," Anschütz gave a three-page, two-section introduction. The discussion of Abs. 1 is relatively minimal: just over four pages containing sections 3, 4, and 5. The discussion of Abs. 2 through 5 covers sections 6 through 19, while Abs. 5 was virtually ignored. In the introduction Anschütz emphasized that the two different matters needed to be kept separate and noted that the dictatorial powers discussion really excluded Abs. 5. He mentioned that in the early discussions regarding the Weimarer Verfassung, the two parts were dealt with in separate articles. It was with the third reading that the two were combined into Art. 48. Anschütz regarded this move to be a mistake because, as he repeated, they deal with separate issues. Much of his 1933 exploration of Art. 48 was devoted to showing how these two issues were focused on two different concerns—one on the relationship between Reich and "Land" and the other on the use of presidential dictatorial force. He reminded his readers that Abs. 1 regulates the conduct of the Reich if and when a "Land" does not fulfill its obligations. It makes no mention of the legitimate use of dictatorial powers to restore "public security and order." The one passage that is shared between Abs. 1 and Abs. 2 is the phrase "with the help of weaponized power" ("mit Hilfe der bewaffneten Macht"). He pointed out that these "measures" may be used against the cause of the disruption of public security regardless of what or who is the cause. He clarified that this applied not only to the single person who has caused this disturbance but under certain circumstances also to the "Land." He noted that "in other words" it can be used to apply to anyone that the Reichspräsident has deemed "responsible" (Anschütz 1933: 267–270). Section 1 was the theoretical context and the pre-history of the article. Section 2 was a detailed a historical overview beginning in 1920 and continuing to around 1932.

In the short Part I on the "Reichsexekution," Anschütz noted that the term "duties" did not apply to all duties but only to those in relation to the Reich. They did not apply to private duties or even public duties such as the police and fire protection. He spells out that these are particular duties that a "Land" has in relationship to the "Reich." This is the basis for the term "Reichsexekution"—the execution of the Land's duties as a member of the Reich. Anschütz does not criticize Abs. 1 explicitly; his complaint is two-fold: these "duties" are not specifically identified and the decision regarding what they are and how they are not being fulfilled is left solely up to the Reichspräsident—which makes it fundamentally the dictator's decision. Yet, he added that the Reichspräsident's decisions need to be ratified by the parliament (Anschütz 1933: 271–275).

Part II is not only much longer than Part 1; it also has a far lengthier title: "The Dictatorial Force of the Reichspräsident and the 'Land' Government" ("Die Diktaturgewalt des Reichspräsident und der Landesregierungen"). Section 6 is mostly historical, and Anschütz turned to the effects of the modern dictatorship laid out in Art. 48 Abs. 2 and Abs. 4. He insisted that there were numerous differences between dictatorial measures that were justified by war and the claims that Art. 48 applied during times of peace. Furthermore, he complained that under Art. 48 the Reichspräsident could claim that he was entitled to use such force as he deemed necessary without the normal approval of parliament. Furthermore, he criticized it on the grounds that it did not specify to what extent the police could use force in their intervention in a "Land." Finally, referring back to his response to the use of Art. 48 in respect to minimizing German debt and maximizing German credit, he questioned how that article could have applicability to monetary issues and credit crises (Anschütz 1933: 275–279). Moreover, there is a genuine problem with the term "temporary" ("Vorübergehende"). It would be dictatorially illegal to claim that it is unlimited since Abs. 2 indicates that Abs. 2 applies only to the restoration of "public security and order." Anschütz insisted that what counts as "temporary" cannot be determined by the Reichspräsident but can be ascertained only by the courts. He insisted that this was not a subjective matter for a single individual but must be addressed "scientifically" by an objective tribunal. Anschütz added that he would return to this issue in Section 18 (d) (Anschütz 1933: 280–282).

Sections 11 and 12 are brief single paragraphs and are composed primarily of remarks on works by other scholars (mainly Grau's and Nawiasky's) and on the phrase "fully unrestricted" ("völlig unbeschränktes"). In contrast, Section 13 is almost two pages in length and has two subsections: (a) is a single paragraph but is important because Anschütz contends with the expression "with help of weaponized force" ("mit Hilfe bewaffneten Macht"). It is not very clear what any of this phrase means, but he believed that it referred to the "Reich's military" ("Reichswehr"). He noted that that made no sense because the "Reichswehr" was intended to defend Germany against foreign invaders and not internal agitators. Anschütz paid considerable attention to the two terms "Verordnungen" and "Notverordnungen," but both terms are difficult to translate. "Verordnungen" are decrees, ordinances, or commands; "Notverordnungen" are emergency decrees, emergency ordinances, or emergency commands. The problem is that regular orders are determined by parliament and then carried out by the executive branch. But emergency orders cannot be deliberated over by parliament because measures must be taken immediately—there is no time for extensive discussions. Thus, the Reichspräsident has supposedly been granted the capacities of the parliament as well as by those from his own office. Just as important, he argued, is that there is a contrast between what legal measures the Reichspräsident has in relation to the parliament to deliberate over "greater, stronger emergency law" ("vergrößertes, verstärktes Notverordnungsrecht") (Anschütz 1933: 281–284). Anschütz then announced that he would be discussing how an emergency situation could apply to four individual cases.

The first example was a contentious one and, as Anschütz pointed out, was a subject of considerable controversy. On one side, some legal scholars contended that certain emergency decrees needed to be in accordance with normal laws, whereas on the other side, other legal experts maintained that any emergency decree superseded any normal law. In other words, the dispute centered (again) on how unrestricted or restricted the Reichspräsident's emergency dictatorial powers were. Much of this discussion focused on the apparent distinction between "law" ("Gesetz") and "Reichs-law" ("Reichsgesetz"). Anschütz named Thoma and Giese as two who interpreted this to mean restrictions and listed Schmitt and Grau as among those who advised an unrestricted interpretation (Anschütz 1933: 284–288).

The second example was also contentious and revolved around the question of setting aside the seven "basic rights." While many, like Grau and Schmitt, saw no difficulties in setting aside these "basic rights," Thoma, and here Anschütz, contended that the setting aside the freedom of opinion and of the press and the sacredness of one's dwelling could not be legally sacrificed for the vague claim of restoring "public security and order" (Anschütz 1933: 288–290).

The third example was bound with the second and covered the extent to which power could be appropriated. Anschütz clarified that the application of laws was not just a matter for the Reich but was also an issue for the individual "Land." As such, the appropriation of power was not simply a matter for the Reich but also an issue for the various "Lands."

The fourth example was the dispute of whether there could be an emergency court. This was not a minor question but went to the issue of control. As Anschütz argued, Abs. 3 did not mention anything about the courts; the Reichspräsident's measures could be continued or stopped by parliament, not any court (Anschütz 1933: 290–295).

Anschütz then moved to discuss Abs. 4 and here, even more so than with the other paragraphs, he made it clear on which side he agreed. While Abs. 1, 2, and 3 focused on the Reich, Abs. 4 was concentrated with the "Land" governments. As expected from previous writings, Anschütz's sympathies lay with the "Land"—in his opinion, Nawiasky was right and Grau was wrong. Anschütz emphasized that Art. 48 spoke about "provisionally" and that these measures were not to be considered long-term, much less, permanent. Anschütz concluded his examination of Art. 48 by insisting that the "Land" had the right to insist on rejecting the Reichspräsident's extraordinary measures if the "Land" believed that those measures intruded upon the sovereignty of the "Land." In fact, Anschütz questioned whether there was ever the need to invoke Art. 48 and that even in abnormal circumstances, the proper authorities need to base their actions on normal laws (Anschütz 1933: 288–299). It seems that Anschütz approached the examination of Art. 48 in much the way that he discussed all the other articles—as a legal scholar and a constitutional expert, he respected the law and he approached it from an "objective" viewpoint. This sense can be detected throughout—as much as he disagreed with people like Grau and Schmitt, he believed that they based their understanding of constitutional issues on legal grounds. What he had not yet realized was that his constitutional opponents were not speaking as legal experts but as political agitators.

The cautious optimism found in Anschütz's "Vorwort" to the 1933 edition of his commentary had not materialized; however, his pessimism had been realized. By the end of March of that same year, he had recognized how hopeless it was to believe that the rule of law mattered and how teaching about constitutions was no longer viable. In his memoir, Anschütz recollected that he was able to teach German law under the monarchy and then in the republic. But now he questioned the possibility of teaching law in a state that did not believe in law. He quoted from his letter of resignation that he submitted to the Baden minister of culture and asked to be granted emeritus status. He expected that this be granted because he had not only reached the year of eligibility for retirement (65) but had exceeded it (67). Anschütz's request was granted. He wrote at the end of *Aus mein Leben* that he had begun his academic career in 1896 and had devoted 36 years to German law. In order to be released from lecturing, he had to submit a request to be granted "inactive full professor" ("inaktiven ordentlichen Professor")—and it had never even occurred to him in all those 36 years that he would ever seek such a release from his teaching duties (Anschütz 1993: 328–329).

The End of the Weimar Era

The history and the causes of the end of the Weimar Era lay beyond the scope of this book. Experts and specialists have been debating how and why the Weimar Republic failed for almost an entire century (see Büttner's overview, 498–500; Blasius 2006: 158–161; Bracher, Sauer and Schulz 1960: 1–8, 31–32). These people were, and are, better suited to continue to discuss and even debate the causes. But it is not out of place to sketch briefly the first two months of 1933 and to provide some conclusions drawn from the work of others.

On January 4, 1933, Hitler met Papen at a banker's residence, which appeared to mark a growing acceptance of the leader of the NSDAP. The party was successful in the small "Land" of Lippe on January 15.[8] Between January 17 and January 29, Papen and Hindenburg met Hitler in secret. On January 28, Schleicher's cabinet was dissolved and two days later Hitler was named Kanzler (Büttner 2008: 490–491, 495–497, 798; Schafer 1995b: 416–417).

Robert Chr. van Ooyen has recently suggested that Weimar failed because it was a "democracy without democrats." However, he also suggested that there were a number of legal scholars who did believe in democracy. Ooyen counted Preuß, Anschütz, Thoma, Kelsen, and Hermann Heller among them (Ooyen 2019: 19, 23). But Preuß was dead, Kelsen and Heller were soon forced to flee, and Thoma and Anschütz were forced to withdraw from public life. In contrast, Schmitt, Jacobi, and Billfinger not only thrived but also (at least for a short while) were feted (Blasius 2006: 106). Peukert reminded us that there were only seven years from the time that Hitler gained power and the beginning of the Second World War. Peukert also insisted that much of the blame lay on the Nazis but also a fair proportion of the blame fell on Germany itself. The political and social institutions were never strong enough to overcome the

8 Lippe is now part of Nordrhrein-Westfalen.

problems that Weimar faced from its earliest days. Hitler was smart and adept enough to take advantage of these institutional weaknesses, and Weimar did not have guardrails strong enough to reign him in. Peukert also hints at the naivety of Hindenburg and those who still had fond memories of the Kaiser era (Peukert 1987: 263–264).

Concluding Comments

Weimar began 1930 under storm clouds. It was threatened by economic, political, and social problems. Some of these were massive and affected every German household; some were smaller and concerned fewer people. But virtually everyone was preoccupied with the dire straits of Germany after the tenth anniversary of the founding of the Weimar Republic and the ratification of the Reichsverfassung. The year 1931 yielded few improvements in the conditions under which Germans lived and worked; if anything, if they had not actually deteriorated but seemed as if they had. The Müller government was the longest lasting government but it was the final one of the SPD. The SPD could be accused of many things, but they believed in democracy and the rule of law. Those things could not be said about the Brüning, Papen, and Schleicher regimes, and it is instructive that none of the three lasted very long. By early 1932, things were at an impasse and so Hindenburg and the Kanzler sought a way out of the darkness. But the imposition of the Reich decrees under the guise of Art. 48 did little to change things for the better. The end of January 1933 revealed some hints about the future. But Germans were too tired of Weimar and the past; Hitler promised a new government and offered hope for the future. Unfortunately, those who comprehended what that future would be were ignored and their warnings went unheeded. It would not be until May 1945 that Germans would look at the rubble of Hitler's reign and would reclaim some of the democratic hopes that Weimar had once promised.

References

Anschütz, Gerhard (1921) *Der Verfassung des Deutschen Reichs vom 11. August 1919.* Berlin: Verlag von Georg Stilke.

Anschütz, Gerhard (1929) *Der Verfassung des Deutschen Reichs. vom 11. August 1919.* Berlin: Verlag von Georg Stilke. Dritte Bearbeitung. 11. Auflage (32. Und 33. Tausend).

Anschütz, Gerhard (1933) *Der Verfassung des Deutschen Reichs. vom 11. August 1919.* Berlin: Verlag von Georg Stilke. 14. Auflage.

Anschütz, Gerhard (1993) *Aus Meinem Leben.* Herausgegeben und eingeleitet von Walter Pauly. Frankfurt am Main: Vittorio Klostermann.

Anschütz, Gerhard und Jellinek, Walter (1932) *Reichskredite und Diktatur. Zwei Rechtsgutachten.* Tübingen: Verlag von J.C.B. Mohr (Paul Siebeck).

Anschütz, Gerhard und Thoma, Richard, Herausgebern (1930) *Handbuch des Deutschen Staatsrechts.* Tübingen: Verlag von J.C.B. Mohr (Paul Siebeck). Erster Band.

Anschütz, Gerhard und Thoma, Richard, Herausgebern (1932) *Handbuch des Deutschen Staatsrechts.* Tübingen: Verlag von J.C.B. Mohr (Paul Siebeck). Zweiter Band.

Blasius, Dirk (2006) *Weimars Ende. Bürgerkrieg und Politik 1930–1933.* Göttingen: Vandenhoeck & Ruprecht.

Boldt, Hans (1993) "Der Artikel 48 der Weimarer Reichsverfassung—Sein historischer Hintergrund und seine politische Funktion." In *Die Weimarer Republik.* Herausgegeben von Michael Stürmer. Frankfurt am Main: Hain. 288–309.

Bracher, Karl Dietrich (1979) *Die Deutsche Diktatur. Entstehung-Struktur-Folgen des Nationalsozialismus.* Frankfurt am, Berlin and Wien: Verlag Ullstein. 6. Auflage.

Bracher, Karl Dietrich, Sauer, Wolfgang and Schulz, Gerhard (1960) *Die nationalsozialistische Machtergreifung. Studien zur Errichtung des totalitären Herrschaftssystems in Deutschland 1933/34.* Köln und Oplanden: Westdeutscher Verlag.

Brecht, Dr. (1933) *Preussen contra Reich vor dem Staatsgerichtshof.* Stenogrammbericht der Verhandlungen von dem Staatsgerischtshof in Leipzig vom 10. bis 14, und vom 17. Oktober 1932. Mit einem Vorwort von Ministerialdirektor Dr. Brecht. Berlin: Verlag J.H.W. Dietz Nachfolger.

Büttner, Ursula (2008) *Weimar. Die überforderte Republik 1918–1933. Leistung und Versagen in Staat, Gesellschaft, Wirtschaft und Kultur.* Stuttgart: J.G. Cotta'sche Buchhandlung Nachfolger.

Civis (1932) "Ein Nachwort zu Professor Kelsens Kritik am Urteil des Staatsgerichtshof." *Die Justiz.* VIII. Band. Doppelheft 2–3. 91–106.

Fraenkel, Ernst (1932a) "Chronik." *Die Justiz.* VIII. Band. Heft 1. 53–58.

Fraenkel, Ernst (1932b) "Chronik." *Die Justiz.* VIII. Band. Doppelheft 2–3. 133–139.

Fraenkel, Ernst (1932c) "Chronik." *Die Justiz.* VIII. Band. Heft 4. 189–193.

Fraenkel, Ernst (1932d) "Chronik." *Die Justiz.* VIII. Band. Heft 5–6. 281–284.

Grau, Richard (1932a) "§ 80. Die Diktaturgewalt des Reichspräsidenten." In Anschütz und Thoma. 1932. 274–295.

Grau, Richard (1932b) "§ 81. Die Diktaturgewalt der Landesregierungen." In Anschütz und Thoma. 1932. 295–300.

Grimm, Dieter (2018) "Weimars Ende und Untergang." In *Das Wagnis der Demokratie. Eine Anatomie der Weimarer Reichsverfassung.* Herausgegeben von Horst Dreier und Christian Waldhoff. München: C.H. Beck. 263–287.

Grund, Henning (1976) *"Preußenschlag" und Staatsgerichtshof im Jahre 1932.* Baden-Baden: Nomos Verlagsgesellschaft.

Holtmann, Everhard, Koordinator (1995) *Die Weimarer Republik. Das Ende der Demokratie. Band 3 1929–1933.* München: Bayerische Landeszentrale für politische Bildungsarbeit.

Jasper, Gotthard (1995) "Die großen Koalition 1928–1930." In Holtmann. 1995. 19–45.

Jones, Larry Eugene (2022) "From Democracy to Dictatorship. The Fall of Weimar and the Nazi Rise to Power, 1930–1933." In Rossol and Ziemann. 95–116.

Kelsen, Hans (1932) "Das Urteil des Staatsgerichtshofs vom 25. Oktober 1932." *Die Justiz.* VIII. Band. Heft 2–3. 65–91.

Kolb, Eberhard (2002) *Die Weimarer Republik.* München: R. Oldenbourg Verlag. 6. überarbeitete und erweiterte Auflage.

Mommsen, Hans (2001) *Aufstieg und Untergang der Republik von Weimar. 1918–1933.* München: Econ Ullstein. 2. Ausgabe.

Nawiasky, Hans (1930) "*Handbuch des Deutschen Staatsrechts.*1–4 Lieferung." *Archiv des öffentlichen Rechts.* Neue Folge 18. Band. Der Ganzen Folge 57. Band. 235–236.

Nawiasky, Hans (1931) "*Handbuch des Deutschen Staatsrechts.*1–4 Lieferung. 5–15." *Archiv des öffentlichen Rechts.* Neue Folge 20. Band. Der Ganzen Folge 59. Band. 298–301.

Ooyen, Robert Chr. van (2019) *Demokratiesche Staats- und Verfassungslehre der Weimarer Republik.* Frankfurt am Main: Verlag für Verwaltungswissenschaft.

Peukert, Detlev J.K. (1987) *Die Weimarer Republik.* Frankfurt am Main: Suhrkamp Verlag.

Pyta, Wolfram (2009) *Hindenburg. Herrschaft zwischen Hohenzollern und Hitler.* München: Verlagsgruppe Random House.
Rossol, Nadine and Ziemann, Benjamin, editors (2022) *The Oxford Handbook of the Weimar Republic.* Oxford: Oxford University Press.
Ruck, Michael (1995) "Wirtschaft und Arbeitsgesellschaft im Zeichen der Großen Krise." In Holtmann. 1995. 131–170.
Schafer, Rainer (1995a) "Parlamentarische Lähmungskrise und Etabilierung der Präsidialkabinette." In Holtmann. 1995. 315–353.
Schafer, Rainer (1995b) "Das Kabinett Papen." In Holtmann. 1995. 355–390.
Schildt, Axel (1995) "Das Kabinett Kurt von Schleicher." In Holtmann. 1995. 391–444.
Stibbe, Mathew (2022) "Coalition-Building and Political Fragmentation, 1924–1930." In Rossel and Ziemann. 2022. 72–94.
Stürmer, Michael, Herausgebern (1993) *Die Weimarer Republik.* Meisenheim: Verlag von Anton Hain. 3. Auflage.
Sweet, Pamela E. (2022) "The Industrial Working Class." In Rossol and Ziemann. 2022. 474–497.
Wright, Jonathan (2022) "Foreign Policy: The Dilemmas of a Revisionist State." In Rossol and Ziemann. 2022. 242–263.

7 Concluding Comments

Introduction

Having traced the use (and abuse) of Art. 48 of the Weimarer Reichsverfassung from its lengthy development during most of 1919 and ending in early 1933, it is now time to offer some brief reflections on Art. 48 and its history. This short chapter is composed of three sets of concluding comments. The first set of comments concerns the main themes of the previous chapters and offers a unifying theme. The second set contains some concluding comments about a handful of books and several essays which have been published since the end of World War Two. These works have, in varying degrees, appeared to have dealt with Weimar and with Art. 48. As one might have expected, there are not many of them and almost all of them are in German. As also expected, there are those who take a scholarly position as Anschütz and Kelsen did and those who take a political view, like Grau and Schmitt. Both types have revealing comments about what Art. 48 was intended to do and how, and sometimes why, it failed. The third set of concluding comments is basically that: the lessons that I have drawn from the study of Art. 48 during the years that I have been working on this book. These final concluding comments fall into two categories: the ones pertaining to Art. 48 and the ones that suggest what the near future may hold. Hence, this final chapter is not so much a "Conclusion" as it is a final opportunity to reflect on what happened in the 1920s and early 30s, what scholars have thought about that, and how those ideas impact our understanding of public security and order. After all, Art. 48 was intended to be the constitutional remedy to restore security and order.

Concluding Comments I

This book traced the history of Art. 48 of the Weimarer Reichsverfassung from the discussion about what it should cover. Chapter 2 set out the period of gestation during the late spring and summer of 1919 and then the final form taken from August 11, 1919. It noted the debates about what should and should not be included in it and showed how the final version of Art. 48 was composed from two different but related proposed articles. The account

DOI: 10.4324/9781003312796-7

continued with the years 1920 through 1922. It examined some of the writings by several of the long-term participants in the debate concerning Art. 48. These individuals included Gerhard Anschütz, Richard Grau, and Carl Schmitt. Chapter 3 focused mainly on the various papers and articles by many of the participants of the decades-long debate about Art. 48. These included Karl Bilfinger and Erwin Jacobi, as well as Anschütz, Schmitt, and Grau. Most all of these contributions were scholarly papers but clearly revealed the political convictions of the authors. Chapter 4 was devoted to the terrible years of 1923 and 1924 as well as the relative peaceful ones of 1925 and 1926. Much of the first part of that chapter focused on the papers presented at the 1924 conference of the German legal scholars. The second part was concerned with several papers devoted to the issue of Art. 48 in terms of its scope and its use. Again, these essays were scholarly in form but contained political passion in content. Chapter 5 covered the years 1927, 1928, and 1929, and while these were relatively mild compared with the earlier years, there were still critical political and economic issues such as reparations and unemployment. Then the Wall Street crash of October 1929 added to the growing sense of despair in Germany. It is against this changing background that the discussions regarding Art. 48 needed to be interpreted. The essays written during 1927 and 1928 tended to be less political and more reflective of careful analyses of the strengths and weaknesses of Art. 48. The writings of 1929 were reflective of the rapidly changing political situation in Germany and were not just more heated but also seemed more personal. This was especially true regarding the debate between Carl Schmitt and Hans Kelsen. Chapter 6 is almost twice the length of any of the previous chapters and while it was dedicated to the years 1930 through 1932, it had to include brief discussions of works published prior to and after that time frame. The majority of that chapter is devoted to the actions and decisions that led up to the "Preußenschlag" of July 20th, 1932, and the actual invocation of Art. 48. Most of the chapter is an in-depth examination of the legal battles, especially the October trial regarding the legitimacy and the legality of implementing Art. 48 of the Weimarer Reichsverfassung to deal with Prussia's supposed failure to secure public security and order. This book was devoted to the debate about Art. 48 during the Weimar Era, but as noted, it involved discussions about Germany in 1918 as well as 1933. Throughout this entire period, the debate was often contentious, but in the later years it revealed who had the need for power and security as opposed to those who preferred law and independence. History shows whose side won out, but that story is beyond the scope of this book.

Concluding Comments II

There are four books which, in varying degrees, discuss Art. 48 of the Weimar Constitution or are instructive for understanding its history.

The first book by Hans Boldt was published in 1967. The title *Rechtsstaat und Ausnahmezustand* might lead one to think that his book is about Weimar.

But its lengthy subtitle indicates that the book was devoted to the nineteenth century: ***Eine Studie über den Belagerungszustand des bürgerlichen Rechtsstaates im 19. Jahrhundert*** (Boldt 1967). Moreover, Boldt's book is focused predominately on the French Revolution and the uprisings during the nineteenth century. He did discuss the use of law in dealing with Germany's unrest in 1871, and he returned to Germany during the First World War (Boldt 1967: 221–222). Boldt's book is valuable in explaining terminology such as "Kriegsrecht" ("war law") and "loi martiale" ("martial law"). Bolt was also helpful in clarifying the distinction between "exceptions" in institutes and in constitutions. Boldt's book was historical, but as he noted in the "Vorwort" it had modern relevance in part because of the problematic legacy of Art. 48 of the Weimarer Reichsverfassung (Boldt 1967: 5–7). Hans Boldt has been the leading authority on "Ausnahmezustand" as indicated by a few of his articles. The most relevant one is "Der Artikel 48 der Weimarer Reichsverfassung—Sein historischer Hintergrund und seine politische Funktion" (Boldt 1993). Section III of his essay "Ausnahmezustand" is devoted to the notion since the end of the First World War and refers to Schmitt's decisionism that he argued for in *Politische Theologie* (Boldt 1972, especially 371–376). I would be remiss if I did not draw attention to Marc de Wilde's excellent discussion about Art. 48. His article is one of the few that focuses on the 1924 debate about Art. 48.[1]

Gabriel Seiberth's title and subtitle indicate that his concern was with Carl Schmitt: *Anwalt des Reiches. Carl Schmitt und der Prozess "Preußen contra Reich" vor dem Staatsgerichtshof* (Seiberth 2001). Seiberth's book was his dissertation, and that helps explain why the first chapter is a literature review. That also helps explain why the final 100 pages are composed of conclusions, references, and indices. The second, third, and fourth chapters are instructive. Chapter II provides a fairly complete and quite accurate account of the historical context for the Weimar Constitution and especially Art. 48. Chapter III discusses Carl Schmitt's role leading up to the events of July 20, 1932, and how Schmitt was called to help represent the Reich in the court proceedings of October. Chapter IV is a lengthy and detailed account of the court proceedings. As a document concerning a critical part of Schmitt's life, Seiberth's book is rather helpful. But because it is a work dedicated to Schmitt and in defending his role in the trial of the "Preußenschlag," it is slightly less important.

Henning Grund's *"Preußenschlag" und Staatsgerichtshof im Jahre 1932* (Grund 1976) has much to recommend it. It is divided into two parts. In the first part, Grund does a remarkably complete job of providing the context for the "Preußenschlag" and the events and decisions leading up to the decision of July 20, 1932. In the second part he does a credible job of explaining

1 See de Wilde 2010. I want to thank Prof. de Wilde for his early encouragement of me to take up the challenge to write the present book.

key issues; his discussion regarding the relationship between "Exekution" and "Diktatur" is quite helpful. Unfortunately, it was rather brief (Grund 1976: 91–95). This complaint may be made about much of the second part. It is, however, focused just on the year 1932 and so is of limited help in understanding the origins and history of Art. 48. While Grund's book is almost 50 years old, it is still worth reading as an account of the "Preußenschlag."

The fourth volume is in English and was published in 2015. Its title reflects the dispute between Hans Kelsen and Carl Schmitt regarding the guardian of the constitution. *The Guardian of the Constitution* is a translation of the discussion concerning "Der Hüter der Verfassung." This book's subtitle clarifies that the book is indeed about the debate between Kelsen and Schmitt: *Hans Kelsen and Carl Schmitt on the Limits of Constitutional Law* (Vinx 2015). But Lars Vinx's volume is not a treatise on the discussion but a translation of portions of some of Kelsen's and Schmitt's writings. Vinx's "Introduction" is focused on the differences that Kelsen and Schmitt had regarding the issue of constitutional law. Kelsen was heavily in favor of a constitutional court that could legitimately decide constitutional questions, whereas Schmitt insisted that the Reichspräsident was the one entitled to make these decisions. Thus, Vinx's "Introduction" discussed the "Preussenschlag" (Vinx's spelling) and while it is useful in helping to explain the two sides, it is an oversimplification of a complex matter. Within these limits, Vinx's "Introduction" and his translations are worth reading. It is to Vinx's credit that he recognized the importance of the conflict between Kelsen's appeal to courts and Schmitt's predilection for executive power and that he provides a rather good translation of some of the key documents of the fight between the supporters of the Reich and the defenders of Prussia.

Concluding Comments III

In writing this book, I was continually impressed with the degree of accuracy of many of those who struggled to understand Germany's position during the Weimar Era and what realistic measures could be taken to address the real and pressing issues that Germany encountered in the decade following its loss in 1918. I have also been impressed with the combination of despair of the moment and the hope for the future that those involved in the debates regarding the Weimar Constitution had. It appears that that combination was often reflected in the general population in Germany. That impression may or not be based on a real understanding of Germany's history between 1919 and 1932. Yet, it seemed that Germans had a strong sense of the value of the history of their country coupled with a faith that it could regain its rightful position among the major nations of the world. Finally, with few exceptions, it appeared to me that most German scholars and many German politicians were honestly intent on finding mutually suitable solutions to its pressing problems. Democracy lost in Germany, and it underwent a terrible 13-year period in which it inflicted as much damage on the world as it did to itself. But it did begin to return to its democratic roots after 1945. In that, there is hope for other countries who turn their backs on the fundamental values of freedom, dignity, and democracy.

For much of my scholarly career I have followed Max Weber's dictum to distinguish between "Sein" and "Sollen"; that is, between "is" and "ought" or between facts and values (Weber 1922: 157–158). His advice has often been misunderstood; he did not insist that there can be no value judgments in scholarly work, but he did insist that one needed to make it evident to others (and to one's self) when one is moving from the realm of facts to the kingdom of values. In this book, I have attempted to keep my values out of my discussion of the facts. But in these concluding comments I am stressing that these are my opinions and values.

For much the modern period there has been an insistence on progress and in the belief in equality. More recently, there has been an insistence on democracy as the best form of government and the belief in the fundamental rule of law. The twentieth century saw both the continuation of those convictions and the rejection of them. The twenty-first century has seen a further erosion in these modern principles. Russia and China have elections; however, very few people believe those elections are open and fair. Hungary and Turkey have governments that by and large proclaim their illiberal values and promote businesses and groups that share their outlook. Other European countries have far-right parties that are opposed or even hostile to democratic values. What makes some of these countries and parties more dangerous is that they use democratic means to undermine democratic values. Rather than placing their trust in congress or parliament as the voice of the people, many place their faith in the power of a president as the ultimate authority. As I write this, Donald Trump has not yet been inaugurated into his second term as president of the United States of America.[2] He has stated more than once that he will be a dictator on the first day. Whether that will be the case remains to be seen, as is whether he will restrict his dictatorial impulses to just Day One or whether he will extend them. The relevance to this book is the following: governments are entrusted with the public security and order of their countries but there are times in which governments have used that trust to go beyond public security and to impose their own ideas and values. Such was the case with Art. 48 of the Weimarer Verfassung. The Weimar Constitution guaranteed all Germans a number of basic rights. But Art. 48 gave a government a legal instrument which could take away even those basic rights in the

2 As I am writing this chapter in December 2024, the president of South Korea just declared martial law. He claimed that the imposition of martial law was necessary to counter some unspecified threat from North Korea and to overcome the political opposition from congress. Whether any of this is true, congress defied him and he has backed down. How this plays out in the coming days and weeks remains to be seen. But commentators have pointed out that whenever an executive calls for a state of exception, it diminishes the guardrails that the constitution and democracy have in place. In essence, no one wins and almost everyone loses.

service of "restoring" "public security and order" (öffentlichen Sicherheit und Ordnung"). Von Hindenburg, von Papen, and von Schleicher were basically monarchists and they believed in a strong central government. Hindenburg and Papen used Art. 48 to undermine the force of democracy and to further weaken the rule of law. Historians can debate how much their convictions and their actions led to Hitler's rise and the Nazi domination of Germany from 1933 until 1945. But the story that I have tried to tell about the origins and the history of Art. 48 should be considered as an example of how legal means have been used to help destroy the legal order. The story of Art. 48 is not just a historical story, but is a stark warning for the present and the future. It points to the use of a constitution to undermine itself; it is a clear and present danger. It is my hope that readers of this book will be prompted to think about the Weimar Era and will be prompted to reflect on the tension between freedom and security. For many people, security is more important than freedom; but for others, freedom is more valuable than order. For people such as Carl Schmitt, Erwin Jacobi, and Karl Bilfinger, order is preferable to freedom. For others, such as Gerhard Anschütz, Hermann Heller, and Arnold Brecht, order must always be subservient to freedom.

References

Boldt, H. (1967) *Rechtsstaat und Aufnahmezustand. Eine Studie über den Belagerungszustand des bürgerlichen Rechtsstaates im 19. Jahrhundert.* Berlin: Duncker & Humblot.

Boldt, H. (1972) "Ausnahmezustand." In *Geschichtliche Grundbegriffe. Historisches Lexikon zur politisch-sozialen Sprache in Deutschland.* Herausgegeben von Otto Brunner, Werner Conze and Reinhart Koselleck. Stuttgart: Ernst Klett Verlag. Band 1A-D. 343–376.

Boldt, H. (1993) "Der Artikel 48 der Weimarer Reichsverfassung—Sein historischer Hintergrund und seine politische Funktion." In *Die Weimar Republik.* Herausgebern von Michael Stürmer. Frankfurt am Main: Hain. 3. Auflage. 288–309.

de Wilde, M. (2010) "The State of Emergency in the Weimar Republic: Legal Disputes Over Article 48 of the Weimar Constitution." *Tijdschrift voor Rechtgeschiedenis/The Legal History Review.* 78. May. 135–158.

Grund, H. (1976) *"Preußenschlag" und Staatsgerichtshof im Jahre 1932.* Baden-Baden: Nomos Verlag.

Seiberth, G. (2001) *Anwalt des Reiches. Carl Schmitt und der Prozess "Preußen contra Reich" vor dem Staatsgerichtshof.* Berlin: Duncker & Humblot.

Vinx, Lars (2015) *The Guardian of the Constitution: Hans Kelsen and Carl Schmitt on the Limits of Constitutional Law.* Translation, introduction and notes by Lars Vinx. Cambridge: Cambridge University Press.

Weber, M. (1922) "Die Objektivität sozialwissenschaftlicher und sozialpolitischer Erkentnis." In *Gesammelte Aufsätze zur Wissenschaftslehre.* Tübingen: Verlag von J.C.B. Mohr (Paul Siebeck). 146–214.

Index

FSC
www.fsc.org
MIX
Papier | Fördert gute Waldnutzung
FSC® C083411

Kolibri 360 GmbH
Ferdinand-Jühlke-Straße 7
99095 Erfurt, Deutschland
produktsicherheit@kolibri360.de